The ADD Hyperactivity Handbook for Schools

Effective Strategies for Identifying and Teaching Students with Attention Deficit Disorders in Elementary and Secondary Schools

Second Edition

Specialty Press, Inc.
Plantation, Florida

Library of Congress Catalog Card Number 92-070275
Parker, Harvey C.
    The ADD Hyperactivity Handbook for Schools
    p. 330 cm.
    Summary: Effective strategies for identifying and
    teaching students with ADD in elementary and
    secondary schools.

    ISBN 0-9621629-2-2 (paper)

    1. Attention deficit disorder-Treatment
2. Attention-deficit/Hyperactivity Disorder-Treatment

Published by:
Specialty Press, Inc. (formerly Impact Publications, Inc.)
300 N.W. 70th Ave., Suite 102
Plantation, Florida 33317
(954) 792-8100 • (800) 233-9273
(954) 792-8545 Facsimile
Internet: http://www.addwarehouse.com

Manufactured in the United States of America

To my family

Roberta, Michelle, and Julie

Preface

Current interest in attention deficit disorder (ADD) is soaring. Magazine articles, newspaper reports, network newscasts, and television talk show hosts have found this to be a popular topic. Scientific journals report numerous studies of ADD children and adolescents, and ADD support groups continue to grow at an astounding rate as parents seek to learn more about this disorder to help their youngsters succeed at home and at school.

While some of the interest in ADD arose from the controversies surrounding this condition, the growing recognition that ADD can be a seriously debilitating disorder with lifelong consequences has fueled concern. Controversy about ADD revolves around disagreements as to the nature of the disorder as well as differing opinions regarding treatment. Apprehension with respect to the dispensing of medication to ADD children began to capture media attention in the mid to late 1980's. Disagreements as to the educational needs of ADD children, and whether they should be eligible to receive special education services when their disorder severely impacts upon their academic performance, have been hotly debated issues.

In the past five years there have been numerous books written about ADD. Some of them address concerns of parents, others inform health care professionals, and still a few others are directed at teachers of ADD students and the children themselves. The information gap about ADD is finally closing as scientific knowledge becomes available to parents and teachers, enabling them to better assist ADD children and adolescents to grow and lead healthy, productive lives.

ADD children make up three to five percent of the population of students attending school within the United States. With approximately 2 million students with ADD, most likely every classroom has 1 to 2 children with the disorder. Most teachers have had experience teaching students with attentional problems and they can probably recall the different challenges that these students posed. Students with ADD are not easy to teach. They test the limits of an educator's patience, skill, and professionalism. Their inattentiveness, distractibility, frequent hyperactivity, and poor organizational skills result in rushed assignments that are often haphazardly done and incomplete when turned in, despite repeated reminders to "take your time," "be careful," and "write neatly." Teachers use different methods to correct these problems. They move the student closer to them, they call parents in for a conference, they provide greater supervision and more positive reinforcement to the child. The ADD student responds to some degree, but improvements are generally not longlasting without continued support.

Nobody has all the answers to help students with ADD. We do, however, have years of research and the results of thousands of psychological, behavioral, and educational studies of these students to call upon for some solutions. Based upon these investigations, we realize that the school performance problems of ADD students are probably the result of physical make-up rather than intentional misbehavior, lack of interest, or emotional difficulty. It is important to understand the causes of this disorder as well as the conditions that aggravate and relieve symptoms. There is no cure for ADD. There are no easy, foolproof teaching strategies either. However, with greater understanding of the disorder, teachers can more effectively help the ADD student in the classroom.

This handbook is designed to provide educators with the tools they need to identify, evaluate, and teach ADD children and adolescents. The handbook is meant to be used by educational administrators interested in developing service delivery models for ADD students, by school psychologists, guidance personnel, exceptional student education specialists, and by regular and special education teachers. For ease of reference, the handbook is divided into two parts.

Part one, Understanding Attention Deficit Disorders, contains a description of the characteristics of children with ADD, presumed causes of ADD and contributing factors, how ADD affects children at different ages, methods of assessment, and a review of medical treatments along with discussions of self-monitoring, problem-solving, and social skills training. School psychologists, intervention specialists, guidance personnel, and others interested in learning more about ADD will find that part one provides a comprehensive overview of the disorder.

Part two of the handbook, Teaching Children with ADD, is designed specifically for classroom teachers and for educators who are responsible for implementing classroom interventions. Part two looks at ADD as an educational disorder and contains a review of teaching strategies useful in the management of students with ADD in both regular and special education settings. The importance of teachers developing partnerships with the parents of their ADD students is discussed. Classroom accommodations and strategies that have been found to be helpful for students with ADD are provided to offer practical solutions for teachers. Proven and unproven/disproven methods of treatment for ADD are reviewed and a listing of support groups and resources for parents are included in part two.

To assist the teacher with practical application of the accommodations and strategic interventions discussed, student activity worksheets are distributed throughout the handbook and are contained in the Appendix. The student activity worksheets may be reproduced for student use. Handouts for teachers to give to parents of ADD children are also included in the Appendix and may be reproduced for classroom use.

I would like to thank Lynn Barker, Lynn Wolf, and Roberta Parker for their helpful comments in preparing this manuscript. My thanks as well go to Sandra F. Thomas, Russell Barkley, Michael Gordon, Jim Swanson, Mary Fowler, Sam Goldstein, David Aronofsky, Hugh Leichtman, and Fran Rice for the knowledge they have each imparted during our many discussions over the past few years and for the spectacular efforts they have made on behalf of children with attention deficit disorders.

My most heartfelt appreciation and devotion goes to Roberta, my wife, and to my children, Michelle and Julie, for their support and love.

Harvey C. Parker, Ph.D.
February 4, 1992

Table of Contents

Table of Contents

The ADD Hyperactivity Handbook for Schools

Part I

Understanding Attention Deficit Disorders

Chapter 1
Characteristics of Children with Attention Deficit Disorder

The primary characteristics found in children with attention deficit disorder (ADD or ADHD), namely, inattention, impulsivity, and hyperactivity are exhibited by all children to some degree. What distinguishes ADD children from others is that these characteristics are prevalent to a far greater degree, and in a wider range of situations and circumstances, than would be true of children without this disorder.

Problems with Attention Span

Children with ADD have shorter attention spans compared to others their age. While an attention span deficit is not as visible as hyperactivity or impulsivity, it is usually the symptom of ADD which causes the most problems in school. In the classroom, the inattentive child shifts from one activity to another and is usually unable to stay focused long enough to finish assignments. Inattentive children have trouble following the teacher's directions and they often drift off and lose their place. Distracted by other stimuli in their environment, or by their own internal thoughts, ADD children often begin more things than they end. Tasks begun are left undone.

Although frequently inattentive, the ADD child is not incapable of attending to situations which appeal to his interests. He usually has a ready supply of attention while performing highly enjoyable activities, such as playing video games or watching television. Novel or unusual situations can capture an ADD child's attention for lengthy periods of time as can special projects or hobbies. In addition, during one-on-one situations, wherein the ADD child is being closely observed, attention span may seem quite normal.

Problems with Impulsivity

Most children with ADD have problems with impulse control. This refers to the child's inability to regulate emotions and behavior. They act quickly, without giving sufficient forethought to the consequences of their behavior. As Dennis the Menace described himself, "By the time I think about doing something, I've already done it".

In school, spur of the moment decision-making causes the child with ADD to rush through assignments without taking the time to read the directions and to make more than his share of careless errors. In the classroom, other children are frequently disrupted by the ADD child's calling out as he gets carried away and forgets to raise his hand before speaking. The impulsive student loses books, breaks pens and pencils, and leaves homework and classwork everywhere, except where it is supposed to be. He does these things not maliciously, but unthinkingly.

Social impulsivity leads to loss of friendships with no understanding as to why. Children with ADD have a knack for getting on other peoples' nerves. Even other children find their behavior annoying because they never seem to realize when enough is enough.

Problems with Hyperactivity

Not all ADD children are hyperactive. A good many, in fact, show normal activity levels or may even be underactive. You can't miss the ones who are hyperactive though. "Faster than a speeding bullet," one mother said about her hyperactive four year old who literally didn't stay still for one minute all day long. Preschool ADD children are always touching something, darting about, never satisfied, never sticking with one thing for very long, always curious, and needing supervision. Fortunately, hyperactivity is often at its worst in young children. As hyperactive children get older they tend to slow down some.

In elementary school, the child's activity level changes from running to restless. Fidgeting, squirming, shuffling feet, drumming fingers, playing with something all the time, talking, making noises, tipping the chair back, getting up, walking around the room, etc. are typical descriptions by teachers of the hyperactive children in their class. Hyperactive girls may express their energy in less physical ways, primarily through non-stop talking.

As the ADD child goes through adolescence, obvious characteristics of hyperactivity may give way to more subtle signs. A wagging foot, tapping pencil, excessive talking, etc. may signify the teenager's restlessness. Hyperactive adolescents usually like to stay busy and they can have trouble settling down to the speed of most other teens.

The important thing to remember is that not all children with attention deficit disorder are hyperactive.

ADD Name Changes

During the 1960's and afterwards, inattentive and hyperactive children became popular subjects for research studies which focused on identifying characteristics of such children. With new information constantly being discovered about them, the name given to this group of children changed through the years to keep up with our growing body of knowledge.

Different Names For Attention Deficits/Hyperactivity Through the Years

1940 —— Minimal Brain Syndrome

1957 —— Hyperkinetic Impulse Disorder

1960 —— Minimal Brain Dysfunction (MBD)

1968 —— Hyperkinetic Reaction of Childhood (DSM II)

1980 —— Attention Deficit Disorder (DSM III)
with hyperactivity
without hyperactivity
residual type

1987 —— Attention-deficit Hyperactivity Disorder
(DSM III-R)
Undifferentiated Attention Deficit Disorder
(DSM III-R)

1994 —— Attention-Deficit/Hyperactivity Disorder
(DSM IV)
Predominantly Inattentive Type
Predominantly Hyperactive-Impulsive Type
Combined Type

Attention-Deficit/Hyperactivity Disorder

Currently, the Diagnostic and Statistical Manual of Mental Disorders (DSM IV), published by the American Psychiatric Association (1994), specifies criteria that need to be met to be diagnosed as having Attention-Deficit/Hyperactivity Disorder. These criteria are listed on page 5. There are three subtypes of the disorder: combined type; predominantly hyperactive-impulsive type; and predominantly inattentive type.

The combined type and predominantly hyperactive-impulsive type make up the majority (around two-thirds) of individuals with this disorder. Individuals with the combined type have symptoms of inattention and hyperactivity or impul-

Characteristics of Children with Attention Deficit Disorder

Diagnostic and Statistical Manual of Mental Disorders Fourth Edition
Attention-Deficit/Hyperactivity Disorder

A. Either (1) or (2):

  (1) six (or more) of the following symptoms of **inattention** have persisted for at least 6 months to a degree that is maladaptive and inconsistent with developmental level:

  Inattention

  (a) often fails to give close attention to details or makes careless mistakes in schoolwork, work, or other activities

  (b) often has difficulty sustaining attention in tasks or play activities

  (c) often does not seem to listen when spoken to directly

  (d) often does not follow through on instructions and fails to finish schoolwork, chores, or duties in the workplace (not due to oppositional behavior or failure to understand instructions)

  (e) often has difficulty organizing tasks and activities

  (f) often avoids, dislikes, or is reluctant to engage in tasks that require sustained mental effort (such as schoolwork or homework)

  (g) often loses things necessary for tasks or activities (e.g., toys, school assignments, pencils, books, or tools)

  (h) is often easily distracted by extraneous stimuli

  (i) is often forgetful in daily activities

  (2) six (or more) of the following symptoms of **hyperactivity-impulsivity** have persisted for at least 6 months to a degree that is maladaptive and inconsistent with developmental level:

  Hyperactivity

  (a) often fidgets with hands or feet or squirms in seat

  (b) often leaves seat in classroom or in other situations in which remaining seated is expected

  (c) often runs about or climbs excessively in situations in which it is inappropriate (in adolescents or adults, may be limited to subjective feelings of restlessness)

  (d) often has difficulty playing or engaging in leisure activities quietly

  (e) is often "on the go" or often acts as if "driven by a motor"

  (f) often talks excessively

  Impulsivity

  (g) often blurts out answers before questions have been completed

  (h) often has difficulty awaiting turn

  (i) often interrupts or intrudes on others (e.g., butts into conversations or games)

B. Some hyperactive-impulsive or inattentive symptoms that caused impairment were present before age 7 years.

C. Some impairment from the symptoms is present in two or more settings (e.g. at school [or work] and at home).

D. There must be clear evidence of clinically significant impairment in social, academic, or occupational functioning.

E. The symptoms do not occur exclusively during the course of a Pervasive Developmental Disorder, Schizophrenia, or other psychotic disorder and are not better accounted for by another mental disorder (e.g. Mood Disorder, Anxiety Disorder, Dissociative Disorder, or a Personality Disorder). (pp. 83-85)

Code based on type:

  314.01 Attention-Deficit/Hyperactivity Disorder, Combined Type: if both Criteria A1 and A2 are met for the past 6 months

  314.00 Attention-Deficit/Hyperactivity Disorder, Predominantly Inattentive Type: if Criterion A1 is met but Criterion A2 is not met for the past 6 months.

  314.01 Attention-Deficit/Hyperactivity Disorder, Predominantly Hyperactive-Impulsive Type: if Criterion A2 is met but Criterion A1 is not met for the past 6 months.

sivity (see page 5), whereas for individuals with the hyperactive-impulsive type, symptoms of inattention are not present to a significant extent. To be diagnosed with ADD, predominantly hyperactive-impulsive type or combined type, symptoms must have been present before age seven, impairment from these symptoms must be present in two or more settings (i.e., at school, work, and at home) and must not be the result of another medical or psychiatric disorder.

Individuals with the predominantly inattentive type of ADD have problems with attention span, but not hyperactivity or impulsivity. To be diagnosed with this type, symptoms of inattention (see page 5) must have been present before age seven, impairment from these symptoms must be present in two or more settings (i.e., at school, work, and at home) and must not be the result of another medical or psychiatric disorder.

The premoninantly inattentive group accounts for approximately one-third of all children with ADD. They have slow tempo in completing tasks and they often become overfocused on their thought processes. Teachers tend to describe them as daydreamers, confused, lethargic, and sluggish. They are an important group of children for teachers to know about since studies indicate that this group of children are at high risk for academic failure. Children with predominantly inattentive type have a higher rate of learning problems than the hyperactive-impulsive group and may develop emotional difficulties related to depression, anxiety, and low self-esteem more easily than the others. Dr. Benjamin Lahey, an expert in this group of attention deficient children, describes their peer acceptance level to be better than their hyperactive-impulsive counterparts, but they tend to be on the periphery of social groups rather than centrally involved.

To remain consistent with public policy, all types of attention-deficit/hyperactivity disorder: combined, hyperactive-impulsive, and inatttentive will be referred to throughout this handbook as ADD.

Prevalence of ADD

Prevalence of ADD within the United States school-aged population could conservatively be estimated to be between 3% and 5%. With 1987 census data indicating that 45 million children are enrolled in public and private schools, the number affected by ADD in the United States could range from 1.35 to 2.25 million.

Differences between boys and girls have been found, with boys being anywhere from 4 to 9 times more likely than girls to have ADD. Compared to ADD girls, boys with the disorder are more aggressive, impulsive and disruptive than ADD girls. Because they tend to be underidentified and thus underserved, ADD girls may be at risk for long term academic, social, and emotional difficulties.

Co-Existing Disorders

Unfortunately, children who have attention deficit disorder also have a greater likelihood of having other problems, the most notable being problems with learning, behavior, and social or emotional development.

ADD and Learning Disorders

In terms of learning, ADD children have a greater likelihood than other children of having a learning disability. Children with learning disabilities commonly show their greatest weaknesses in the basic psychological processes involved in understanding or in using spoken or written language. For learning disabled students, such weaknesses may result in reading, writing, spelling, or arthmetic skill deficits.

There has been considerable confusion, and some controversy, regarding the relationship between learning disabilities and attention deficit disorders. Some would say that these two and attention deficit disorders. Some would say that these two conditions are one in the same, with ADD merely being a subtype of learning disability. Others would argue that they are separate and distinct disorders with a fairly high degree of co-existence in children. In the past, it was generally accepted that the incidence of learning problems and underachievement within the population of children with ADD was quite high, with estimates ranging from 43% to 92%. While theoretically these figures may seem to make sense, in practical application they greatly overestimate the numbers of children with ADD that would qualify for help in school with a co-existing learning disability diagnosis. Most state departments of education have specific criteria that need to be met in order for a student to be classified as learning disabled. Almost always, this criteria includes heavy emphasis on academic functioning and requires the student to manifest a discrepancy between potential (often measured by IQ) and achievement (often measured by an individually administered achievement test). Studies by Drs. Sally and Bennett Shaywitz found that when such an ability/ achievement discrepancy formula was used to classify students as learning disabled, only 11% of their sample of 445 ADD children in grades kindergarten through third could be classified as learning disabled in reading or arithmetic. Since there is a significant overlap between ADD and learning disabilities, school personnel identifying students with ADD should also be alert for signs of co-existing learning disabilities within these students.

ADD and Behavior Disorders

In terms of behavior, ADD children have a greater likelihood than other children of having behavior disorders. It is estimated that between 40% and 60% of children with ADD will show signs of a co-existing oppositional defiant disorder (ODD) and half of those children, in turn, will develop a conduct disorder (CD).

The child with ODD is characterized by a pattern of negativistic, defiant behavior and irritable mood and is often descibed as difficult, although without the more serious aggressive components of behavior typically found in children with conduct disorder. The CD child or adolescent exhibits behavior which more dramatically transgresses social and legal norms. CD behavior is more profoundly aggressive and frequently can manifest itself in stealing, running away, lying, fire-setting, school truancy, destruction of property, or physical cruelty.

Parents of ADD children with ODD complain about the strong-willed, stubborn, and argumentative aspects of their child's behavior as much or more than they do about the inattentive, impulsive, and hyperactive components. It is also quite common for teachers to find the ADD/ODD child's defiance more disagreeable than his short attention span and hyperactivity. A large part of the treatment planning for the ADD/ODD child invariably addresses the oppositional aspects of the disorder. And indeed such treatment planning is extremely important, for if oppositional defiant disorder develops into conduct disorder the prognosis for outcome is much less favorable. It is estimated that such children are four times more likely to be retained in school and eight times more likely to drop out of high school before graduation. They have a greater likelihood of developing adult anti-social personality, substance abuse disorder, and other psychiatric and social problems.

ADD and Emotional Disorders

ADD children tend to also develop secondary emotional problems stemming from the frustration, rejection, and failure that frequently results from their attentional disorder. It is likely that there is a higher incidence of low self-esteem, anxiety, depression, and socialization problems in ADD children. Due to lack of success in school, within the family, or in social relationships, ADD children can become extremely demoralized leading to apathy, irritability, and withdrawal.

Although the development of such problems can easily occur in hyperactive as well as nonhyperactive inattentive children, they are more likely to occur within the nonhyperactive sub-group both because of their tendency to internalize rather than externalize stress and their seemingly more passive, sensitive nature.

Recognition of ADD children's vulnerability to emotional problems is extremely important. Treatment of their emotional needs obviously requires considerable understanding on the part of parents and teachers in order to provide them with the needed emotional support necessary to foster a more positive attitude towards self and others.

It is important to note that although ADD can lead to problems in emotional functioning causing greater anxiety and depression, so too can anxiety and depression lead to diminished motivation and interfere with cognitive processes involved in the regulation of attentiveness, concentration, and mood. Children and adolescents suffering from anxiety or depression may show behavioral signs which closely resemble ADD symptoms. Sometimes this is a sudden, temporary reaction to an environmental situation involving family, school, or peer problems. In other cases, the emotional disorder is more chronic and pervasive, the origin of which may lie in the family or biological history of the individual. It is certainly not difficult to understand how children with problems on their mind would have difficulty paying attention in school and may become restless and impatient. Therefore, the symptoms alone cannot tell us the whole story. Understanding the whole child including family, home environment, and previous background is essential before intervention is attempted.

As with the behavior disorders of conduct and oppositionality, it is sometimes difficult to differentiate emotional disorders from ADD because they can co-occur so often within the same individual. The differentiation of ADD from emotional disorders of depression and anxiety may be made by taking a thorough clinical history which would establish the age of onset of the behavior (ADD must be present before age seven), the chronicity of the behavior (ADD children show a continuous pattern of symptoms), and the pervasiveness of the behavior (ADD children usually show symptoms in a variety of settings including family, school, and social environments).

In summary, although the name has changed for ADD over the years, the symptoms which characterize the disorder have not. The cardinal symptoms of inattention, impulsivity, and often, hyperactivity have been described in ADD children over several decades. In the last 10 years, however, we have realized that most problems of children with ADD are caused by their inattentiveness and that not all ADD children are hyperactive. ADD is often complicated by other learning, behavior, or emotional problems.

Chapter 2
Causes of ADD and Contributing Factors

Most experts agree that ADD is a biological disorder which can have multiple causes. The available evidence suggests that various genetic, neurologic, neurochemical, dietary, and toxic factors may cause ADD. Other factors, such as other medical conditions, medication side effects, familial functioning, or environmental conditions may contribute to the disorder or to the development of ADD-like problems in some children.

Genetics

Heredity is regarded as the most frequent cause of ADD. It is not uncommon for ADD children to have one or more biological relatives with ADD. Thus the disorder may run in families with a significant number of fathers of ADD children citing that they also had characteristics of the disorder as children themselves, and fewer, but still a significant number of mothers also reporting ADD characteristics as children.

Heritability of the disorder is further substantiated since the incidence of ADD in biological families, where there is an ADD offspring, is greater than in adoptive families. Researchers have found a higher rate of ADD among first and second-degree biological relatives of ADD children than in families wherein the ADD child was adopted.

Studies of adopted monozygotic (identical) twins further support the heredity notion of causality. Hyperactivity in one twin was highly correlated with hyperactivity in the other even if they were raised in separate families.

Fetal Development and Birth Factors

A number of investigators share the view that ADD in some children may be the result of some type of prenatal or perinatal stress. Such stress could result in brain dysfunction. Damage to a developing fetus may result from infection, trauma or other complications during pregrancy. Premature delivery or complications during the birth process might also cause potential problems. However, large scale studies offer no conclusive evidence that difficulties during pregnancy, length of labor, type of delivery, the child's weight at birth, or its Apgar score are risk factors for ADD.

Maternal Use of Alcohol During Pregnancy

Women who consume alcoholic beverages during pregnancy are at a higher risk to have children with characteristics of hyperactivity and attentional deficits.

Abnormalities of Brain Structure, Arousal, and Neurochemical Functioning

Although only about 5% of ADD children have any hard evidence of neurological impairment, there is emerging evidence to suggest that ADD children may have some form of dysfunction occurring in regions of the brain associated with the control and regulation of attention, arousal, and activity.

The brain is a complex information network made up of billions of nerve cells called neurons which transmit information to each other in much the same way as signals are transmitted electronically in a telecommunications network. However, messages within the brain are transferred by electrical conduction within a nerve cell and by chemical conduction between nerve cells.

Once a message is carried along the axon (cell body) of a sending nerve cell, it has to cross a small space called a synapse to reach a receiving cell. At the tip of the axon are tiny sacs that contain neurotransmitter chemicals which are automatically released by the sending nerve cell. These neurotransmitter chemicals excite the receiving nerve cell, causing that cell to fire and thus once again propel the message along the axon to receptors in the next nerve cell. Once the message is received the neurotransmitter chemical is deactivated or taken up from the synapse and stored in sacs so as not to cause repeated firing of the receiving cell.

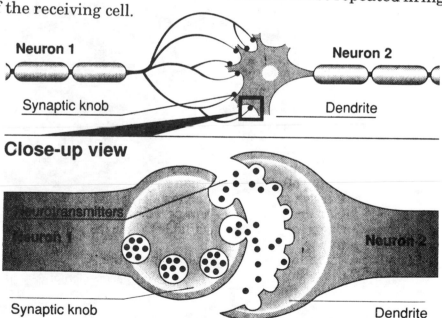

Neuron 1   Neuron 2

Synaptic knob   Dendrite

Close-up view

Neurotransmitters

Neuron 1   Neuron 2

Synaptic knob   Dendrite

Dopamine, norepinephrine, and serotonin are examples of neurotransmitter chemicals which play such an important part in brain activity. They make up the dopaminergic, noradrenergic, and serotonergic chemical systems which regulate our senses, thinking, perception, mood, attention, and behavior. The malfunction of any of these neurotransmitter systems can have a wide ranging impact on how an individual behaves.

Problems in neurological functioning can be directly measured by analyzing brain structure or electrical and chemical activity within the brain. Structural abnormalities, which could result from brain injury due to trauma, infection or disease, probably account for only a small percentage of the population of those with ADD. Using sophisticated technologies such as computerized axial tomography (CT) scans and magnetic resonance imaging (MRI), scientists have tried to determine structural abnormalities in the brains of those with ADD. Findings have been inconclusive. Another line of research investigating electrical activity in the brain's cortex using electroencephalogram (EEG) or evoked potential responses also has not been conclusive.

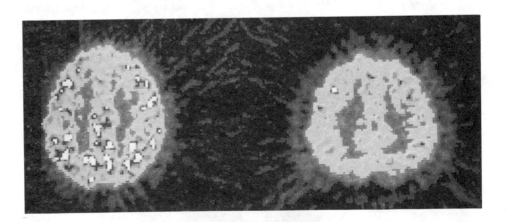

Non-ADHD Adult   ADHD Adult

Reprinted by permission of *The New England Journal of Medicine, 323, 20,* 1990 and with permission of Alan J. Zametkin, M.D.

However, researchers who are studying the chemical activity within the brain are coming up with interesting findings regarding the nature of ADD. Alan Zametkin M.D. (1990) recently published a study using positron emission tomography (PET) scans of the brain showed differences in the way glucose is metabolized in ADD adults and normal controls. These findings gave further credence to neurochemical theories. Research indicates that the frontal area of the brain may be most involved.

Lead Poisoning

While it does not seem likely that lead poisoning accounts for more than a very small portion of children with ADD, an association between elevated blood lead levels and hyperactivity has been demonstrated in a number of studies. Children are thought to acquire elevated lead levels through eating lead-based paint or through exposure to lead fumes from automobile emissions.

Food Allergies

Benjamin Feingold's 1975 publication, *Why Your Child is Hyperactive,* advised parents to put their hyperactive children on an elimination diet wherein foods containing artificial flavorings and natural salycilates would be avoided. Dr. Feingold's early theories have yet to be scientifically validated, but the notion that hyperactive behavior is strongly related to the intake of sugar, food additives, food dyes and preservatives is probably the most widespread and false belief about ADD that is held today.

If diet has a specific effect on behavior or on activity level it is probably minimal or short-lived at best. Early studies by Keith Conners, Ph.D. found little relationship to what children eat and how they act. More recent studies by Conners, however, point to a link between carbohydrate intake and hyperactivity and suggest that protein may lessen the effect that carbohydrates may have in increasing hyperactive behavior.

Other Medical Conditions

Other medical conditions can cause symptoms that look like ADD, but which really are not.

Hyperthyroidism, a disorder resulting in overproduction of a hormone produced by an overactive thyroid gland, can result in accelerated heart rate and hyperactive behavior. Treatment with medication to reduce the production of thyroid hormone will improve this condition.

There are some types of seizure disorders which result in episodic periods of inattention characterized by prolonged staring, brief loss of conscious awareness, eye blinking, and sometimes, tremor. While such occurrences can happen several times a day, the seizure disorder should not be mistaken for ADD. In such cases where a seizure disorder is suspected the child should receive a thorough neurological examination.

Child and adolescent psychiatrist, Dr. Charles Popper, cautions that there are other psychiatric disorders, such as anxiety disorders, depression, or bi-polar disorders, which can occur in children or adolescents . These disorders may result in ADD-like characteristics but should not be confused for ADD.

Mental retardation, autistic disorder, and Gilles de la Tourette syndrome are additional neuropsychiatric disorders which could produce symptoms of inattention, distractibility, and impulsivity and could be confused with attention deficit disorder.

Medication Side Effects

Certain medications may cause ADD-like behavior.

Phenobarbital and Dilantin, anti-convulsants used to treat children with seizure disorders, may give rise to inattention and hyperactivity. Children taking Theophylline for asthma treatment may exhibit signs of ADD-like behavior due to the medication's side effects. These effects are short-lived and disappear when the medication wears off.

Familial Factors

Studies investigating parenting style and methods of discipline in families of hyperactive and normal children do not indicate that parents, by virtue of their parent-child interactions, cause their children to develop attention deficit disorder.

However, most people would agree that children who live in families which lack structure, routine, discipline, and order may have a greater likelihood of developing disruptive behavior disorders which can result in symptoms of inattention, impulsivity, and hyperactivity. Children from homes with chaotic family interactions will often demonstrate poor organizational skills, difficulty with self-regulation, failure to accept responsibility for their actions, and so on. Behavior of this sort, resulting from difficulties in family functioning should not be confused with attention deficit disorder which is a biologically-based disorder, not primarily caused by familial factors.

In summary, researchers would agree that ADD can have multiple causes. Most children with ADD have probably inherited the disorder from one of their parents. A small number of ADD children were probably victims of head injury, infection or disease which affected brain functioning. Neurological research is ongoing and promises to yield more definitive answers in the future. Research into dietary causes of ADD, however, have failed to be convincing as to any definitive role that food allergies play in giving rise to the disorder. Other medical conditions and psychosocial factors can contribute to problems of ADD children or can cause problems that look like ADD, but which are manifestations of other disorders.

Chapter 3
Developmental Course of ADD

The Preschool Child with ADD

It is customary for preschool age children to be overactive and impulsive. Their attention is captured only by things that interest them and only for as long as their interest lasts. Their shifts from one activity to another are considered quite normal and appropriate for their young age. We expect preschoolers to be demanding, impulsive and self-centered in their emotional wants and generally we don't get too upset when their frustration leads to temper outbursts or crying spells. We anticipate their impatience, plan for their short attention span, and vary their daily preschool curriculum enough to sustain their interests.

Parents of ADD preschoolers typically describe their children as much more overactive than normal. They are constantly moving, climbing, and curiously getting into things. These children demand constant parental surveillance as their high activity, drivenness, and insatiable appetite for stimulation require an ever watchful eye. They are often given to moodiness, irritability and temper outbursts. Hitting and biting others is not an uncommon reaction to frustration as they tend to be more aggressive than most other children their age.

At what point does activity exceed the bounds of normalcy and become hyperactivity? When is inattentiveness considered attention deficit? Where does common immaturity end and extreme impulsivity begin? Unfortunately there are no objective answers to these very important questions. For preschoolers, in general, we have no measures that differentiate between what is normal toddler or "terrible 2's" behavior and what is abnormal. Parents of young children typically report concerns as to disobedience, increased activity, and temper outbursts during this developmental period, and we do not have any means by which to differentiate those children for whom these behaviors are simply a normal temporary phase of their development from those for whom these behaviors are indicative of a more long-lasting problem.

The Preschooler with ADD at School

Parents of ADD preschoolers often describe themselves as exhausted by the child rearing process. The typical methods of discipline such as time-out, positive reinforcement, and punishment don't work as well for these children. Parents are often left without an effective means of behavioral control.

Teachers of ADD preschoolers end up equally frustrated. Disruptive behavior, especially aggression towards other children, becomes a chief concern for the teacher and preschool director.

In those preschoolers with severe hyperactivity, behavior modification works, but often with poorer results than we would like. Successful control over their behavior is hampered by the children's lack of internal requisite controls necessary to contain themselves even with the promise of immediate rewards or the threat of punishments. Parents of the more seriously involved kids are frequently asked to withdraw their child from the preschool only to end up in a desperate search for another school that will be able to handle their child's problems. Such places are rare, and often the parent ends up relying on the good graces of another preschool director or teacher who is willing to give their child a second (or third) chance.

Fortunately, the majority of the preschool age children described by their parents as inattentive and overactive will show improvement in these areas as they mature. However, for those children whose hyperactivity and conduct problems persist for at least one year, there is a much stronger likelihood that they will have continuing difficulty in these areas and may more likely receive a diagnosis of attention deficit disorder or oppositional defiant disorder in the future.

The Elementary School-Aged Child with ADD

Most ADD children will be identified by the time they reach third or fourth grade in school. By this time they have had school problems for several years with consistent reports of short attention span, distractibility, organizational difficulties, hyperactivity, and self-control problems. They may have been retained in a grade or placed in a transitional program such as "prefirst" or "kindergarten plus" to give them more time to strengthen weak developmental skills, but nevertheless, their problems will persist despite such interventions.

The course of their disorder in school may improve or deteriorate from year to year, depending to some extent upon a teacher's classroom style and attitude. However, as academic demands requiring attentiveness, organization, planning, and independent work increase, the elementary school-aged ADD child's problems generally multiply.

Learning disorders, which may have gone unnoticed up to now, begin to emerge. Up to 25% of ADD children will exhibit serious learning impairments or learning disabilities which affect their academic achievement. These problems may show themselves in an inability to read well, write correctly, or solve mathematical problems. Communication disorders, either oral or written, may become obvious as more demands are placed on the child to comprehend information and use language.

Daily completion of classwork may become a problem. For the ADD child who is unable to attend to a teacher's instructions, getting started on assignements can become a troublesome activity. For the ADD child who is unable to stay focused on a task, either because they are distracted by other aspects of the classroom environment or because they distract themselves with their own thoughts, unfinished work piles up higher and higher. For the ADD child who has organizational problems and cannot find paper to write on, pencils to write with, or the proper books to use, the process of completing a task from begining to end becomes too complicated to resolve.

Homework can become a parent's nightmare as well as a child's drudgery. The many skills it takes to do homework (e.g. write the homework assignment in class, bring the proper books and materials home, settle down after school to concentrate on work, put the completed homework away in the proper place, remember to bring it to school the next day, retrieve the work from a notebook or folder to hand to the teacher) may challenge the organizational and attentional skills of an ADD child.

Socialization plays an increasingly important part in the daily life of a child as he progresses through elementary school. Researchers who have studied the social behavior of ADD children indicate that hyperactive children tend to be disliked by their classmates. Their behavior is too much even for other children to tolerate. They have a tendency to be bossy, disruptive, and immature. They cannot read social cues well and become overly intrusive with other children, ignoring social conventions such as waiting one's turn, exhibiting modesty about oneself, sharing in an activity, etc.. These are learned social skills that are easily acquired by most children in elementary school, but which are not well demonstrated by

ADD children.

At home, depending on whether the elementary school-age ADD child is hyperactive or not, he will present various management problems as well. If the child is primarily inattentive, but not necessarily hyperactive, he will leave a trail of unfinished tasks: uncovered toothpaste in the bathroom, clothes scattered about the floor of the bedroom, bed unmade, toys and books left wherever they were last used, games started and unfinished, tomorrow's math homework paper mixed in with last month's spelling, dresser drawers bulging from unfolded clothes, and on and on. If hyperactivity is also present along with impulsivity the picture at home becomes even more chaotic: toys scattered and broken, walls marked up, frequent family arguments over listening, meals disrupted by fighting, shopping trips marred by relentless demands, sibling conflicts, and frayed nerves.

Patterns of academic frustration and failure, social rejection, and criticism from parents and teachers build in elementary school to the point where other disorders associated with ADD begin to appear. As noted earlier, approximately 60% of these children will develop oppositional disorder characterized by defiant and non-compliant behavior. Frustrated by their lack of success, these children may become irritable and sullen. About half of this group of oppositional children will develop an even more serious behavior disorder in adolescence, namely conduct disorder (CD). Many ADD children will suffer low self-esteem due to their inability to achieve the same levels of success as their peers. Still others will develop serious depression.

The Adolescent with ADD

We used to think that ADD children outgrew the disorder in adolescence. We now know that this is not the case. Long-term follow-up studies clearly indicate that many children diagnosed as having ADD in childhood will continue to have marked symptoms of the disorder well into adolescence and even into adulthood. Dr. Russell Barkley estimates that over 80% of children diagnosed with ADD in early childhood will continue to have symptoms of overactivity, inattention and impulsivity through their adolescence.

As the child matures, ADD symptoms change qualitatively. The most striking difference is in motor activity. Hyperactivity, often so apparent in the young ADD child, has usually lessened by adolescence to the point where the ADD teenager may be indistinguishable from normal teens in that respect. Dr. Gabrielle Weiss and colleagues followed a large number of ADD children over time. When they were seen in adolescence at nearly 14 years of age, most of them still had symptoms of ADD. Though they were better than when they were younger, they still showed impulsive cognitive styles, difficulties with attention, and were having significant academic problems as well. Low self-esteem, poor peer relationships, depressive symptoms, and problems with anti-social behavior can be characteristic of ADD adolescents.

School problems can intensify in middle and high school. Greater demands are placed on students in secondary schools. They have more teachers to cope with, more work to be responsible for, more activities to organize, and they tend to be less closely supervised by teachers and parents. The ADD adolescent starts middle school with several teachers each of whom probably has two hundred or more students to keep track of. It is easy to get lost in the shuffle.

Teens with ADD show significantly higher rates of academic performance problems than non-ADD adolescents. According to a recent outcome study, they are much more likely to fail a grade or receive a suspension from school and are also more likely to be expelled or to drop out. Furthermore, their scores on academic achievement tests generally fall below average.

However, the most troublesome outcomes for ADD adolescents occur for those who develop a conduct disorder. Teens with conduct disorder are much more likely to lie, steal, abuse alcohol and drugs, be truant from school, and eventually drop out. Dr. Russell Barkley followed ADD children through their teenage years. He found that approximately 43% of the ADD adolescents exhibited signs of conduct disorder as compared to less than 2% of a control group. Teens who showed evidence of ADD (but who did not develop conduct disorder) had substantially more difficulty in school than non-ADD adolescents, but had a much better outlook than the ADD/conduct disorder group.

There are several factors which are associated with more positive outcomes for adolescents with ADD. Higher family socioeconomic status and higher intellectual ability affects outcome positively. ADD teens who are less aggressive do better than those who exhibit aggressive behavior. ADD adolescents whose families show low rates of family dysfunction and who have less conflict with their parents have greater chances for future success. Finally, those ADD teens who do well academically will have better outcomes than those who do not.

In summary, symptoms of attention deficit disorder which appear in the young preschool child may persist throughout childhood and adolescence. Extreme hyperactivity, aggressive behavior, and impulsive responding to frustating or exciting stimulation can create innumerable problems in the management of the preschooler at home or in school. While behavior can begin to settle down in the elementary school years, demands from school on attention span, organization, and persistence continue to create problems for the ADD pre-teen. Adolescence brings a lessening of hyperactivity, but even greater school demands. ADD adolescents may develop serious behavioral and emotional problems. The course of the disorder can continue into adulthood as up to 40% of ADD adolescents will retain symptoms of the disorder into their adult years.

Chapter 4
Assessment of ADD

The primary characteristics of ADD are not difficult to spot in a classroom. However, not all children who exhibit signs of inattention, impulsivity, or hyperactivity have attention deficit disorder. These same symptoms can be the result of numerous factors. Children who are frustrated by difficult schoolwork may display inattention. Students who are preoccupied by problems at home, with friends, or elsewhere may have trouble staying focused and concentrating. Nervousness can produce restless, fidgeting behavior. Unmotivated students often do not complete assignments or pay attention. Certain medical conditions can result in inattention. Many of these problems are commonly found in children and should not be confused with ADD.

For example:

1. Difficulty with school assignments can cause inattention.

Joseph had trouble in school ever since he transferred from Norcross Elementary across town to his new school. Fifth grade was fifth grade his mother had told him, and he didn't have to worry about being able to do the work. However, Joseph was having more trouble now than he ever had before. He used to be the first one in his class to raise his hand and now he hardly ever knows the right answers. He's getting discouraged and finds himself daydreaming a great deal. He can't seem to get his work finished and he wishes he could return to his old school.

2. Being worried or depressed can cause inattention.

Susan's parents were recently separated. Since then her life hasn't been the same. Her father moved out and found an apartment, her mother got a new job with better pay, but longer hours, and Susan's grandmother moved in with them to help out. Susan misses her father and worries about him being alone. She frequently hears her mother telling others that they have financial problems, and she knows her mother doesn't like working so hard. Susan wishes things were back the way they were before her parents split up, but deep down inside she knows that won't happen. With all these problems on her mind, Susan is having difficulty concentrating in school.

3. Some medications can cause inattention and hyperactivity.

Jeff has suffered from asthma since he was a preschooler. It got so bad sometimes that breathing became very difficult. Things got better after his doctor diagnosed his condition and gave him medication which improved his respiration. However, whenever he takes the asthma medication he gets "hyper" and gets in trouble in school.

4. Students who are learning English as a second language may have trouble paying attention.

English is a second language for Ana. She just moved to this country from South America and her family always spoke Spanish. She's having a hard time catching on in seventh grade and most of the time she doesn't understand the teacher or the other students. Being bored her mind wanders, and she often cannot force herself to pay attention to things she doesn't understand.

5. Lack of motivation to succeed in school can cause inattention and acting out.

Every year Robert's teachers say the same thing, that he is just not working up to his ability. He doesn't seem to care. Robert sits in class and talks to others, fools around, and disrupts the class, but he doesn't pay attention or complete assignments. Homework is never done, and when it is completed it usually contains numerous mistakes. Robert's teachers send notes home almost every other day, but they never hear from his parents. It sometimes seems that his parents don't care whether Robert receives a good education or not.

For many children the factors that cause inattention, impulsivity or hyperactivity may be immediately obvious and do not require any extensive investigation. However, a significant number of children who exhibit ADD-like behavior will need further assessment to determine if they really have an attention deficit disorder.

Experts recommend that an educational assessment of children who are suspected of having an attention deficit disorder should be a two-tiered process (PGARD, Notice of Inquiry Response, 1990). Tier 1 of the assessment should determine whether a child meets criteria for a diagnosis of attention deficit disorder. If the tier 1 assessment confirms the presence of ADD, then a tier 2 evaluation would be required. Tier 2 of the assessment should determine the degree to which the ADD child's educational performance is impaired. Tier 2 assessments will help determine what types of educational services are necessary to assist the student.

Tier 1: The Diagnostic Evaluation for ADD

Physicians, clinical and school psychologists, social workers, regular education teachers, guidance counselors and others might all participate in providing information about the child suspected of having an attention deficit disorder. The diagnosis of ADD should be made by professionals certified to make such a diagnosis. Unless restricted by law, properly trained school personnel who are currently conducting evaluations of children suspected of having other disabling conditions may be capable of doing tier 1 diagnostic assessments for ADD.

Diagnosing attention deficit disorder requires gathering information about the child from a number of sources and in a variety of ways. Medical information, parent or guardian descriptions of the child's physical, mental, social, and emotional development, school information, descriptions of social behavior and classroom adjustment, and assessment of the child's cognitive functioning are essential to making a diagnosis. Procedures for collecting such information include direct assessment of the child through medical examination, interviews with the child, interviews with parents or guardians and teachers, and cognitive testing. Each of these methods of information gathering will be discussed in the following sections.

Medical Evaluation of the Child

The child's pediatrician or family physician is often the first person parents talk to when they suspect their child is having a problem. The physician, usually familiar with the child's medical history and already having some knowledge of the family through previous treatment contact, is in a good position to help the parent. However, depending on what the doctor says, the assessment process may begin or end with this first request for help.

In the past, physicians have been criticized either for not taking parents seriously enough when they believed their child had a significant attention or behavior problem or, at the other extreme, for being too quick to prescribe medication to take care of the problem without first having a comprehensive assessment done. Many physicians, even pediatricians, have not had a great deal of training in child psychology or education during medical school, internship or residency programs. On one hand, the doctor may overlook a potential problem and just give well-meaning advice to the parent when indeed much more is needed to help the child and the family adjust. Parents go home and follow the doctor's advice, but to no avail as the child continues to have problems. The parents end up feeling even more frustrated and will often question their own adequacy in parenting the child. On the other hand, the doctor may prematurely offer medication for the child as a means of handling the problem without doing a full assessment. In such circumstances the parent who gives the child medicine does so without a full understanding of the child's problem and without being aware of other treatments the child may need. This often results in misconceptions about ADD, and compliance to medication usage in such cases is usually only short-term.

The process of "advising" or "prescribing" without comprehensive assessment is much less common now than it has been in the past. Physicians, like other professionals, have become more knowledgeable about attentional deficits and are more careful about obtaining comprehensive assessments prior to treatment planning. They often will start by interviewing the parent about the child's adjustment and behavior at home, in school and with peers. They will also spend considerable time reviewing the child's genetic background, early birth history, and developmental and medical history. Taking a careful medical history may alert the doctor to previous health problems which could account for the development of ADD-like symptoms. In rare circumstances, the ADD may be related to some previous injury, head trauma, central nervous system infection, or cerebral-vascular illness.

The physician will usually proceed by physically examining the child. Routine physical examinations of ADD children are often normal and provide little help in diagnosis or management of the disorder, but they are definitely needed to rule out the unlikely possibility of another medical illness which could cause ADD symptoms. For instance, the child may be having absence seizures, a neurological disorder which could account for problems with inattention. Or the child may be taking medication which could cause or aggravate attentional difficulties. Certain asthma medications, Theophylline, for example, are known to affect children's attention span. Or the child may have other health problems which would preclude the use of certain medications to manage the ADD. For example, a personal or family history of tic disorders or Gilles de la Tourette's syndrome may make one cautious about the use of stimulant medication for the child. In addition, the presence of high blood pressure or cardiac problems may give concern about the use of stimulants or some anti-depressants, since these medications can affect the cardiovascular system.

Although no specific laboratory test is available to diagnose ADD, the physician may want certain laboratory tests done to determine the overall health of the child. However, such tests as chromosome studies, electroencephalograms (EEGs), magnetic resonance imaging (MRI), or computerized axial tomograms (CT scans) should not be used routinely for evaluation of ADD. Such procedures may be necessary when the physical examination of the child or the medical history suggests that a genetic syndrome or other health problem may be present. In such cases, referrals to other medical specialists such as neurologists, psychiatrists, or endocrinologists may be needed. Consultation with non-medical specialists such as clinical or school psychologists, speech and language therapists, and psychoeducational specialists may also be needed to provide additional information about the child's level of adaptive functioning in a variety of areas and to rule out any other potential problems.

Since ADD is now considered by the U.S. Department of Education to be a health impairment, some states may require that children suspected of having ADD who are being evaluated for special education receive a medical evaluation, even though the new federal policy does **not** require a medical diagnosis (Schrag, 1992 Personal communication). This will require a strengthening of school-community professional partnerships. Teachers and physicians, previously unaccustomed to talking with one another directly about student (patient) performance, will need better communication if accurate data is to be obtained for purposes of medical diagnosis and follow-up care.

The Parent Interview

The interview done with the child's parent (or guardian) is probably the most important component of the assessment process. Having witnessed the child in a variety of situations over a number of years, parents have a unique perspective on their child's previous development and current adjustment. More than any other adult, the child's parents have the fullest view of the child, therefore the information they provide is vital to the assessment process.

However, parents bring more than just information about the child to the interviewer. Usually they also bring with them a mixture of emotions about themselves, their child, and the school. For some parents the interview will be their first attempt at getting help for the child and will be the first time they've ever talked to anyone outside the family about their child's problems. Other parents will be "old hats" at discussing these issues, having sought help for their son or daughter many times in the past. In either case, the parents are likely to have been deeply affected by their son's or daughter's problems. The interviewer will need to be sensitive, understanding, and nonjudgmental in talking to the child's parents. Given such understanding, the parents are likely to establish a positive rapport with the interviewer and may benefit from the opportunity to express the difficulties and worries they have faced over the years in raising their child.

Usually done by a health care professional, school psychologist, or properly trained member of the school's child study team, the parent interview is intended primarily to document important events from the child's medical, developmental, social, and academic history relevant to the assessment of ADD. Additionally, however, the interview process also provides an opportunity to learn more about relationships among family members, the type of parent-child interactions which exist in the home, the parents' perceptions of the child's problems, outcomes of other attempts to obtain help for the child, and a host of other information. The interview should optimally be held with both parents as informants. It can take one or two hours to collect a complete history, depending on the complexity of the child's problems.

Document the Presenting Problems

One portion of the interview should focus on whether the child exhibits characteristics of ADD behavior in the home and school environment. The age of onset of these problems, their duration and intensity, and the situations within which ADD characteristics occur should be documented.

Frequently the interview will start with a review of current difficulties. Often parents of children or adolescents with ADD will report that their child has had a long history of school related problems. Consistent reports from teachers frequently describe difficulties with attention, work completion, and social or behavioral adjustment. Typically statements such as, "Jason's teachers say he has trouble paying attention...he doesn't finish his work...he talks too much and he's very distractible" are commonly expressed during the initial parent interview. Parents will report additional problems which typify children with poor impulse control: "He can't control his temper...is bossy with others...is impatient...doesn't think before he acts." Comments such as, "He can't sit still...always has to be busy doing something....She constantly talks" refer to the hyperactive component of the syndrome. Parents typically describe difficulties with rule-following and with listening at home which, in adolescence, may turn into more serious behavior problems. Parents of non-hyperactive ADD children, on the other hand, describe less oppositional behavior and report little hyperactivity at home, but are concerned about the child's chronic inattention, spacey, daydreamy state of mind, and generally passive or anxious disposition. This group of ADD children may have even more trouble finishing assignments in school, as they lack the drive to compete and seem to work in slow motion much of the time.

Document the Developmental and Medical History

Another portion of the parent interview should review the early birth, developmental, and medical history of the child. Questions should be asked about previous illnesses, accidents, and hospitalizations that the child may have had. Does the child take any medications that could result in ADD-like symptoms? Was he evaluated and treated before? If so, by whom, and what was that professional's conclusions and recommendations?

It is also important to determine if either biological parent has had a history of attentional difficulties or learning problems in school. Frequently problems with inattention, reading, handwriting, etc. may have existed in other biological relatives, but were not diagnosed as attention deficit disorder or a specific learning disability.

Document Information About the Family

This portion of the interview should document the family's socioeconomic status, ethnic or minority status, amount of exposure the child has had to the language of educational instruction, and any significant family problems or stressors which affect family functioning.

The interviewer should take a detailed history of the child's family make-up. The marital history of the parents and their educational and occupational backgrounds, ages of the child's siblings and their adjustment history, the atmosphere in the home and how family members get along are all important factors for which to account. Determine what stressors, if any, exist in the family and how the family adjusts to such pressures. Frequently life with an ADD child can be quite stressful resulting in marital disharmony, depression, and tension in the home.

It is important to document how the family has coped with the child's difficulties up to now. To this end, it is helpful to understand the quality of family relationships within the home, parental discipline styles, behavioral interventions currently utilized by the parents, consistency of parental interaction with the child, quality and quantity of time spent with the child, and other factors related to the home and family.

Document Information About the Child in School

The interview should document the parents' perceptions as to the child's previous academic performance in school. Going through the child's school history, grade by grade, and asking about school performance, learning problems, and socialization each year may reveal a pattern of chronic inattention, impulsivity, and overactivity common to hyperactive ADD children. Parents of ADD children without hyperactivity usually do not report significant behavioral difficulties, but typically recall teachers describing their child as inattentive, spacey, and excessively quiet in class.

Document Information About the Child and Peers

Questioning parents about the child's friends often reveals problems the child may have in getting along with others. Such problems may be due to the ADD youngster's impatient and intrusive social style. It is common for hyperactive ADD children to play with kids younger than themselves since their immaturity is likely to be better accepted by younger children. In the case of children who have ADD without hyperactivity, social problems may be due to lack of assertiveness and social withdrawal.

The interviewer should prepare a written summary of the relevant findings of the interview which should become part of the evaluation report. Dr. Russell A. Barkley (1990) and Dr. Sam Goldstein (1990) have each written texts on the subject of attention deficit disorder which contain lengthy discussions about the parent interview process. For more detail the reader should consult these sources. They have each also developed comprehensive questionnaires to be completed by parents prior to coming to the interview, or by the interviewer as he discusses the family history with the parents. These textbooks and interview forms are available through the ADD WareHouse (800-ADD-WARE, 300 Northwest 70th Avenue, Plantation, Florida 33317).

The Teacher Interview

ADD assessments should include teacher interviews regarding the student's classroom performance. Brief interviews of teachers either over the phone or in person are frequently done during the course of evaluating a child. However, such interviews have typically been an informal and unsystematic part of the assessment process. They frequently provide useful information about how the child is functioning in the classroom, but often do not result in accurate problem identification or the identification of environmental events that trigger or maintain academic or social behavior problems in school settings.

Teachers, although being an important source of information about the child, are not utilized as well as they should be in the assessment process. This may be because of the emphasis that has been placed on using standardized, norm-referenced tests of intelligence, perception, personality, and academic achievement and on the failure of psychology training programs to include training in doing teacher interviews. For quite some time the perception has existed that data gathered from testing methods was superior to data obtained from teachers, resulting in an overreliance on test data for placement considerations.

Drs. Frank Gresham and C.J. Davis (1988), in a review of interview procedures, discuss the differences between the traditional teacher interview and the behavioral interview format which is recommended as part of a curriculum-based assessment process. The behavioral interview focuses on the specification and delineation of target behaviors, the identification and analysis of environmental conditions surrounding target behaviors, and the use of this information to formulate, implement and evaluate interventions. In a behavior interview, information is obtained regarding the student's skill strengths and weaknesses and other social, emotional, or behavioral characteristics. The student's adjustment in class should relate to aspects of the instructional environment, namely: the curriculum in which the student is working; teacher's expectations for the class and for the individual student; methods of instruction employed by the teacher; incentives for work completion; methods of teacher feedback to students; and comparative performance of other students in the class. The traditional teacher interview, by comparison, is more vague and does not focus upon current environmental conditions that may be maintaining problem behavior, but instead focuses on historical information about the child.

Behavioral interviews with the child's teacher have several advantages over other assessment procedures such as rating scales, cognitive testing, and direct observation. First, the behavioral interview offers flexibility as to the type and amount of data one could receive regarding the student. The interviewer has the flexibility to explore areas of interest as they come up which could provide additional understanding of the child's problems. This flexibility is not available in other assessment methods. Second, the interview process is not only an opportunity to collect information about the child, but also serves as a starting point for the interviewer to assess the teacher's receptivity to intervention strategies and to evaluate any misconceptions or unrealistic expectations that the teacher may have concerning the child.

During the interview process the teacher and interviewer seek to organize information about the child, and as they do so the problem situation tends to get clarified. In some cases it may become apparent that the child is having attentional problems because he is being asked to do work which is at his frustration level, or perhaps the child is being influenced by other factors in the classroom. Those readers who would like more information on specific methods by which to conduct behavioral interviews should consider Sylvia Rosenfeld's book *Instructional Consultation* (1987).

The Child Interview

An interview with the child is an indispensable part of the assessment process. Depending upon the child's age and intellectual development, one or more interviews will be held with the child in order to make observations about behavior, appearance, and development and to obtain information about how the child perceives himself in relation to others.

Observations made during the interview sessions about the child's behavior, level of activity, attentiveness, or compliance with the interviewer's requests should not be taken as true of the child in other settings. Most ADD children behave well during such interviews and can exhibit excellent attention and self-control. Rarely do they act out or display hyperactivity or impulsive behavior at these times. However, normal behavior in a one-on-one setting does not decrease the likelihood of the child being ADD. Unfortunately, some practitioners place greater weight on their own observations of the child than on the descriptions of behavior received from the parents or the teacher. The, "He looked fine to me" (there must be something wrong with how you're raising him or teaching him) mentality can be highly destructive to the assessment process and sends a message to the parents or the teacher that their perceptions of the child are invalid.

Often the interview with the child will begin by asking the child the purpose for his coming to the interview that day. Most children who are interviewed in a clinical office have been told by their parents what to expect and are able to offer some explanation of their problems to the interviewer. With careful listening and frequent reassurance, the interviewer can spend a brief time encouraging the child to talk about some of his difficulties. The initial tension the child feels can then be relaxed by turning to lighter topics for discussion, such as: the child's interests, pets in the family, trips taken, and favorite television shows or movies.

After a while the child may be asked to provide factual information about family members, school, and friendships. Light questioning of this sort provides more structure to the interview, gives direction to the child, and encourages the child to get into a conversational mode. As the interview proceeds, more open-ended questions may be asked in an effort to obtain the child's impressions and feelings. Typically questioning of this type would involve discussion of family, school, and social interactions. During this time the interviewer can gently probe deeper into problem areas which the parents may have brought up earlier. The purpose of this line of questioning would be to ascertain whether there is agreement between parent and child as to specific problems and to determine the child's perception as to the cause or severity of such problems.

It is important to help the child feel comfortable during the interview process. The interviewer needs to take great care not to be accusatory, judgmental, or unhappy with the child's reports, but should instead be concerned, interested, and helpful. As the child relaxes, questioning can proceed in the area of affective disclosure. Asking the child to talk about things he worries about, feels sad about, or things that make him upset or angry, helps the interviewer gain information about emotional factors which could contribute to the child's adjustment and behavior.

Before ending the interview the child should be reassured that the information he provided will be helpful in understanding him better. If further evaluation is going to be done, the child should be given a brief description of what he can expect the next time he comes to the office. The interview should end on a positive note with the child feeling that his participation in the assessment process is important and that the end result of all this effort will be to provide help to him and his family.

Behavior Rating Scales

A variety of rating scales have been developed over the past twenty-five years to determine whether a child is having adjustment problems and, if so, the severity of such problems. Earlier scales developed in the 1960's and 1970's, were normed on small samples and lacked rigorous standardization. Newer scales provided much more superior measures because they utilized a broader pool of items, employed newer rating formats, and were developed on larger samples of subjects, therefore resulting in better standardization.

Behavior rating scales can offer valid and reliable information about a child, thus providing a means by which to compare a child's behavior to that of others of the same sex and age. Most of the rating scales used to assess ADD provide standardized scores on a number of factors, usually related to attention span, self-control, learning ability, hyperactivity, aggression, social behavior, anxiety, etc.. In some respects rating scale measures may be superior to more informal methods of data collection. They provide a standard set of behaviors to be evaluated thereby reducing variability in the information that is obtained about the child and ensuring that specific target behaviors will be assessed. They offer a means by which to evaluate the frequency and severity of specific behaviors and provide age and sex-graded norms to determine whether reported behaviors are appropriate or deviant in relation to normal peers. Rater bias and subjectivity of responding is reduced by using a standardized presentation of questions. Compared with other assessment procedures such as psychological testing, direct observation, or interviewing, rating scales are simple, quick, and economical in terms of cost and expenditure of professional time.

Although they are a quick and easy method by which to gather information, rating scales have significant shortcomings and, therefore, should not be overly relied upon. First, data obtained from such ratings rely totally on the rater's familiarity with the child and, to some extent, upon the rater's familiarity with normative behavior of other children of the same sex and age. Thus, elementary school teachers, who spend several hours a day with a student, for example, may be more familiar with the student's behavior than a middle or high school teacher whose contact with the student is limited to one period per day. Therefore, in secondary education settings it is essential to receive ratings from several teachers so as to accurately assess behavior throughout the day. Second, rating scales are also subject to rater bias based upon other characteristics of the child, e.g. likeable children may be rated less negatively on scales of hyperactivity and inattention than aggressive/stubborn children. Third, rating scales can be subject to rater bias based upon characteristics of the rater as well, e.g. mothers who are depressed rate their children as having greater behavior problems than do non-depressed mothers.

Despite these shortcomings, behavior rating scales can offer important information which is helpful in the ADD assessment process. Separate scales have been developed for parents and teachers since each informant will rate behaviors relevant to their areas of involvement with the child.

Rating Scales To Be Completed by Teachers

Some of the more popular rating scales developed to assess a child's behavior are:

- Conners Teacher Rating Scale (CTRS)
- IOWA-Conners Rating Scale
- SNAP Rating Scale
- ADD-H:Comprehensive Teacher Rating Scale (ACTeRS)
- ADHD Rating Scale (Parents and Teachers)
- Child Attention Profile
- School Situations Questionnaire
- Home Situations Questionnaire
- Child Behavior Checklist (CBCL)
- Academic Performance Rating Scale (APRS)

None of these scales directly measure the student's behavior in the classroom, but instead provide a measure of the teacher's appraisal of behavior.

The Conners Teacher Rating Scales

The Conners Teacher Rating Scale-39 (CTRS-39) was the first standardized rating scale designed to assess teacher perceptions of hyperactivity and other learning and behavioral problems. The scale contains 39 descriptors of behavior which are rated by the teacher along a continuum of frequency from not at all, just a little, pretty much, very much. Ratings are coded as 0, 1, 2, 3 respectively. The CTRS -39 contains five factors: Daydreaming-Inattentive, Hyperactivity, Conduct Problems, Anxious-Fearful, and Sociable-Cooperative. The Conners Teacher Rating Scales -28 (CTRS-28) is a shortened version of the 39 item scale and is scored in the same manner, but provides four factors: Conduct Problem, Hyperactivity, Inattentive-Passive, Hyperactivity Index.

The CTRS-39 was originally developed by Dr. Keith Conners in 1969 to evaluate changes in behavior for children being treated with medication. For the past twenty years Conners rating scales have been used in numerous studies and are very widely used in clinical practice. Normative data is available on children as young as three years of age and up to age seventeen. With the newly published quick-scoring forms these scales are very easy to use.

The Abbreviated Symptom Questionnaire (ASQ-T) is a brief scale composed of the ten items making up the Hyperactivity Index of the CTRS-39 and CTRS-28. Several versions of this scale have been used. The ASQ-T may be useful in obtaining follow-up data on the student when time does not permit for more extensive assessment by the teacher. A portion of the ASQ-T can be found on page 52.

The CTRS-39, CTRS-28, and ASQ-T are available through the ADD WareHouse (800) ADD-WARE or through the scales' publishers, Multi-Health Systems, Inc., 908 Niagara Falls Boulevard, North Tonawanda, New York 14120-2060.

Criticism of the Conners Rating Scales, particularly the 10-item Abbreviated Symptom Questionnaire, centers around the scales' difficulty in distinguishing children who have problems with inattention versus problems with aggression. Because of this, several other scales have evolved from the Conners and were developed to more aptly discriminate children with primary problems related to inattention from those with aggression-related problems.

The IOWA-Conners Rating Scale

The IOWA-Conners Rating Scale was developed in 1981 by Jan Loney and Richard Milich due to concerns that the original Conners was not able to sufficiently discriminate ADD children from children with aggression or conduct disorders. The IOWA-Conners contains 10 items from the original 39-item Conners, five of which measure attention/overactivity and five of which measure aggression, but which are not correlated with inattention.

The SNAP Rating Scale

In 1984, a team of researchers developed the Swanson Nolan and Pelham (SNAP) Rating Scale as an alternative measure to the CTRS and the IOWA-Conners. The SNAP contains items which evaluate core symptoms of ADD, namely, inattention, impulsivity, and hyperactivity as well as additional items to assess peer-related aggression. SNAP items are based on the DSM III criteria for attention deficit disorder. The SNAP Rating Scale (and normative data) is contained on pages 62-63 with the permission of Dr. James Swanson.

The ADD-H Comprehensive Teacher Rating Scale (ACTeRS)

The ADD-H: Comprehensive Teacher Rating Scale (ACTeRS) by Rina K. Ullmann, M.Ed., Esther K. Sleator, M.D. and Robert L. Sprague, Ph.D. was developed for identifying and monitoring the behavior of children from kindergarten to fifth grade who manifest deficits in attention span or demonstrate unusually active or restless behavior in the classroom.

The ACTeRS scale contain 24 items relevant to classroom behavior. The items are rated on a five-point scale and yield four factors: Attention, Hyperactivity, Social Skills, and Oppositional Behavior. The ACTeRS is easy to complete and to score. The ACTeRS is available through the ADD WareHouse (800) ADD-WARE, MetriTech, Inc., 111 North Market Street, Champaign, IL 61820, or Psychological Assessment Resources, Inc. 800-331-TEST.

The ADHD Rating Scale

The ADHD Rating Scale, developed by George DuPaul (1990), lists the 14 DSM III-R characteristics of ADD. Respondents are asked to rate the severity of these characteristics on a scale ranging from Not at all to Very Much. The scale can be completed by parents and teachers with separate norms available for each set of respondents. The ADHD Rating Scale (and normative data for both teachers and parents) is contained on pages 53-55 with the permission of Dr. George DuPaul.

The School Situations Questionnaire

The School Situations Questionnaire was developed as a means of assessing situational variability and the severity of behavior problems in a school setting. The scale consists of 12 situations and teachers are asked to what degree the child exhibits behavior problems in each one. The scale provides two scores: number of problem areas in which the child has trouble behaving, and the severity of behavior problems. The School Situations Questionnaire (and normative data) is contained on pages 56 - 57 with the permission of Dr. Russell A. Barkley.

The Child Attention Profile (CAP)

The Child Attention Profile (CAP) is composed of twelve items taken from the Inattention and Nervous-Overactive scales of the Child Behavior Checklist Teacher Report Form (CBCL-TRF). The CAP has two primary factors: Inattention and Overactivity. This scale is useful in subtyping ADD children into those with and without hyperactivity. The Child Attention Profile (and normative data) is contained on pages 60-61 with the permission of Dr. Craig Edelbrock.

The Child Behavior Checklist (CBCL-Teacher)

The Teacher Report Form of the Child Behavioral Checklist (CBCL-TRF), developed by Thomas Achenbach, Ph.D. and Craig Edelbrock, Ph.D., contains 118 items to be completed by the child's teacher. Separate scoring profiles are standardized for each sex at ages 6-11 and 12-16. Although not specifically developed to evaluate ADD the CBCL has been widely used for this reason and is a favored scale due to its comprehensiveness.

The CBCL-TRF yields eight problem scales: Anxious, Social Withdrawal, Depressed, Unpopular, Self-Destructive, Inattentive, Nervous-Overactive, and Aggressive. The CBCL-TRF provides global scores for internalizing and externalizing behaviors. A major strength of the CBCL-TRF is its usefulness for assessing affective disorders such as anxiety and depression in addition to factors related to behavioral disorders. In addition, the Inattentive and Nervous-Overactive scales have been found to identify children who meet criteria for ADD.

The CBCL-TRF is available through T.M. Achenbach, Ph.D., University Associates in Psychiatry/Dept. of Psychiatry, University of Vermont, 1 South Prospect St., Burlington, VT 05401.

Rating Scales To Be Completed by Parents

The Conners Parent Rating Scales

There are two forms of the Conners Parent Rating Scale. The CPRS-93 and CPRS-48 contain descriptors of behavior which are rated by the parent along a continuum of frequency from not at all, just a little, pretty much, very much. Ratings are coded as 0, 1, 2, 3 respectively. The newly published manual recommends that the CPRS-48 be used for clinical diagnostic applications. The scale provides six subscales: Conduct Problem, Learning Problem, Psychosomatic, Impulsive-Hyperactive, Anxiety, and Hyperactivity Index. Normative data is available on children as young as three years of age and up to age seventeen. As with the teacher versions of the scale, scoring is very easy. The CPRS-93 and CPRS-48 are available through ADD WareHouse (800) ADD-WARE or through the scale's publisher, Multi-Health Systems, Inc., 908 Niagara Falls Boulevard, North Tonawanda, New York 14120-2060.

The Home Situations Questionnaire

The Home Situations Questionnaire (Barkley, 1987) was developed as a means of assessing situational variability and severity of behavior problems in the home. The scale contains 16 home situations and asks the parent to rate the degree to which the child demonstrates problems with behavior in each situation. The scale provides two scores: number of problem situations and severity of behavior problems. The Home Situations Questionnaire (and normative data) is contained on on pages 58-59 with the permission of Dr. Russell A. Barkley.

The Child Behavior Checklist (CBCL-Parent)

The parent version of the Child Behavioral Checklist

(CBCL/4-16) contains 113 items to be completed by the parent and is designed to obtain standardized data on children's competencies and problems. The CBCL yields eight problem scales: Anxious, Social Withdrawal, Depressed, Unpopular, Self-Destructive, Inattentive, Nervous-Overactive, and Aggressive. The Inattentive and Nervous-Overactive scales have been found to identify children who meet criteria for ADHD.

A major strength of the CBCL is its usefulness for assessing affective disorders such as anxiety and depression in addition to factors related to behavioral disorders. Available for younger children is the CBCL/2-3, which was standardized on children two to three years old. Comprehensive manuals are published reviewing standardization, reliability, and validity data.

The CBCL is available through T.M. Achenbach, Ph.D., University Associates in Psychiatry/Dept. of Psychiatry, University of Vermont, 1 South Prospect St., Burlington, VT 05401.

The Personality Inventory for Children (PIC)

The Personality Inventory for Children (PIC), developed by Robert Wirt, Ph.D., David Lachar, Ph.D., James K. Klinedinst, Ph.D. and Philip D. Seat, Ph.D. is a parental report inventory. The PIC contains up to 600 items and provides descriptions of child behavior, affect, and cognitive functioning, along with factors relevant to family characteristics for children ages three to sixteen. The manual compares profiles of hyperactive and non-hyperactive children across various scales of the inventory.

While yielding considerably more information about personality functioning than some of the shorter rating scales, the PIC may not be as sensitive a measure of ADD characteristics and is not used as often as some of the other scales for the identification of ADD and assessment of treatment effectiveness. The PIC is available from Western Psychological Services, 12031 Wilshire Boulevard, Los Angeles, CA 90025.

ABBREVIATED SYMPTOM QUESTIONNAIRE -TEACHERS*

Child Rated:_____   Rater:_____

Day: _____   Date: _____   Time: _____ *am pm*

Instructions

Read each item below carefully, and decide how much you think your student has been bothered by this problem today/this week/this month. For each behavior described below, circle one number to indicate how much of a problem that behavior was for your student.

Not at All	Just a Little	Pretty Much	Very Much	
0	1	2	3	Restless in the "squirmy" sense
0	1	2	3	Temper outbursts, unpredictable behavior
0	1	2	3	Distractibility or attention span a problem
0	1	2	3	Disturbs other children
0	1	2	3	Pouts and sulks
0	1	2	3	Mood changes quickly and drastically

*Six out of ten items printed.

Reprinted with permission of Multi-Health Systems, 908 Niagara Falls Blvd., North Tonawanda, NY 14120-2060 (800) 456-3003.

ADHD RATING SCALE

Child's Name_____ Age_____ Grade_____

Completed by _____

Circle the number in the one column which best describes the child.

	Not at all	Just a little	Pretty much	Very much
1. Often fidgets or squirms in seat.	0	1	2	3
2. Has difficulty remaining seated	0	1	2	3
3. Is easily distracted	0	1	2	3
4. Has difficulty awaiting turn in groups.	0	1	2	3
5. Often blurts out answers to questions.	0	1	2	3
6. Has difficulty following instructions.	0	1	2	3
7. Has difficulty sustaining attention to tasks.	0	1	2	3
8. Often shifts from one uncompleted activity to another.	0	1	2	3
9. Has difficulty playing quietly	0	1	2	3
10. Often talks excessively	0	1	2	3
11. Often interrupts or intrudes on others.	0	1	2	3
12. Often does not seem to listen	0	1	2	3
13. Often loses things necessary for tasks	0	1	2	3
14. Often engages in physically dangerous activites without considering consequences.	0	1	2	3

Note: From "Parent and teacher ratings of ADHD Symptoms: Psychometric properties in a community-based sample by G. J. DuPaul, *Journal of Clinical Child Psychology, 20,* 245-253. Reprinted with permission.

ADHD RATING SCALE SCORING INSTRUCTIONS

For Teachers:
Three scores are calculated for the scale:
Total Score: Sum items 1 - 14
Inattention-Restlessness: Sum items 1-3, 6-8, 12-14
Impulsivity-Hyperactivity: Sum items 1, 2, 4, 5, 9-11, 14

Means and Standard Deviations: Teacher-Completed ADHD Rating Scale by Gender and Age

Age	Boys			Girls		
	Total	Factor I	Factor II	Total	Factor I	Factor II
6 years (n = 55)						
M	12.04	7.88	6.19	8.69	5.83	4.31
SD	12.17	7.60	6.64	9.88	5.97	5.87
7 years (n = 89)						
M	13.46	8.41	7.17	10.47	7.12	5.40
SD	11.52	7.58	7.65	11.37	7.36	6.10
8 years (n = 102)						
M	10.81	6.52	6.00	8.54	6.00	3.86
SD	9.94	6.23	5.94	9.36	6.21	5.26
9 years (n = 89)						
M	13.46	8.17	7.34	9.67	5.85	5.21
SD	12.41	7.51	7.09	10.22	6.26	6.13
10 years (n = 84)						
M	11.82	7.67	5.82	7.44	5.15	3.34
SD	10.46	6.98	5.92	8.44	6.10	4.44
11 years (n = 96)						
M	13.98	8.93	6.90	7.18	4.36	3.78
SD	13.25	7.81	7.71	9.29	5.71	5.51
12 years (n = 36)						
M	12.10	7.05	6.50	7.19	4.75	3.31
SD	8.12	5.55	4.54	8.14	5.22	4.32

Note: From "Parent and teacher ratings of ADHD Symptoms: Psychometric properties in a community-based sample by G. J. DuPaul, *Journal of Clinical Child Psychology, 20*, 245-253. Reprinted with permission.

ADHD RATING SCALE SCORING INSTRUCTIONS

For Parents:
Three scores are calculated for the scale:
Total Score: Sum items 1 - 14
Inattention-Restlessness: Sum items 1-3, 6-8, 12-14
Impulsivity-Hyperactivity: Sum items 1, 2, 4, 5, 9-11, 14

Means and Standard Deviations: Parent-Completed ADHD Rating Scale by Gender and Age

Age	Boys			Girls		
	Total	Factor I	Factor II	Total	Factor I	Factor II
6 years (n =113)						
M	13.71	8.54	8.08	11.50	7.18	6.56
SD	9.66	6.58	5.70	9.51	6.42	5.44
7 years (n = 117)						
M	13.69	8.96	7.69	10.65	6.67	5.83
SD	11.89	8.06	6.90	8.95	5.72	5.08
8 years (n = 108)						
M	16.21	10.70	8.96	10.92	6.92	5.77
SD	10.97	7.60	6.01	8.71	5.97	4.72
9 years (n = 94)						
M	14.08	9.19	7.65	11.23	7.26	5.93
SD	10.40	7.11	6.08	9.27	6.34	4.96
10 years (n = 105)						
M	13.71	9.65	6.73	10.68	6.64	5.66
SD	10.22	7.75	5.25	10.18	6.39	6.01
11 years (n = 80)						
M	13.91	9.22	7.34	7.34	4.63	3.63
SD	11.69	8.08	6.58	9.25	6.06	4.90
12 years (n = 52)						
M	15.34	10.79	7.21	7.70	5.22	3.65
SD	10.72	7.59	5.57	10.15	6.42	5.69

Note: From "Parent and teacher ratings of ADHD Symptoms: Psychometric properties in a community-based sample by G. J. DuPaul, *Journal of Clinical Child Psychology, 20*, 245-253. Reprinted with permission.

SCHOOL SITUATIONS QUESTIONNAIRE

Child's Name_____   Date_____

Name of Person Completing This Form_____

Instructions: Does this child present any behavior problems for you in any of these situations? If so, indicate how severe they are.

Situations	*Yes / No* (Circle one)	*If yes, how severe?* Mild (Circle one) Severe
While arriving at school	Yes No	1 2 3 4 5 6 7 8 9
During individual deskwork	Yes No	1 2 3 4 5 6 7 8 9
During small-group activities	Yes No	1 2 3 4 5 6 7 8 9
During free play time in class	Yes No	1 2 3 4 5 6 7 8 9
During lectures to the class	Yes No	1 2 3 4 5 6 7 8 9
At recess	Yes No	1 2 3 4 5 6 7 8 9
At lunch	Yes No	1 2 3 4 5 6 7 8 9
In the hallways	Yes No	1 2 3 4 5 6 7 8 9
In the bathroom	Yes No	1 2 3 4 5 6 7 8 9
On field trips	Yes No	1 2 3 4 5 6 7 8 9
During special assemblies	Yes No	1 2 3 4 5 6 7 8 9
On the bus	Yes No	1 2 3 4 5 6 7 8 9

Office Use Only: No. of problems _____   Mean severity _____

Reprinted with permission of Russell A. Barkley, Ph.D.

Norms For The School Situations Questionnaire

Age Groups (in years)	n	Number of problems settings	Mean severity
Boys			
6 - 8	170	2.4 (3.3)	1.5 (2.0)
9 - 11	123	2.8 (3.2)	1.9 (2.1)
Girls			
6 - 8	180	1.0 (2.0)	0.8 (1.5)
9 - 11	126	1.3 (2.1)	0.8 (1.2)

Note: Table entries are means with standard deviations in parentheses. From *Factor Structures of the Home Situations Questionnaire (HSQ) and the School Situations Questionnaire (SSQ)* by M.J. Breen and T.S. Altepeter, 1990.

HOME SITUATIONS QUESTIONNAIRE

Child's Name_____   Date_____

Name of Person Completing This Form_____

Instructions: Does your child present any problems with compliance to instructions, commands, or rules for you in any of these situations? If so, please circle the word Yes and then circle a number beside that situation that describes how severe the problem is for you. If your child is not a problem in a situation, circle No and go to the next situation on the form.

Situations	Yes/No (Circle one)	If yes, how severe? Mild (Circle one) Severe
Playing alone	Yes No	1 2 3 4 5 6 7 8 9
Playing with other children	Yes No	1 2 3 4 5 6 7 8 9
Mealtimes	Yes No	1 2 3 4 5 6 7 8 9
Getting dressed/undressed	Yes No	1 2 3 4 5 6 7 8 9
Washing and bathing	Yes No	1 2 3 4 5 6 7 8 9
When you are on the telephone	Yes No	1 2 3 4 5 6 7 8 9
Watching television	Yes No	1 2 3 4 5 6 7 8 9
When visitors are in your home	Yes No	1 2 3 4 5 6 7 8 9
When you are visiting someone's home	Yes No	1 2 3 4 5 6 7 8 9
In public places (restaurants, stores church, etc.)	Yes No	1 2 3 4 5 6 7 8 9
When father is home	Yes No	1 2 3 4 5 6 7 8 9
When asked to do chores	Yes No	1 2 3 4 5 6 7 8 9
When asked to do homework	Yes No	1 2 3 4 5 6 7 8 9
At bedtime	Yes No	1 2 3 4 5 6 7 8 9
While in the car	Yes No	1 2 3 4 5 6 7 8 9
When with a babysitter	Yes No	1 2 3 4 5 6 7 8 9

Office Use Only: No. of problems _____   Mean severity _____

Reprinted with permission of Russell A. Barkley, Ph.D.

Norms For The Home Situations Questionnaire

Age Groups (in years)	n	Number of problems settings	Mean severity
Boys			
4 - 5	162	3.1 (2.8)	1.7 (1.4)
6 - 8	205	4.1 (3.3)	2.0 (1.4)
9 - 11	138	3.6 (3.3)	1.9 (1.5)
Girls			
4 - 5	146	2.2 (2.6)	1.3 (1.4)
6 - 8	202	3.4 (3.5)	1.6 (1.5)
9 - 11	142	2.7 (3.2)	1.4 (1.4)

Note: Table entries are means with standard deviations in parentheses. From *Factor Structures of the Home Situations Questionnaire (HSQ) and the School Situations Questionnaire (SSQ)* by M.J. Breen and T.S. Altepeter, 1990.

CHILD ATTENTION PROFILE

Child's Name_____   Child's Age_____

Filled Out By _____   Child's Sex [ ] M [ ] F

Directions: Below is a list of items that describe pupils. For each item that describes the pupil **now** or within the past week, check whether the item is **Not True, Somewhat or Sometimes True**, or **Very or Often True**. Please check all items as well as you can, even if some do not seem to apply to this pupil.

	Not true	Somewhat or Sometimes true	Very or often true
1. Fails to finish things he/she starts	[ ]	[ ]	[ ]
2. Can't concentrate, can't pay attention for long	[ ]	[ ]	[ ]
3. Can't sit still, restless, or hyperactive	[ ]	[ ]	[ ]
4. Fidgets	[ ]	[ ]	[ ]
5. Daydreams or gets lost in his/her thoughts	[ ]	[ ]	[ ]
6. Impulsive or acts without thinking	[ ]	[ ]	[ ]
7. Difficulty following directions	[ ]	[ ]	[ ]
8. Talks out of turn	[ ]	[ ]	[ ]
9. Messy work	[ ]	[ ]	[ ]
10. Inattentive, easily distracted	[ ]	[ ]	[ ]
11. Talks too much	[ ]	[ ]	[ ]
12. Fails to carry out assigned tasks	[ ]	[ ]	[ ]

Please feel free to write any comments about the pupil's work or behavior in the last week.

Reprinted with permission of Craig Edelbrock, Ph.D.

Norms For The Child Attention Profile

Normative cutoff points for Inattention, Overactivity , and Total Score.

Inattention (Sum of items 1, 2, 5, 7, 9, 10, 12, each scored 0, 1, or 2, range: 0 -14)

	Total (1100)	Boys (550)	Girls (550)
Median	1	2	0
69%ile	3	4	2
84%ile	6	7	5
93%ile	8	9	7
98%ile	11	12	10

Overactivity (Sum of items 3, 4, 6, 8, and 11, each scored 0, 1 or 2, range: 0 - 10).

Median	0	1	0
69%ile	1	2	1
84%ile	4	4	2
93%ile	6	6	5
98%ile	8	8	7

Total Score (Sum of all items 1 - 12, each scored 0, 1, or 2, range: 0 - 24).

Median	2	4	1
69%ile	6	7	4
84%ile	10	11	8
93%ile	14	15	11
98%ile	19	20	16

Note: Numbers in parentheses are n's. Table entries are raw scale scores that fall at or below the designated percentile rank.
The 93rd percentile is the recommended upper limit of the normal range. Scores exceeding this cutoff are in the clinical range. All scores are based on teacher reports.

SNAP RATING SCALE

Child's Name_____ Age_____ Grade_____

Completed by _____
Check the one column which best describes the child.

	Not at all	Just a little	Pretty much	Very much
Inattention				
1. Often fails to finish thing he or she starts	___	___	___	___
2. Often doesn't seem to listen	___	___	___	___
3. Easily distracted	___	___	___	___
4. Has difficulty concentrating on school work or other tasks requiring sustained attention	___	___	___	___
5. Has difficulty sticking to a play activity	___	___	___	___
Impulsivity				
1. Often acts before thinking	___	___	___	___
2. Shifts excessively from one activity to another	___	___	___	___
3. Has difficulty organizing work (this not being due to cognitive impairment)	___	___	___	___
4. Needs a lot of supervision	___	___	___	___
5. Frequently calls out in class	___	___	___	___
6. Has difficulty awaiting turn in games or group situation	___	___	___	___
Hyperactivity				
1. Excessively runs about or climbs on things	___	___	___	___
2. Has difficulty sitting still or fidgets excessively	___	___	___	___
3. Has difficulty staying seated	___	___	___	___
4. Moves about excessively during sleep	___	___	___	___
5. Is always "on the go" or acts as if "driven by a motor"	___	___	___	___
Peer Interactions				
1. Fights, hits, punches, etc.	___	___	___	___
2. Is disliked by other children	___	___	___	___
3. Frequently interrupts other children's activities	___	___	___	___
4. Bossy, always telling other children what to do	___	___	___	___
5. Teases or calls other children names	___	___	___	___
6. Refuses to participate in group activites	___	___	___	___
7. Loses temper often and easily	___	___	___	___

Note : From "Methylphenidate Hydrochloride Given With or Before Breakfast: Behavioral, Cognitive, and Electrophysiologic Effects" by J. M. Swanson, C.A. Sandman, C. Deutsch, and M. Baren, 1983, *Pediatrics.*, 7, 49 -54. Reprinted with permission of J. M. Swanson, Ph.D.

NORMS FOR THE SNAP

Scoring:

Each item in the SNAP is rated on a 0 to 3 scale (Not at All = 0, Just A Little = 1, Pretty Much = 2, and Very Much = 3). The item scores are summed for each subscale and then expressed as an Subscale Score, that is the sum of all the items in the subscale divided by the number of items in the subscale. Inattention has 5 items; Impulsivity has 6 items; Hyperactivity has 5 items; and Peer Interactions has 7 items. In general, a subscale score of over 1.5 may be considered to be high.

Normative Data:

	Inattention	Impulsivity	Hyperactivity	Peer Interaction
Males Age				
6 - 7	1.29 + .85	1.10 + .86	1.00 + .90	.75 + .75
8 - 9	.95 + .88	.76 + .77	.81 + .79	.60 + .60
10 -11	.90 + .79	.68 + .71	.48 + .61	.42 + .54
Females Age				
6 - 7	.82 + .85	.63 + .79	.51 + .67	.55 + .69
8 - 9	.54 + .78	.34 + .53	.31 + .53	.28 + .50
10 -11	.43 + .63	.26 + .54	.27 + .41	.28 + .53

Psychometric Testing

Psychometric testing is an important and necessary part of a diagnostic assessment of ADD. Data relevant to a child's intellectual ability, information processing skills, and academic achievement is obtained through psychometric testing. This information is helpful in understanding the student's learning style, whether or not there are any signs of a learning disability, or if there are academic achievement deficits which could be the result of non-cognitive factors.

Psychometric testing may involve evaluating intellectual ability, attention span, visual-motor skills, paired-associate learning, impulsivity, short-term memory, and a number of other cognitive functions. These tests are frequently administered by a clinical, school, or educational psychologists who are specially trained to administer such tests and interpret test results. Test findings are usually communicated in a written report which outlines information about the child's presenting problems, the developmental and social history, the test data, interpretation of the test results in terms of specific strengths and weaknesses of the child, and recommendations for interventions when necessary. Teachers are frequently asked to read such reports for a better understanding of the student.

Intelligence Testing

Intelligence testing is frequently done to obtain an overall measure of the student's intellectual ability. The four tests that are used most often for this purpose are: Wechsler Preschool and Primary Scale of Intelligence-R (WPPSI-R), Wechsler Intelligence Scale for Children-R (WISC-R), Wechsler Intelligence Scale for Children III (WISC-III), and the Stanford-Binet Intelligence Scale: Fourth Edition. The WPPSI-R, WISC-R, and WISC-III provide information about verbal and non-verbal information processing resulting in a Verbal I.Q., Performance I.Q. and a Full Scale I.Q.. The Stanford-Binet provides scores for Verbal Reasoning, Abstract/Visual Reasoning, Quantitative Reasoning, and Short-term Memory.

In much the same way as the degree of discrepancy between ability and achievement (I.Q. test scores compared to achievement test scores) is important in determining the extent to which a student may exhibit a learning disability, the ability-attention span discrepancy may be important in determining the extent to which a student may have attentional deficits. Thus, by knowing the intellectual ability of the child one can make a determination as to whether attention span (as measured by parent or teacher observations, or as assessed by other procedures) is discrepant from the child's measured mental ability.

Intelligence tests, however, offer little information which is uniquely relevant to ADD. For example, there is no single pattern of subtest scores on the WISC-R that is common to ADD children. Earlier research had suggested that a child's collective performance on the Arithmetic, Digit Span, and Coding subtests, which make up the so-called Freedom From Distractibility Scale, or when the Information subtest is included, the "ACID" profile, could be useful measures of attentional ability, but they turn out not to be. Difficulties with attention, concentration, and alertness are characteristic of a number of major disorders of childhood. In actuality, low Freedom From Distractibility scores are more commonly found in children with reading disability. These profile patterns have **not** been demonstrated to be typical of children with a specific diagnosis, and should not be relied upon to confirm or to rule out the presence or absence of ADD.

Achievement Testing

Tests of academic achievement are routinely incorporated in the ADD assessment. Since many of the problems of children with ADD are school related, and since a significant number (less than 25%) of ADD children also have a co-existing learning disability, it is important to examine the child's achievement skills to assess weaknesses in areas of reading, arithmetic and written language.

Standardized tests used for this purpose include such instruments as: Woodcock-Johnson Psychoeducational Test Battery: Tests of Achievement, Wide Range Achievement Test (WRAT-R), Test of Written Language (TOWL), Kaufman ABC (K-ABC), Woodcock Reading Mastery Test, Key Math, and others.

Other Psychometric Tests

In a review of several other tests of neuropsychological functioning which have been purported to be of value in the assessment of ADD, Dr. Russell Barkley (1990) found that neither the Matching Familiar Figures Test (Kagan, 1966) or the Wisconsin Card Sort Test (Grant & Berg, 1948) were of value in discriminating ADD from non-ADD children. However, the Stroop Word-Color Association Test and the Hand Movements Test, a subtest of the Kaufman Assessment Battery for Children (Kaufman & Kaufman, 1983), may be somewhat sensitive in picking up difficulties found in ADD children.

Computerized Attention Testing

Computerized assessment of attention span had been used for over thirty years in laboratories doing research on hyperactive children. The first such computerized assessment device was the Continuous Performance Test (CPT) (Rosvold, Mirsky, Sarason, Bransome & Beck, 1956). This test required the child to attend to a screen and selectively respond to a specific pair of flashing letters presented in sequential combination over a fixed period of time. Many years of research indicated that children with attentional disorders tended to do less well on such a task. However, the CPT was too bulky and expensive to use in clinical practice.

Left: The Gordon Diagnostic System (GDS). Right: The Test of Variables of Attention (T.O.V.A.). Both are computerized measures which evaluate a person's attention span and impulsivity.

Dr. Michael Gordon developed a portable CPT called the Gordon Diagnostic System (GDS). The GDS is a computerized instrument which can easily be programmed to administer any of three tasks to a child. The Delay Task, for example, provides a measure of impulse control. On this task the child sits before the GDS and is instructed that he can earn points by repeatedly pressing a button on the GDS console. However, in order to earn points the child must press the button, wait awhile, and press it again. The child is not told how long he should wait between button presses, but if he waits long enough, he will earn additional points which accumulate on a visual display for feedback. The Vigilance Task measures sustained attention. On this task the child sits before the GDS and is instructed to look at the display whereon numbers flash on and off. The child is told to press the button on the console when he sees a specific number (or sequence of numbers) come up on the display. Sustained attention is measured by number of correct responses the child is able to make when the targeted numbers appear and by the number of errors he makes either by neglecting to respond when he should have (errors of omission) or by not suppressing a response (errors of commission). The Distractibility Task measures sustained attention when distracting stimuli are present.

The T.O.V.A.™, Tests of Variables of Attention, is another continuous performance test which can be used as part of a multi-modal assessment for ADD. It is also being used to determine response to medication and to monitor pharmacotherapy in ADD children. This easily administered test, programmed for use with IBM compatibles and Macintosh personal computers was developed by Dr. Lawrence Greenberg at the University of Minnesota.

The Continuous Performance Test Computer Program (for IBM compatibles) developed by C. Keith Conners, Ph.D. is also popular among clinicians for assessment of ADD and medication effects. Similar to the other CPTs, results can be accessed by computer immediately after administration.

Continuous performance tasks such as the Gordon Diagnostic System, T.O.V.A.™, and the Continuous Performance Test Compuater Program are becoming more widely used as part of a larger battery of procedures in the assessment of ADD and in determining responses to medication. While they may provide information which is useful to the assessment process, the data obtained from such methods should be used in conjunction with other information in determining whether a child has attentional problems. The GDS, T.O.V.A.™, and Conners Continuous Performance test Computer Program are available through the ADD WareHouse (800-ADD-WARE).

Testing for Other Conditions

As indicated earlier, there are a number of conditions which a child could have which might result in characteristics of ADD. For example, some children have significant problems with achievement either due to an underlying learning disabilty or due to environmental or cultural disadvantage, English as a second language, or other problems. Such achievement problems, whatever their cause, could have serious impact on the child's ability to attend to an assignment.

Furthermore, children with emotional problems may show difficulties with inattention, impulsivity or overactivity similar to the behavior of an ADD child. In children where there is suspicion of an emotional disturbance being at the root of these difficulties an assessment of emotionality should be done.

Tier 2 Evaluation: Severity of Impact on Academic Performance

If the tier 1 diagnostic evaluation results in the child receiving a diagnosis of ADD, then the tier 2 evaluation should be done to determine to what extent the child's attention deficit disorder impacts on academic performance.

For a number of reasons, school personnel play an important role in collecting data for this stage of the assessment. Teachers, being in a position to compare the ADD child to that of a normal peer group, are best able to describe the child's functioning in comparison to other classmates and may be best able to document the degree of impairment of academic performance the child exhibits in class. Additionally, in contrast to clinicians who observe the ADD child over relatively short periods of time, teachers see the child over a long period, as much as six hours a day, five days a week, for forty weeks a year, thereby enabling them to be in a better position to make judgments about the child's academic performance.

In addition to the use of assessment procedures to evaluate impairment of academic performance, tier 2 evaluations should include the implementation of trial interventions in the regular education classroom. The inclusion of such trial interventions is recommended because doing so will provide information as to the severity of the child's ADD characteristics as manifested in the classroom and will also provide an estimate as to how successful regular education interventions in the child's classroom might be.

Direct Observation of the Student

Direct observation is a useful method by which to assess a child's performance and behavior in the classroom. Data of the classroom and of the child's activities within the classroom can provide objective information for documenting the degree to which the child with ADD exhibits impairments in academic performance. Direct observational data can confirm teacher's reports via interview or rating scale methods about a student's functioning and can add more information about the ecology of the classroom itself and its effect upon the student.

The advantage of direct observation procedures is that they reduce bias in ratings of students as data are unaffected by teacher perceptions. One disadvantage of direct observation procedures is that they are typically the most costly of school-based assessment methods because they involve a great deal of time in training and data collection. A second disadvantage of direct observational data is the lack of standardization of data collected which could then be interpolated as scores to be used in a norm-referenced way to determine degree of severity of problems.

Traditionally, classroom observation is often done in a casual, anecdotal fashion. The following exerpt from an observation of a kindergarten child illustrates typical anecdotal observational data:

10:00 a.m.

Charles is at the math center. He is standing at his seat using a geoboard. The other children at the center are using pattern blocks to create designs and/or figures. He uses rubberbands on the geoboard. One rubberband flies across the room. A girl from his table goes to Ms. Walker and tells her Charles is "shooting rubber bands". Ms. Walker tells Charles he is not supposed to be using the rubber bands and geoboard; she instructs him to put it away; he does.

10:12 a.m.

Charles begins playing with blocks. He builds and "flicks" his bombs (Here comes a bomb!") till his blocks knock into a neighbor's. A child tells the teacher that Charles is knocking over their buildings/designs. Ms. Walker monitors. Charles says to the children again, "Want to make a bomb?"

10:14 a.m.

Charles builds a three dimensional structure; moves it towards his neighbor's; talks with his neighbor; reaches to the center of the table for additional blocks. He stands and talks.

10:15 a.m.

Ms. Walker turns out the lights; Charles stands. When instructed to clean up, Charles argues with 2 other children at the table who were designated as the "cleanup people". As these 2 children begin putting away the blocks on the table, Charles argues with them. He continues building. Ms. Walker tells Charles he needs to come to the group on the floor. He knocks down his building in anger.

10:17 a.m.

Charles goes to the group area, does not sit, bounces up and down, bending at the knees. The children are told to find their own personal space. He goes inside the "barn" area (he is the only child in the "barn"). The children begin moving around the room to the music on a record. Charles appears to dance to the music rather than move around the room as the other children are doing. He freezes when the music stops (as he should do).

10:19 a.m.

When other children come to the "barn" area Charles leaves and moves very freely across the room. He continues to freeze when appropriate (and the observation continues).

In recent years systematic behavioral observation techniques have become more popular. School psychologists have probably received more training in this procedure than other groups.

Systematic direct observations can focus on the specific characteristics of ADD (inattention, impulsivity, hyperactivity) that are manifested in the classroom during performance of independent seat work or during times when direct instruction is presented by the teacher. When using such a procedure, behavioral manifestations of ADD in the classroom are typically coded as: off-task (e.g. not attending to work or instruction); fidgeting (e.g. repetitive, purposeless, task-irrelevant behavior); out of seat (e.g. gets up from chair without permission); vocalizes (e.g. talks without permission, makes noises); plays with objects (e.g. manipulating objects in a way which is not directly associated with assigned work).

One of the early classroom observation codes to reliably identify hyperactive children was developed by Howard Abikoff, Rachel Gittelman-Klein, and Donald Klein (1977) at Long Island Jewish Hospital in New York. Using their method, observers were trained to rate both hyperactive and "average" students in a class every 15 seconds on 14 different categories of behavior (e.g. calling out, interruption of others during work periods, off task, minor motor movement such as in-chair restlessness, noncompliance with teacher commands, etc.). Their code has been shown to be reliable in differentiating hyperactive from non-hyperactive children.

Procedures for collecting data systematically by direct observation usually involve several steps:

1. The observer discusses with the teacher the academic problems of the child and they decide on an appropriate time to observe the child. The observation should be done at a time when an activity will be ongoing that is related to the child's referral problem.

2. The observer should enter the room discreetly without notice given to the child that s/he is being observed. It is best for the observer to use a signalling device such as an audio tone with an ear plug which signals at predetermined fixed intervals to indicate rating time.

3. For purposes of reliability more than one observation

should be done, however, it will be necessary to consider time constraints of the observer as frequent observations could become a lengthy process. Enough observations need to be scheduled to get an accurate picture of the child's behavior within the instructional environment.

4. Observation of other students in the class is important so as to enable the observer to compare the behavior of the referred child to peers within his or her classroom. Such comparison observations can provide a class norm which could be very helpful in determining how much the behavior of the child falls outside the typical behavior of other children in the classroom.

5. Observational data will then need to be organized in a systematic way so that the results can be interpreted and presented in a report.

Edward Shapiro (1989) provides a detailed review of several methods of direct observation. Methods vary greatly in complexity from simply counting specific behavioral acts within a pre-defined period of time to more complex systems based on time-sampling procedures and interactions with the classroom environment.

Another early observation method developed by a group of researchers at the State University of New York at Stony Brook has also been used in studies examining students with a diagnosis of hyperactivity. In this method observers were asked to rate nine categories of behavior such as out of chair, playing with objects, noise, and aggression and were able to successfuly discriminate hyperactive from non-hyperactive children.

The State-Event Classroom Observation System (SECOS) developed by Saudargass and Creed (1980) allows for the assessment of 15 student and 6 teacher behaviors. The SECOS is available by writing to Richard A. Saudargas, Ph.D., Department of Psychology, University of Tennessee, Knoxville, TN 37916.

The Ristricted Academic Situation coding system developed by Barkley (1981) targets many behaviors commonly exhibited by ADD children and is easy to learn how to use. As an observational system, it has been shown to be sensitve to stimulant drug effects and to discriminate between hyperactive and nonhyperactive students. The complete form and instructions can be found in *Attention-Deficit Hyperactivity Disorder: A Clinical Workbook* (Barkley, 1991) available through Guilford Press or the ADD-WareHouse.

The National Association of School Psychologists publishes *Behavior Assessment for School Psychologists* (1983). This detailed manual describes the process of doing direct observation data collection. Prepared by Galen Alessi and James Kaye, the manual is designed to facilitate the training of individuals in methods of direct observation.

Alessi and Kaye developed The Classroom Observation Record Form for recording observational data. A sample of the form is shown on the following page. The beginning of the form contains identifying information about the child, the reason for observation, and the classroom activity ongoing when the observation is done. The middle section of the form contains a coding system for noting various behaviors, classroom events, and teacher and peer reactions. The bottom half of the form contains twenty blanks, each one representing either an interval for observation or a time sample frame. Each blank line has a space on which to record the behavior of the referred student and comparison pupils, anecdotal reports about the incident, the class grouping at the time, and the teacher's and peers' reactions to the incident. Data is summarized at the bottom giving, in this case, frequency data about time on-task for the referred student and comparison peers. For those interested in learning more about this procedure, consult *Behavior Assessment for School Psychologists* by Alessi and Kaye.

Assessment of ADD

Western Michigan University
School Psychology Program
CLASSROOM OBSERVATION RECORD PROTOCOL

Pupil: _Phoebe S._   Comparison: _C. J._   Observer: _School Psychologist (L.C.)_
Age: _6-10_   Age: _6-7_   Reliability: _Social Worker (E. S.)_
Grade: _2ND_   Class size: _26_
School: _Westwood_   Class type: _Regular Ed._
Teacher: _Mrs. Kaput_   Time Stop: _9o:23_
Date: _16 / 10 / '78_   Time Start: _10:13_
day month year   Total Time: _:10_

Reason for observation (What questions do we want to answer?):
To confirm the reported discrepancy between Phoebe's behavior and that of her classroom peers.

Classroom Activity and explicit rules in effect at time of observation:
Activity: math. — See notes below for details. Rules: 1. Follow teacher's directions; 2. Work quietly; 3. complete work.

Description of Observation Techniques: (internal or time sample and length)
30" interval for many and comparison, 2 minute time-sample for class scan-check

Behavior Codes:
T = On Task
V = Verbal Off task
M = Motor Off task
P = Passive Off task
=
=
=

Grouping Codes:
L = large group
S = small group
O = one-to-one
I = independent Act.
F = Free-time
=
=

Teacher and Peer Reaction Codes:
AA = attention to all
A+ = positive attention to pupil
A- = negative attention to pupil
Ao = no attention to pupil
An = neutral attention to pupil
=
=

	Time	Pupil	Comparison	Class Scan Check	Anecdotal notes on behavior	Grouping	Teacher Reaction	Peer Reaction
1.	10:13	P	T		Ph not responding to teacher	L	An	Ao
2.		M	T		Standing up - others sitting	L	Ao	A+
3.	10:14	M	T		Tr leads Ph back to desk	L	An	Ao
4.		M	I	80%	Standing up	L	Ao	A+
5.	10:15	P	T		Sitting staring at others	L	Ao	A+
6.		T	N		Looking at teacher	S	Ao	Ao
7.	10:16	T	N	76%	Sitting quietly and listening	S	Ao	Ao
8.		T	T		Working at desk	S	Ao	Ao
9.	10:17	P	T		Looking out window	L	Ao	Ao
10.		T	T	93%	Copying math problems	L	Ao	Ao
11.	10:18	P	T		Staring at board	L	Ao	Ao
12.		M	T		On floor getting pencil	L	Ao	Ao
13.	10:19	M	T	80%	On floor getting pencil	L	Ao	A+
14.		M	N		On floor looking at others	L	Ao	A+
15.	10:20	P	T		In seat staring	L	Ao	Ao
16.		P	T	88%	In seat staring	L	Ao	Ao
17.	10:21	T	T		writing math	S	AA	Ao
18.		T	T		writing math	S	Ao	Ao
19.	10:22	M	T	80%	Walking in class	S	Ao	A+
20.		T	T		writing in class math	S	Ao	Ao
		35%	85%	81%		L=13; S=7	Ao=17 An=3	Ao=14 A+=6

Summary: 7/20 17/20
Reliability = 93%

Note: From *Behavior Assessment for School Psychologists* by G.J. Alessi and J.H. Kaye, p.13. Copyright 1983 by the National Association of School Psychologists. Reprinted by permission of the publisher.

75

Academic Performance Measures

Measures of academic performance can be useful indicators as to whether or not the student is educationally impaired and, if so, to what degree. Academic performance refers to the amount of work a child produces in the classroom and the accuracy of such work. There are a number of measures which can provide an indication of academic performance. For example, grades recorded in a teacher's grade book provide an indication of the quality of the student's academic performance. Representative samples of a student's work collected over a predetermined period of time (e.g. 10 days or so) may provide measures of how well the student performs with respect to amount of work completed and accuracy of work relative to other students in the class.

The Academic Performance Rating Scale

The Academic Performance Rating Scale (APRS), recently developed by Drs. George J. DuPaul, Mark D. Rapport and Lucy M. Perriello (1991), provides information about the quality of a student's academic performance in the classroom. Unlike previously discussed rating scales which specifically target the frequency of problem behaviors, with few, if any, items related directly to academic performance, the APRS provides important data as to the student's academic productivity in terms of amount of work completed and accuracy of work done. The following scores can be tabulated: Total Score, Learning Ability, Impulse Control, Academic Performance, and Social Withdrawal (Barkley, 1991).

Rating scales like the APRS may be helpful in identifying children in need of special help in school. A copy of the APRS (and normative data) is contained on pages 77-80 with the permission of Dr. George DuPaul.

ACADEMIC PERFORMANCE RATING SCALE

Student _____   Date _____

Age _____   Grade _____   Teacher _____

For each of the below items, please estimate the above student's performance over the **PAST WEEK**. For each item, please circle **one** choice only.

1. Estimate the percentage of written **math** work *completed* (regardless of accuracy) relative to classmates.	0-49%	50-69%	70-79%	80-89%	90-100%
	1	2	3	4	5
2. Estimate the percentage of written **language arts** work *completed* (regardless of accuracy) relative to classmates.	0-49%	50-69%	70-79%	80-89%	90-100%
	1	2	3	4	5
3. Estimate the *accuracy* of completed wirtten **math** work (i.e., percent correct of work done).	0-64%	65-69%	70-79%	80-89%	90-100%
	1	2	3	4	5
4. Estimate the *accuracy* of completed **written language** arts work (i.e., percent correct of work done).	0-64%	65-69%	70-79%	80-89%	90-100%
	1	2	3	4	5
5. How consistent has the quality of this child's academic work been over the past week?	Consistently poor	More poor than successful	Variable	More successful than poor	Consistently successful
	1	2	3	4	5
6. How frequently does the student accurately follow teacher instructions and/or class discussion during *large-group* (e.g., whole class) instruction?	Never	Rarely	Sometimes	Often	Very Often
	1	2	3	4	5
7. How frequently does the student accurately follow teacher instructions and/or class discussion during *small-group* (e.g., reading group) instruction?	Never	Rarely	Sometimes	Often	Very Often
	1	2	3	4	5
8. How quickly does this child learn new material (i.e., pick up novel concepts)?	Never	Rarely	Sometimes	Often	Very Often
	1	2	3	4	5

9. What is the quality or neatness of this child's handwriting?	Poor	Fair	Average	Above Average	Excellent
	1	2	3	4	5

10. What is the quality of this child's reading skills?	Poor	Fair	Average	Above Average	Excellent
	1	2	3	4	5

11. What is the quality of this child's speaking skills?	Poor	Fair	Average	Above Average	Excellent
	1	2	3	4	5

12. How often does the child complete written work in a careless, hasty fashion?	Never	Rarely	Sometimes	Often	Very Often
	1	2	3	4	5

13. How frequently does the child take more time to complete work than his/her classmates?	Never	Rarely	Sometimes	Often	Very Often
	1	2	3	4	5

14. How often is the child able to pay attention without you prompting him/her?	Never	Rarely	Sometimes	Often	Very Often
	1	2	3	4	5

15. How frequently does this child require your assistance to accurately complete his/her academic work?	Never	Rarely	Sometimes	Often	Very Often
	1	2	3	4	5

16. How often does the child begin written work prior to understanding the directions?	Never	Rarely	Sometimes	Often	Very Often
	1	2	3	4	5

17. How frequently does this child have difficulty recalling material from a prevous day's lessons?	Never	Rarely	Sometimes	Often	Very Often
	1	2	3	4	5

18. How often does the child appear to be staring excessively or "spaced out"?	Never	Rarely	Sometimes	Often	Very Often
	1	2	3	4	5

19. How often does the child appear withdrawn or tend to lack an emotional response in a social situation?	Never	Rarely	Sometimes	Often	Very Often
	1	2	3	4	5

Note: From "Teacher Ratings of Academic Skills: The Development of the Academic Performance Rating Scale" by George J. DuPaul, Mark D. Rapport, and Lucy M. Perriello, 1991, *School Psychology Review, 20,* 284-300. Reprinted with permission.

ACADEMIC PERFORMANCE RATING SCALE NORMS

Total score: Sum items 1 -19 with the following items reverse-keyed: 12, 13, 15, 16, 17, 18, 19.
Learning Ability: Sum items 3 - 5, 8, 10, 11, 15, 17 with items 15 & 17 reverse-keyed.

Impulse Control: Sum items 6, 7, 9, 12, 14, 16 with items 12 & 16 reverse-keyed.
Academic Performance: Sum items 1 - 7, 13, 14 with item 13 reverse-keyed.
Social Withdrawal: Sum items 13, 15, 17 - 19 with all items reverse-keyed.

MEANS AND STANDARD DEVIATIONS FOR THE ACADEMIC PERFORMANCE RATING SCALE BY GRADE AND GENDER

Grade	Total score	Learning Ability	Impulse Control	Academic Performance	Social Withdrawal
			Boys		
Grade 1 (n = 42)					
M	71.95	30.19	22.86	35.52	17.88
SD	16.09	7.22	5.02	8.85	4.50
Grade 2 (n = 45)					
M	67.84	28.44	20.79	33.80	16.64
SD	14.86	7.11	4.59	8.43	5.10
Grade 3 (n = 49)					
M	68.49	28.39	20.90	34.71	17.67
SD	16.96	7.31	5.47	9.08	4.73
Grade 4 (n = 41)					
M	69.77	28.50	21.78	34.36	18.40
SD	15.83	7.51	4.90	8.40	4.21
Grade 5 (n = 35)					
M	63.68	26.00	19.86	32.09	16.56
SD	18.04	8.15	5.17	9.83	5.15
Grade 6 (n = 39)					
M	65.24	26.64	20.08	33.22	16.78
SD	12.39	6.52	3.86	6.39	4.05

ACADEMIC PERFORMANCE RATING SCALE NORMS

Total score: Sum items 1 -19 with the following items reverse-keyed: 12, 13, 15, 16, 17, 18, 19.
Learning Ability: Sum items 3 - 5, 8, 10, 11, 15, 17 with items 15 & 17 reverse-keyed.

Impulse Control: Sum items 6, 7, 9, 12, 14, 16 with items 12 & 16 reverse-keyed.
Academic Performance: Sum items 1 - 7, 13, 14 with item 13 reverse-keyed.
Social Withdrawal: Sum items 13, 15, 17 - 19 with all items reverse-keyed.

MEANS AND STANDARD DEVIATIONS FOR THE ACADEMIC PERFORMANCE RATING SCALE BY GRADE AND GENDER

Grade	Total score	Learning Ability	Impulse Control	Academic Performance	Social Withdrawal
			Girls		
Grade 1 (n = 40)					
M	67.02	27.15	21.05	33.98	16.83
SD	16.27	8.41	4.46	8.49	4.83
Grade 2 (n = 46)					
M	72.56	29.89	22.59	36.46	18.26
SD	12.33	6.44	3.91	6.22	4.37
Grade 3 (n = 43)					
M	72.10	28.62	23.00	35.93	18.77
SD	14.43	6.85	4.92	7.34	3.82
Grade 4 (n = 38)					
M	67.79	27.29	22.15	33.32	17.41
SD	18.69	8.57	5.27	9.28	5.08
Grade 5 (n = 44)					
M	73.02	29.39	23.58	37.00	18.31
SD	14.10	6.90	4.07	6.43	4.44
Grade 6 (n = 31)					
M	74.10	30.13	23.00	36.74	19.17
SD	14.45	7.28	4.31	7.09	3.71

Trial Interventions

It is recommended that a program of trial interventions be planned and implemented for the ADD child in the regular classroom setting. Such interventions may result in improved academic performance. Trial interventions should be carefully documented giving information about the objectives of the interventions, the strategies that will be utilized, the methods of implementation, and the process by which results will be evaluated to determine outcomes.

The outcome of such trial interventions could provide additional information as to the child's need for services. While successful outcomes from trial interventions should not rule out the child possibly being considered for special education services, an unsuccessful outcome could be a strong indication that the ADD child's impairment may be significant enough to warrant consideration for special education services.

Chapter 5
Medical Treatment for ADD

Following the diagnosis of ADD in a child or adolescent, appropriate treatment needs to be pursued in order to facilitate proper adjustment. Treatment of ADD, like diagnosis, is not a simple, one step process. Usually treatment planning targets identified deficits and often more than one intervention is necessary. Common treatments for ADD children and adolescents may involve one or more of the following procedures: medical management, behavior modification, cognitive-behavior therapy, social skills training, counseling, parent training, and the implementation of appropriate educational interventions. With regard to medical management, the use of medication alone to treat ADD is rarely sufficient. However, when medications are properly prescribed and monitored, the benefits can be quite worthwhile. This chapter will review the medications commonly used to treat ADD and discuss related controversies surrounding the utilization of medication in the treatment of ADD children.

Stimulant Medications

Stimulants have been used to treat hyperactivity for over fifty years and they continue to be prescribed more often than any other classes of medication for this condition.

Dr. Charles Bradley was the first to treat a group of hospitalized children in Rhode Island with the stimulant, Benzedrine, and found substantial improvements in behavior and attention. The stimulant medications received little attention in the psychopharmacology literature, however, until the mid-1950's. Since then they have become the most prevalent therapy for ADD and their use with children has been extensively and carefully studied.

After Ritalin (a form of stimulant known generically as methylphenidate) became commercially available in 1957, its popularity as a treatment for hyperactive children grew, and by 1970 significant numbers of children were taking medication to control their behavior. An erroneous report in the *Washington Post* in the early 1970's, indicating that from 5% to 10% of children in the Omaha, Nebraska school system were being given stimulants, precipitated controversy over their use (Barkley, 1990). This led to a congressional investigation which prompted further scientific investigation into the effects of stimulant medications with children. While the results of these studies clearly demonstrate the efficacy of the use of stimulants for ADD children in the short-term, the long-term benefits of these medications is yet to be clearly established.

The specific action that the stimulants have on brain functioning is unclear. It is generally assumed that they increase arousal (alertness) by enhancing catecholamine activity in the central nervous system. This is presumed to result from greater availability of specific neurotransmitter chemicals, perhaps norepinephrine and/or dopamine, at the synapse between neurons. The specific areas of the brain in which such change occurs is also controversial as some investigators report the area of the brain stem to be most affected while others suggest frontal lobe functioning to be the cite of action by these medications.

The end result in behavior seems to be to enable the child to better focus attention, control impulsiveness, decrease motor activity, improve visual-motor coordination, and, in general, exhibit more purposeful, goal-oriented behavior. It is estimated that over 70% of ADD children taking stimulant medication show improvement.

Of the stimulants, methylphenidate (Ritalin), Adderall, and dextroamphetamine (Dexedrine) are most often prescribed. Each is taken orally and, in general, for children taking these medications, their effects can be seen within thirty to ninety minutes after ingestion. However, in the standard form their duration of action is usually only three to six hours, often requiring the child to take a second and sometimes a third dose during the day. Ritalin comes in a sustained release form as does Dexedrine. The duration of effects on behavior using these forms is much longer, approximately eight to ten hours. Dosage typically is adjusted for each child depending on such factors as the severity of symptoms targeted for improvement and the time of day when the medication is needed (i.e., at school, for homework, etc.). Even at doses in the lower range some children exhibit what is called a "rebound effect" which can occur a few hours after the last dose was taken. This "rebound effect" is due to withdrawal from the medication and can result in the child temporarily displaying more severe signs of hyperactivity, sensitivity, and irritability than originally seen. While most parents tolerate this rebound of symptoms (it doesn't occur in all children) some find it intolerable and discontinue use of medication.

Pemoline (Cylert) is another stimulant commonly used to treat ADD. Cylert has the advantage of a longer duration of action (lasting 8 to 12 hours), but the disadvantage of taking as long as 4 to 6 weeks before it reaches its maximum level of effectiveness. Cylert is administered once a day in the morning. Dosage levels of Cylert have not been as well investigated as Ritalin. Periodic evaluation of liver enzymes is recommended. Due to concerns regarding effects on the liver, the FDA has advised Cylert should no longer be a first line medication to treat ADD.

In comparison to other psychoactive medications commonly used to treat children, the stimulants are probably the safest and least toxic, resulting in the fewest adverse side effects. Of the side effects usually seen with the use of stimulants, the most common include appetite reduction and sleep difficulties and to a substantially lesser degree irritability, nausea, headaches, and constipation. These side effects can lessen or disappear entirely on their own within a few weeks or diminish if the dosage is reduced. There is no strong evidence of significant growth retardation for either children or adolescents who have taken stimulants for long periods.

Movement disorders such as benign tics or, in more serious cases, Tourette's syndrome (a more chronic tic disorder which includes the presence of both vocal and motor tics) may appear in a small percentage of children treated with stimulants. In such cases the parent should consult the child's physician as it may be advisable to reduce dose or discontinue the stimulant medication. The doctor may prescribe a different class of medication such as a tricyclic antidepressant or combine the stimulant with another medication which can treat the tic disorder. Furthermore, in those children with ADD whose parents or siblings have a history of tic disorder, caution should be used with regard to taking stimulant medication.

Although the effectiveness of stimulant therapy has been well documented for treatment of ADD in childhood, the efficacy of such treatment with adolescents had been questioned for quite some time. We now know, however, that the commonly held belief that ADD teens don't benefit from taking stimulant medication is false. A number of studies done over the past several years clearly demonstrate that stimulants have similar positive benefits for adolescents with ADD to those shown for children.

Effects of Methylphenidate on Cognitive Skills, Academic Performance, Academic Achievement, Behavior, and Social Interaction

Effects on Cognitive Skills

Methylphenidate has been shown to improve children's performance on laboratory tests of sustained attention, short-term memory, paired-associate learning, impulse control, and visual-motor coordination. In general, the onset of positive effects on cognitive functioning is somewhere around 50 to 60 minutes, with peak enhancement lasting between 2 to 3 hours. Improved performance on cognitive tasks may be due, in part, to drug induced changes in attitude, motivation and self-regulation rather than enhanced information processing.

Effects on Academic Performance and Achievement

Recent studies have focused on how academic productivity and accuracy of work is affected by stimulant medications. Swanson, et al. (1991) described the results of several studies which assessed stimulant (Ritalin) effects on both academic performance and academic achievement. With regard to academic performance measures, there has been general agreement that academic productivity in ADD students can be dramatically (25 to 40%) increased by stimulant medication. These studies evaluated academic performance measures such as amount of work completed and rate and accuracy of performance when students are given assignments in class or in a laboratory setting. These measures seem to be sensitive to medication effects in a positive direction and confirm informal reports from teachers that students on medication tend to improve in performance of tasks.

However, despite improvements in academic performance (productivity) for children taking stimulant medication, the research has been less conclusive as to long-term positive gains in academic achievement made by students. It has yet to be determined that short-term, drug-induced improvements in attention span and academic productivity ultimately translate into long-term improvements in academic achievement. Swanson, however, cautions that the lack of verification of such gains should not be interpreted as meaning that stimulants do not improve learning.

Effects on Behavior

The behavioral effects of stimulant medication have been extensively studied. On medication, ADD children generally show less oppositional behavior, reduced aggression, decreased talkativeness, and more task orientation than they do when unmedicated. These effects may tend to be more observable in structured, desk activity situations than in less structured, free play environments such as during recess or physical education class. However, recent studies of aggressive ADD children enrolled in a summer program for anger control also demonstrated improved self-control and decreased aggression in play situations.

The medication seems to have an indirect effect on the teachers of these children as well since they exhibit less negative behavior towards the child and show increased rates of positive teacher initiated interaction.

Effects on Social Interaction

Stimulants have also been shown to significantly improve social interactions of ADD children. Typically, ADD children are reported to be more immature, intrusive, impulsive and aggressive in social interactions. For some, their aggressive, hyperactive behavior clearly impedes social progress causing them to be alienated from peers. Other ADD children show less interest interpersonally and stay on the periphery of social groups. Studies of small groups of ADD children in social settings indicate that when taking stimulant medication, these children become more focused and compliant with others and are less controlling and less domineering. With medication they are better able to take turns in structured game situations, are less argumentative, and are generally more agreeable.

Participation in organized sports may also be positively affected by stimulant medication. This is particularly important since most ADD children are boys and athletic prowess is often regarded highly by other boys. It is typical that ADD children are selected last and often reluctantly by their peers to be a team member in an athletic activity. In a study on how Ritalin affected the behavior of ADD children during a baseball game, Pelham et al. (1990) demonstrated that while medication had no effect on baseball skills such as batting, throwing, or catching a ball, during the games the medicated ADD children were more alert, attentive and focused on the action of the game. Given the strong relationship between athletic ability and social acceptance, especially in boys, the medication benefits as they affect sports activities may have significant implications for improving peer status and self-esteem.

Indirect Effects on Parents and Teachers

Drug induced improvements in behavior of hyperactive children are accompanied by positive changes in their adult caretakers' attitudes and behaviors toward the children. An early study by Barkley and Cunningham (1979) showed that parents became less controlling, less coercive and more positive with their children when the children took stimulant medication to control their hyperactivity. Other studies have found similar effects, as parents show higher rates of acceptance and positive regard for their child when the child's behavior is managed by medication. Similar changes in attitude and behavior are noted in teachers toward hyperactive children whose behavior changes as a result of medication treatment.

Adjusting Dosage of the Stimulants

Unfortunately, clinicians are unable to predict how an ADD child will respond to stimulant medication, which stimulant will be best for a particular child, or what dose would be most beneficial. Response to stimulants varies from child to child. The physician usually starts by prescribing an initial low dose of one of the stimulants one or two times per day. Reports are obtained from parents, teachers, and the child or adolescent regarding changes in behavior and the presence of any adverse side effects. Dose may be adjusted weekly until the child's behavior improves to an acceptable level.

Ritalin is often the first choice of many physicians because of the success they have had prescribing it and their lengthy experience using this medication with children. Ritalin comes in a standard and sustained release form. The standard form comes in 5 mg, 10 mg, and 20 mg tablets and lasts about four hours. The sustained release form comes in a 20 mg tablet and lasts about six to eight hours. Physicians usually start with an initial dose of 5 mg once a day (usually in the morning) and after a week a second dose (usually at lunchtime) is added. Either dose might be raised by 5 mg increments over the course of the next few weeks depending on the effect on behavior and whether there are any reported adverse reactions.

Dexedrine comes in 5 mg tablets and 5 mg, 10 mg, and 15 mg spansules. Some physicians prefer to prescribe the Dexedrine spansule since it has a longer duration of action than methylphenidate, requiring less frequent dosing during the day. The starting dose of Dexedrine is 2.5 mg to 5 mg once a day in the morning. A noontime dose may be added as needed. Dexedrine doses are usually about half of the Ritalin doses. Dexedrine also has the advantage of being less expensive than Ritalin, but some pharmacists are reluctant to carry it because of its higher abuse potential.

Adderall, mixed salts of a single-entity amphetamine product, is a newer stimulant which is gaining rapid popularity among clinicians for use with ADHD patients. Adderall comes in 5 mg, 10mg, 20 mg and 30 mg tablets. Adderall has the advantage of working quickly as do other stimulants and may last longer than standard Ritalin or Dexedrine.

Cylert comes in 18.75 mg, 37.5 mg, and 75 mg tablets. Cylert requires only once a day dosing in the morning and may last for seven to eight hours or more. The recommended starting dose is 37.5 mg. and it can be gradually increased by 18.75 mg amounts. The maximum daily recommended dose is 112.5 mg. There have been reports of chemical hepatitis and liver failure with the use of Cylert.

Stimulant Medication for ADD Children, Inattentive Type

Children who suffer from the predominantly inattentive ADD are typically described as sluggish, drowsy, daydreamy and apathetic. They may be prone to anxiety or self-esteem problems and may have a higher rate of learning difficulties than do their hyperactive counterparts. These children will respond to stimulant medication with the percentage of nonresponders being somewhat higher than in the hyperactive group. There is also some evidence to indicate that responders may require lower doses of medication for optimal effect than do hyperactive-impulsive ADD children. For those children who display signs of anxiety be alert to possible increases in anxiety with the stimulants. Careful monitoring of medication is recommended and dosage should probably be kept low. As with hyperactive ADD children, medication should not be the sole treatment utilized but should be combined with additional treatment methods.

Tricyclic Antidepressants

Tricyclic antidepressants including imipramine (Tofranil), desiprimine (Norpramine), and amytriptyline (Elavil) have also been prescribed for the treatment of ADD since 1974 when Judith Rapoport, M.D. and a team of researchers documented their usefulness in treating this disorder. They are most often prescribed for those children who did not benefit from stimulant therapy, who had unacceptable side-effects from the stimulants, or who have additional symptoms of low self-esteem and depression along with ADD.

The onset of action of these medications is slower than for Ritalin or Dexedrine as it may take several days for effects to be observed. These medications have been shown to be helpful in improving attention span, decreasing hyperactivity and reducing aggression in up to 70% of ADD children treated.

Long term use of tricyclic antidepressant medications in ADD children has not been well studied. Side effects include:

- constipation (which can be alleviated with stool softeners) and dry mouth (alleviated by sugar free gum or candy)
- elevated blood pressure
- confusion
- possible precipitation of manic-like behavior and inducement of seizures are uncommon side effects of the antidepressants

It is important that the child or teen be carefully evaluated prior to the use of this class of medications and that they be carefully monitored by their physician to determine medication effects while receiving treatment with any of the tricyclic antidepressant medicines.

Clonidine and Guanfacine

Recently, clonidine (Catapress) and guanfacine (Tenex), medications with documented effect in regulating blood pressure, have been shown to be effective for children with ADD. They may be especially useful for the child who has Tourette's syndrome (tics). Furthermore, while Ritalin is probably superior for treatment of the mildly to moderately hyperactive child with primary attentional difficulties (in that it narrows the attentional field and helps the child focus attention), clonidine may be preferable for severely overactive, aggressive ADD children. It is not recommended for treatment of distractibility in children who have ADD without hyperactivity. Usually clonidine may be recommended after stimulants and antidepressants have been tried unsuccessfully or with ADD children who have tics. For those ADD children with severe hyperactivity unaffected by the stimulants alone, Ritalin and clonidine are sometimes used in combination.

Clonidine may be taken orally or can be administered transdermally (skin patch). With transdermal administration, it is the first medication for ADD children that maintains a constant and effective blood level for about five days. This form of administration may be preferred by some children since no pills are involved.

Unlike the near immediate effect that the stimulants have, it takes about two weeks for clonidine to affect ADD symptoms (although sedative effects can be seen rather quickly). Maximal effect may not be seen for two to three months.

The major side effect of clonidine is sedation which occurs about one hour after administration and lasts 30 to 60 minutes, gradually decreasing as the child begins to tolerate the medication. Clonidine may improve sleep and appetite (a benefit for children who may have lost weight on stimulants), and because it is a releaser of growth hormone, it may facilitate growth.

Amino Acid Supplementation

A number of investigators have studied the effects of amino acid supplementation on ADD symptoms. Disturbances in the release or uptake of the neurotransmitters serotonin, norepinephrine, and dopamine are possible contributors to ADD. As precursors to these neurotransmitters, phenylalanine, tryptophan, and tyrosine increased within the body could theoretically result in increased levels of neurotransmitters and thus reduction of attentional deficits. Unfortunately, this has not proven to be an effective treatment for ADD.

Monitoring Medication Effects

Once medication therapy has begun, it is extremely important to take steps to monitor the effects of the medication on the child. Schools play an ever increasing role in the monitoring of medication effects on children. For most children, the primary effects of medication will only be noticeable during school hours so teachers will be very important informants as to how well the medication works and how well the child tolerates it.

Typically small doses of medicine are initially prescribed, and the dosage is gradually increased until the therapeutic level is reached. Careful monitoring of the child's behavior, alertness, attentiveness, and work habits will signal when a child is benefiting from the treatment or appears to be responding in an adverse way. Positive effects to the stimulants Ritalin and Dexedrine can occur within 30 minutes after ingestion, whereas, such effects usually take several days or weeks to be noticed with Cylert or the antidepressant medicines. Adverse side effects may also occur quickly or may only become noticeable after the child has taken the medication for awhile.

Depending on the child's response to the medication and on the reporting by the teacher, changes in dosing and frequency of administration may occur. Typically, Ritalin is taken twice a day, just before school and at noontime. However, for some children the morning dose may last throughout the entire school day, whereas for others, whose bodies metabolize the medication more quickly, a second dose may be needed at mid-morning and a third sometime after lunch.

There are a variety of ways for teachers to determine medication effectiveness. The most commonly used method of evaluating medication response has probably been telephone reports by the teacher to the child's parents or physician. Some practitioners ask teachers to complete behavior rating scales periodically to determine medication effectivenss. The Conners scales were originally designed for that very purpose. Another method of judging medication response is through analysis of student work products. In this way, a teacher could determine whether the quality and/or quantity of a student's work has been affected by medication. Teachers should coordinate their reporting of medication effects with the school nurse, who may have the ultimate responsibility in dispensing and monitoring the medication. Unfortunately, many schools do not have a full-time nurse so the job is often left for teachers to do.

The Medication Effects Rating Scale (on the following page) can be used to assess both unwanted side effects as well as main effects that the child may experience as a result of medication treatment.

MEDICATION EFFECTS RATING SCALE

Name _____ Completed by _____

Date of Birth _____ Age _____ Sex _____ Grade _____

Date form completed _____

Medication(s)   Dosages and Times Administered Per Day

_____   _____

Mark any changes noticed in the following behaviors:

Main Effects on Behavior	Worse	No Difference	Improved a little	Improved a lot
Attention to task	_____	_____	_____	_____
Listening to lessons	_____	_____	_____	_____
Finishing assigned work	_____	_____	_____	_____
Impulsivity	_____	_____	_____	_____
Calling out in class	_____	_____	_____	_____
Organizing work	_____	_____	_____	_____
Overactivity	_____	_____	_____	_____
Restless, fidgety	_____	_____	_____	_____
Talkative	_____	_____	_____	_____
Aggressive	_____	_____	_____	_____
Peer interaction	_____	_____	_____	_____

Mark any side effects which you have noticed or which the child has mentioned.

Side Effects	Comments
_____ Appetite loss	_____
_____ Insomnia	_____
_____ Headaches	_____
_____ Stomachaches	_____
_____ Seems tired	_____
_____ Stares a lot	_____
_____ Irritability	_____
_____ Excessive crying	_____
_____ Motor/ vocal tic	_____
_____ Nervousness	_____
_____ Sadness	_____
_____ Withdrawn	_____

Source: The ADD Hyperactivity Handbook for Schools by Harvey C. Parker, Ph.D. This form may be reproduced for classroom use.

Teachers' Perceptions and Knowledge of Medication

Despite the fact that teachers have increasing responsibility for students who are taking medication for management of their behavior, attention, or emotionality, teachers generally feel that their training and knowledge about drug therapy is weak. This is unfortunate since teachers play such an important role in the the use of medication in school. Oftentimes teachers are called upon to:

- provide the physician with detailed descriptions of the student's school adjustment and behavior,
- help the physician to monitor the therapeutic effects and side effects of medication on the student's behavior in school,
- report changes in behavior to facilitate titration of drugs for proper dosing regimes,
- administer medication in school.

There have been very few studies of teachers' knowledge and perception of medication usage with ADD students. In a recent investigation (Epstein, Singh, Lusbke, and Stout, 1991), the perceptions, knowledge, and opinions of 104 SLD teachers were surveyed regarding medication used with their students. Less than 20% of the teachers surveyed indicated that their professional preservice or inservice training had provided them with sufficient information on the use of medication for students with behavioral or attentional problems. Over half of the teachers surveyed felt that additional training about the use of medications was extremely necessary and should focus on topics such as: what the major effects of drugs would be; what alternatives there are to medication; and, most importantly, how to monitor and evaluate medication effectiveness in students.

When Should Medication Be Considered?

While most clinicians agree that medications can substantially benefit many children or adolescents with ADD, there are no hard and fast rules as to when medication should be administered. Not every ADD child will need medication to manage behavior or attention. Not every child on medication will need to continue on it at the same dosage each year or, in fact, will require medicine year after year after year. The decision to medicate may depend on several factors:

1. Age of the Child
   Generally, medications to treat ADD are less effective with children below the age of five than they are for older children, and young children tend to exhibit greater side effects.

2. Use of Non-medical Interventions
   The utilization of non-medical interventions such as behavior modification, educational accommodations, special education placement, parent training, etc. may be useful to pursue prior to the use of medication. Utilization of such interventions may eliminate or decrease the need for medication.

3. Risk of Side Effects
   None of the medications described above are without potential side effects. Prior history of motor tics or the presence of severe anxiety in a child, for example, may rule out the use of stimulants which may worsen the tics and heighten the anxiety. Before considering medication, one should always ask whether the benefits outweigh the risks for a particular child.

4. Opinion of the Teacher
   Teachers should be surveyed for their opinion as to a student's need for medication to treat a behavioral, emotional, or attentional disorder. Teachers' opinions

are rarely considered in actual practice despite the extremely important role they play in the ongoing medical management of the student.

5. Concerns of the Parents

Parents should maintain a cautious attitude about giving their child medication. They should be educated about ADD and the various treatments available before any decision is made to medicate. Such a decision is extremely important and should only be made in conjunction with the child's physician and other health care professionals.

Input from school personnel is extremely valuable in the decision-making process regarding the use of medication, although the decision to medicate a child is not, and should not be, an educator's decision. Sometimes parents are offended by well meaning teachers and school administrators who advise them to put their child on medication. Still worse, we occasionally hear of a school administrator who threatens that the child cannot come to school unless he is medicated. Such coercive action rarely occurs, but when it does, serious problems of mistrust and alienation result.

The lay press has been filled with non-scientific and purposely deceiving articles portraying the "horrors" of Ritalin without any shred of scientific evidence whatsoever to substantiate these claims. Anti-medication campaigns advocated by groups like the Church of Scientology surface periodically and produce accusations that children are being kept on medication in a dazed-like, zombied state. Some law suits have been filed against the manufacturers of such medications and their prescribers. Although the information spread by anti-medication groups is inaccurate and greatly exaggerates the dangers of using ADD medications, these campaigns have been quite effective in dissuading some parents from even considering the use of medication treatment for their child. With more and more ADD publications and resources available to the public to present accurate information about medical management of ADD, we hope that the false claims of anti-medication zealots will be balanced by scientific fact.

Medication Alone Is Usually Not the Answer

Most of the time we take medication to cure a condition. Unfortunately, there is no known medical cure for ADD. Like other childhood disorders such as asthma or diabetes, the best that medication can do is to alleviate the core symptoms of the disorder: inattention, impulsivity, and overactivity. We aren't even sure that diminishing these symptoms has any substantial long term positive effect on learning, although common sense suggests, and studies tend to indicate, that medication can help learning.

Obviously, parents who are considering the use of medication in treating their child need to make informed decisions and should thoroughly discuss their concerns with their child's doctor. It is important to emphasize that medication for many ADD children is not the only treatment choice. There are numerous other interventions which are often necessary to utilize to treat this disorder. Thorough treatment will almost always include a variety of educational, psychological, and behavioral interventions as well.

For those who are interested in providing parents with facts about medication management for ADD children, we have included a copy of Medication Fact Sheet in Appendix C.

Medication: Use or Abuse?

In response to concern that Ritalin may be overprescribed, a number of studies have focused on the prescribing practices of Ritalin in various states.

Data from a 1987 Maryland study investigating the use of methylphenidate in Baltimore County schools indicated that a total of 3.4% of the school-age children in that county were receiving stimulant medication, 93% of which was methlyphenidate. The majority of the prescriptions were written for elementary school-age children ages 7 - 11 years.

A study of prescribing practices in Suffolk County, New York during 1986 indicated that approximately .4% of children (1 of every 250) in that county aged 3 to 17 years received at least one prescription for methylphenidate (Sherman and Hertzig, 1991). Considering the prevalence of ADD to be 3%-5% of school aged children, this statistic of .4% is not at all alarming and is well below the 3.4% noted in Baltimore County. Most of these prescriptions were written for school age children age 8-11 with a male:female ratio of 6:1. Interestingly over half of the prescriptions were written only once for a given child. The investigators speculated that the reason for this single prescription phenomena may be due to patient noncompliance or due to the fact that the prescribing physician may have been "pressured" into medicating the child by the school and may not have done an adequate initial evaluation or planned for the effective integration of medical management in a more comprehensive treatment program for the child.

In 1990 the Virginia Departments of Education, Health Professions, Mental Health, Mental Retardation and Substance Abuse Services issued a report entitled, "The Effects of the Use of Methylphenidate" in response to concerns of the needs of ADD children as well as the controversy generated by the use of methylphenidate in their treatment.

Summary findings of the Virginia report indicated that there was **no** evidence of widespread abuse or diversion of methylphenidate in Virginia. However, dramatic increases in distribution of the drug to retail outlets over the last decade prompted the task force to recommend the following action be taken to improve the diagnosis and treatment of ADD children and to reduce potential overreliance on medication as a sole treatment procedure:

- Diagnosis, treatment, and planning for children with ADD should involve a multidisciplinary process including medical, psychological and educational professionals and the child's parents.
- Improved educational services for children with ADD.
- Better communication between physicians and educators regarding the use of methylphenidate for school-aged children.
- Appropriate treatment and instructional approaches including behavioral and cognitive therapy and other accommodations should be developed to provide alternatives or to complement drug therapy. Medication should not be used as an isolated treatment and proper classroom placement, behavioral interventions and counseling should be used prior to beginning a program of pharmacotherapy.
- The effects of any methylphenidate treatment should be carefully evaluated by the prescribing physician at least every six months.
- Intensive inservice educational programs should be instituted on the appropriate interventions and special needs of children with ADD for health care professionals, school personnel and parents.

Virginia's solution to any potential abuse in prescribing practices or use of methylphenidate is to improve the quality of methods and procedures used to diagnose children who are suspected of having ADD and to maintain a broad-based, multimodal treatment perspective for the disorder, emphasizing comprehensive training for educators, health care professionals, and parents so that overreliance on a medication approach alone is avoided.

Clearly, other states need to follow Virginia's lead in emphasizing the importance of comprehensive assessment, well balanced treatment, and carefully trained teachers in assisting ADD children.

Chapter 6
Self-Monitoring, Problem-Solving and Social Skills Training

A number of programs have been developed over the past twenty years to teach inattentive, impulsive, hyperactive, and aggressive children ways they could achieve better self-control. The methods used to teach these skills generally involve training children in self-monitoring, problem-solving, and social skills acquisition. These methods seem perfectly suited for the problems of ADD children. Their impulsive cognitive tempo, quick, error-prone decision-making, poor means-end thinking, and lack of purposeful planning would seem to make them ideal candidates for programs which could help them more effectively control their behavior and encourage the development of positive social skills.

Self-Monitoring Procedures

Self-monitoring (also referred to as self-observation, self-assessment, and self-recording) is a valuable treatment procedure for helping children with attentional disorders in school settings. In self-monitoring, children are trained to observe specific aspects of their own behavior and to record their observations. For example, a child may be asked to observe whenever he calls out without raising his hand for permission to speak and is trained to record each time he does so.

Originally, clinicians used self-recording to collect data about their client's behavior when the clients were away from the clinician or when the behavior of the client was unobservable (e.g. thoughts or feelings). Clients were taught to observe their own behavior and to record whenever a specific behavior occurred. It became obvious that the act of recording one's behavior resulted in a change in the frequency of the behavior. Self-recording procedures became popular for management of smoking, overeating, negative thinking, and other habits.

Self-monitoring has also been used in the classroom to help children pay attention, complete academic assignments, improve speed of classroom performance, control behavior, etc.. Because of their simplicity of design and ease of use in a classroom setting, self-monitoring procedures are fairly popular with teachers. Dr. Daniel P. Hallahan's research in the early 1980's is an example of how a self-monitoring procedure can be used to increase a student's attentiveness to assignments in school. Dr. Hallahan placed a tape recorder emitting tones at an average of once every 45 seconds in a self-contained classroom of learning disabled students. Each student, trained as a group by the teacher, asked himself or herself, "Was I paying attention?" at the sound of each tone. Every member of the class then recorded their own assessment by checking a box for "yes" or "no" on a self-recording sheet placed on the child's desk. Improvements in on-task behavior were noted during self-monitoring.

Other self-monitoring procedures simply utilize paper and pencil recording of specific behavior. For instance, a child may be trained to observe how frequently he calls out of turn and to record each instance he does so by making a tally mark on a card or slip of paper. In one study the children in a class were provided a dittoed sheet composed of fifty small squares and were instructed to mark a "+" when they felt they were studying and a "-" when they were not. The recording of their behavior led to greater studying time. Other self-monitoring procedures require that external prompts be given to the student to signal when the student is to record his behavior. Such prompts could be a tap on the shoulder by the teacher, use of a predetermined phrase spoken by the teacher, or an audio tone.

Drs. John Lloyd and Timothy Landrum (1990) reviewed a number of studies using self-monitoring procedures to improve attention-to-task. Overall, the results have shown that the activity of focusing attention on one's behavior and the subsequent self-recording of these observations could result in improved attentiveness in school. Most of the training of pupils to self-monitor attending behavior has been done by teachers in their classrooms. Thus these procedures have real-life applicability. Generally, self-monitoring programs use cues to signal the student to observe his behavior. A tape that played short "beeps" at irregular intervals ranging from 15 to 90 seconds with an average inter-tone interval of approximately 45 seconds was a common cue in some studies while a kitchen timer set to ring every few minutes was also frequently used. Many studies, however, did not use any cues to signal students to self-monitor. Students were simply instructed to record their attending behavior whenever they thought about it. Even without external cueing, student's attention to task and academic productivity continued at high levels.

Interestingly, it doesn't seem to make a difference whether students record their behavior accurately. Most studies that have assessed student accuracy in self-recording attention-to-task behavior have discovered that students overestimate their rate of attention compared to ratings of independent observers. However, regardless of the accuracy of their self-recordings, attention-to-task improves. Thus it is not really important for the teacher to protect against students inaccurately self-recording.

Procedures for directly applying self-monitoring in the classroom will be fully discussed in chapter 9.

Problem-Solving and Self-Instruction Training

A number of programs are now available for direct use with students and to train teachers and clinicians on how to use cognitive-behavioral interventions with children and adolescents. Several of these programs teach problem-solving strategies and the application of these strategies within a social context.

Mary Ann Bash and Bonnie Camp have written curricula for use in classrooms to teach children problem-solving techniques. *Think Aloud* classroom lessons are written for grades one through six. Children are taught to use verbal mediation (talking to oneself to guide problem-solving or other behaviors) and receive training in self-control, self-monitoring, and self-evaluation in their dealings with everyday problem situations. The program contains a small group program and three classroom programs for grades 1-2, 3-4, and 5-6. Some lessons include: generating alternative solutions to problems, identifying emotions in others, becoming aware of different perspectives people may have in seeing a situation, understanding friendships, stopping to think before solving a social problem, learning about different emotions, predicting consequences of behavior, and using means-end thinking.

A recently published text by Drs. Lauren Braswell and Michael Bloomquist entitled *Cognitive Behavioral Therapy with ADHD Children* describes their model of teaching problem-solving and self-instructional skills to small groups of ADD children and adolescents in a clinical setting. Their program focuses on teaching children problem recognition skills, helping children learn to think of alternative solutions to problems, anticipate possible consequences and obstacles to conceived solutions, and to evaluate the results of their planning, once they follow through with action.

Most problem-solving programs teach children and adolescents to use a five-step problem-solving strategy. Once learned, the children talk themselves through problem-solving. The process of learning the five steps to effective problem-solving involves a rather comprehensive program requiring fairly intense training in small groups. These five steps are:

1. Stop! What is the problem?
2. What are some plans?
3. What is the best plan?
4. Do the plan.
5. Did the plan work?

Braswell and Bloomquist demonstrate how the process works through this example:

In this situation, you are sitting behind me in class and you are kicking my chair. OK, start kicking my chair. (*The child pretends to kick the chair.*) **Stop! What is the problem?** The problem is that he is kicking my chair and I am getting mad. **What are some plans?** I could turn around and kick his chair, I could tell the teacher, or I could ignore him. **What is the best plan?** If I turn around and kick him, he might get really mad at me but he might call me a tattletale. If I ignore him, he may stop kicking me. I think I'll try ignoring him. (*The therapist models ignoring while the child kicks his chair.*) **Did my plan work?** Yes, it did. I thought about it; came up with some plans; did the best one, which was to ignore him; and he stopped kicking my chair (p. 151).

Braswell and Bloomquist emphasize that Step 1 in this process, problem recognition, is crucial for the procedure to be effective. They employ role-playing within their small group training sessions to help children recognize cues which signal that a problem exists. These include recognizing various types of body language such as facial expressions, posture, and tone of voice, and being able to identify feelings of others such as sadness, anger, worry, etc.. Problem recognition charades are used wherein two or more children in the group role-play problem incidents after which the therapist questions the group as to what the problem was and what signals led one to believe that there was a problem.

In a small group, the children are trained in Step 2, to generate solutions to problems. These may be written on a chalkboard using brainstorming strategies. After all possible solutions are written down the potential consequences are discussed for each one. Training children to think ahead and anticipate consequences is an important step in the process as it is necessary to evaluate the potential benefits and shortcomings of each plan. Once done, the group is trained to do Step 3, pick the best plan, and finally to execute the plan and evaluate its effectiveness.

Unfortunately, figuring out a workable plan and carrying out that plan are two different things. Researchers have found that ADD children are quite capable of going through Steps 1-3 of the problem-solving, self-instructional strategy, but they often fail to utilize the strategy in naturalistic settings. Therefore, Braswell and Bloomquist emphasize that a great deal of time must be spent role playing the execution part of the plan so as to encourage the children to utilize planned behavior.

The research literature studying the effectiveness of problem-solving training in small groups or individually is discouraging. Treatment effects do not seem to be maintained after the training is finished and rarely do they generalize into the natural environment. Better results may be obtained by training children within the natural setting such as the classroom in which the problem behaviors occur and training caregivers or instructors within these settings, e.g. teachers, aides, etc. to encourage children to apply these problem solving skills.

Social Skills Training

ADD children often experience significant problems with social interaction. The hyperactive child's behavior readily stands out in the classroom and is perceived negatively by other students. These children exhibit more intrusive, aggressive behavior than others. They engage more frequently in teasing and name-calling, are less likely to be cooperative with peers when participating in group activities, exhibit physical aggression more often, and act impulsively. The hyperactive ADD child is frequently rejected by his peers, and, in response to this rejection may become sad, angry, bossy, or withdrawn, thereby, perpetuating the cycle of inappropriate behavior and continued rejection. Over time, difficulties with peer acceptance can cause substantial damage to the hyperactive child's self-esteem.

Children with ADD who are not hyperactive tend to have a somewhat different set of social problems. Characterized by their tendency to be overly passive and somewhat anxious, the non-hyperactive ADD child is likely to have problems in forming and maintaining social relationships due to their timid and unassuming social style. They generally have difficulty approaching others and are often seen as quiet and withdrawn. Rather than dominating social gatherings like hyperactive children, this group tends to go unnoticed and, therefore, may not be included in social activities as frequently as others.

There has been increasing emphasis on training of social skills with ADD children. A number of training programs have been developed and are currently available to mental health professionals and schools in order to provide a systematic approach to helping children develop prosocial behavior. While most of these programs have not been specifically developed for ADD, they do focus on social skills which are commonly lacking in children and adolescents with attention deficit disorder.

Dr. Arnold P. Goldstein's *The Prepare Curriculum* is a

series of coordinated lessons designed to teach social skills to adolescents and younger children. This extensive volume contains practical ideas to use in the classroom or in small groups to train problem-solving, interpersonal skills, anger control, moral reasoning, stress management, empathy, and cooperation.

Skillstreaming In Early Childhood by Dr. Ellen McGinnis and Dr. Arnold P. Goldstein is a social skills training program for children ages 3 through 6. The authors stress the importance of teaching prosocial skills to children at this young age, especially for those who display withdrawal, aggression, problems with behavior, or learning difficulties. The curriculum includes 6 skill areas: Beginning Social Skills, School-Related Skills, Friendship-Making Skills, Dealing with Feelings, Alternative to Aggression, Dealing with Stress. Through modeling and role-playing exercises, children are systematically taught skills that will enhance their relationships with other youngsters. Some examples from the 40 specific skills that children are taught, include: trying when it's hard, joining in, dealing with teasing, knowing when to tell, and waiting your turn. The program is designed to be used in conjunction with a Program Forms Booket which contains homework reports, checklists, recording forms, and awards. *Skillstreaming In Early Childhood* is available through Research Press, 2612 North Mattis Avenue, Champaign, IL 61821 or through the ADD WareHouse, (800) ADD-WARE.

Skillstreaming the Elementary School Child by Ellen McGinnis and Dr. Arnold Goldstein with Dr. Robert P. Sprafkin and Dr. N. Jane Gershaw is a social skills training program designed to provide instruction in small groups, but it can be used in large classrooms as well. The manual addresses the social skill needs of children who exhibit aggression, immaturity, withdrawal, or other behavior problems. It provides a training program which is based on the Structured Learning approach which involves modeling, role playing, performance feedback, and transfer training. The curriculum is divided into the following content areas: Dealing with Feelings, Classroom Survival Skills, Alternatives to Aggression, Friendship-Making Skills, and Dealing with Stress. Within these areas, the program addresses 60 prosocial skills, such as: saying thank you, asking for help, apologizing, dealing with anger, responding to teasing, and handling group pressure. These skills could be included in the curriculum of regular and special education classrooms. Program Forms Booklets include assessment forms for the teacher or group leader, student self-assessment forms, homework report forms, contracts, self-monitoring forms, and award certificates. *Skillstreaming the Elementary School Child* is available through Research Press, 2612 North Mattis Avenue, Champaign, IL 61821 or through the ADD WareHouse, (800) ADD-WARE.

Skillstreaming the Adolescent by Dr. Arnold Goldstein, Dr. Robert P. Sprafkin, Dr. N. Jane Gershaw and Paul Klein contains social skills that can be taught to older children in small groups or in classroom settings. Expressing feelings, maintaining a conversation, setting a goal, apologizing, responding to teasing, and standing up for oneself or a friend are among the 50 prosocial skills presented. As with the program for younger students, a Structured Learning approach which involves modeling, role playing, performance feedback, and transfer training is used to promote learning. *Skillstreaming the Adolescent* is available through Research Press, 2612 North Mattis Avenue, Champaign, IL 61821 or through the ADD WareHouse, (800) ADD-WARE.

Adolescent Curriculum for Communication and Effective Social Skills (ACCESS) (Walker, Todis, Holmes and Horton, 1988) is based on Dr. Hill Walker's work on social competence. Designed to train social skills in small groups, the program is structured over 31 sessions. Skill lessons are composed of 10 steps, some of which include a review of a previously trained skill, the introduction of a new skill, practice of the new skill through role playing, and contracting for skill implementation. The *ACCESS* program is well planned and offers a systematic way for teachers to provide social skills training for groups of students. *ACCESS* is available through PRO-ED, Austin, TX.

Sam Goldstein, Ph.D. and Michael Goldstein, M.D. (1990) present a sample social skills training program specifically for children with ADD in their comprehensive text, *Managing Attention Disorders In Children*. Developed by Goldstein and Pollock (1988), the program teaches 23 skills to improve social competence. It is designed to be administered in six 11/2-hour sessions over a six week period and is best implemented in small group settings containing from 3 to 6 children. Examples of some of the skills taught are: listening, meeting people, beginning a conversation, ending a conversation, joining an ongoing activity, asking questions appropriately, asking favors, seeking help from peers and adults, sharing, interpreting body language, working cooperatively, saying thank you, giving a compliment, apologizing, understanding the impact your behavior has on others, and understanding the behavior of others.

James Swanson, Ph.D. developed a school-based treatment program for children with attention deficit disorder at the University of California, Irvine in conjunction with the Orange County Department of Education. One of the only programs of its kind in the country specifically designed to teach ADD children, Dr. Swanson's program teaches students problem-solving and other prosocial behavior in small group settings. Students' learned social skills and problem-solving behavior are then monitored by the classroom teacher. Through continuous evaluation and reinforcement of these skills within the classroom, at recess, during lunch and throughout the entire school day, children learn to apply these skills better than they would if there were no follow-up by the teacher. Continuous monitoring and reinforcement of cognitive skills and prosocial behavior within the natural setting of the classroom enhances generalization.

In summary, the use of self-monitoring, problem-solving, self-instruction, and social skills training show promise as potentially effective methods by which to help ADD children. Self-monitoring strategies, in particular, have been shown to be successful in cases wherein attention to task has been targeted for improvement. Application of cognitive problem-solving strategies within the natural setting could be enhanced through teaching and rehearsal of problem-solving skills within the child's actual classroom environment. Training in social skill acquisition with follow-up reinforcement of learned social skills in naturalistic settings could be quite important in helping ADD children develop better relationships. A number of programs are available for training students to use self-monitoring, prob-lem -solving, and to acquire social skills.

Part II

Teaching Children with Attention Deficit Disorders

Chapter 7
ADD as an Educational Disorder

For a long time no one seemed to have the answers to help students with ADD in a school setting. Daily reports of poor school performance created heartache and misery for ADD children and their parents, who faced each new school day with the discouraging thought that it would offer no more hope than the day before. Unfortunately, most teachers didn't know what to do with these inattentive, hyperactive children who took up much of their day with poor behavior and even poorer work. For the most part, teachers never had any training in their under-graduate education programs about attention deficit disorders and probably had received little, if any, ADD related in-service training during their teaching career. Books about ADD were not readily available five or six years ago and those that were had been written more for health care professionals and parents than for teachers. With an average of one to two ADD children in every classroom and with teachers unaware of how to reach them, ADD children were in trouble and their parents and teachers knew it.

One of the reasons so few educators knew about ADD was because for many years ADD had not been considered a handi-capping condition in our nation's public schools. No mention of ADD or its cardinal symptoms of inattention, impulsivity, and hyperactivity could be found in the Education of the Handi-capped Act (EHA; PL 94-142) or in its reauthorized form, the

Individuals with Disabilities Education Act (IDEA; PL 101-476). ADD was not considered, in and of itself, a disabling condition, despite the fact that many ADD children experienced substantial problems in school.

Parents Advocate for ADD

Fueled by concern and desperation, parents of ADD children began to meet and organize support groups. The ADD parent support group movement had unprecedented growth between 1987 and 1991. With a strong conviction to find help for their children and to secure a place for them in our country's educational system, parents like Sandra F. Thomas, Mary C. Fowler, JoAnne Evans, Bonnie Fell, Michael and Fran Gilman, Ellen Kosh, Carol Lerner, Pamela Murray, Debra Maxey, Nancy Cornish, Nancy Eisenberg, Tom Phelan, Judy Mitchell, Judy Leonard, Mary Jane Johnson, Jean C. Harrison and many others, worked tirelessly to develop support groups and to spread information about ADD throughout their communities and around the country.

One parent support group, CH.A.D.D., Children With Attention Deficit Disorder, started in 1987 by myself, Fran Gilman, and Carol Lerner took off like a rocket in south Florida. Within six months three chapters of CH.A.D.D. had started and within a year we were planning our first national conference in Orlando with over twenty chapters formed. As of March 1992, there are almost three hundred CH.A.D.D. chapters around the country offering information and support to parents. Similarly, other ADD support groups, like Debra Maxey's HAAD (now part of CH.A.D.D.) in Virginia, Pamela Murray's ADDAG in Colorado, Nancy Eisenberg's ADHD Association of Texas, Judy Mitchell's ADD-IN in Massachusetts, to name just a few, have significantly influenced attitudes about ADD in their states.

Starting in 1989, parents began to tell members of the

United States Congress their stories of heartache and discouragement in trying to get educational help for their ADD children. Their timing was right because the Education of the Handicapped Act, which became law in 1975, had to come before the legislature for reauthorization.

While considering the reauthorization of PL 94-142 the United States Senate became aware that children with ADD were not receiving a free appropriate public education as the law required. Attempting to remedy this situation, the Senate Committee on Labor and Human Resources passed a bill in November 1989 which added ADD to PL 94-142 under the definition of specific learning disability (SLD). While categorizing ADD children within the definition of learning disabled looked like a workable solution to members of the Senate, ADD experts knew that this step would not only be technically inaccurate, but would not help the majority of ADD children, since they do not have learning disabilities.

In order to be considered eligible for special eduation services, a learning disabled child must show a significant discrepancy between tested mental ability and academic achievement. The SLD child must be underachieving relative to his ability level. Since most ADD children did not have academic achievement problems in school, they would not have been eligible to receive services under the SLD category. The Senate's remedy would have been a solution in name only, with little practical benefit to most ADD children who needed special help. Trying to apply an SLD definition to ADD children would not work.

In the Spring 1990 the U. S. House of Representatives' Committee on Education and Labor was also considering their EHA reauthorization bill. Sandra F. Thomas, Mary C. Fowler, and Dr. James Swanson prepared testimony which was heard by the Subcommittee on Select Education. Their testimony led the Subcommittee to recognize, as the Senate did, that ADD children were being denied a free appropriate public education.

They were also made aware of the fact that ADD and SLD were different disorders. The drawbacks of the Senate bill, which was passed six months earlier, became evident. Taking this testimony into consideration, the House passed a bill which would have included ADD in EHA as a handicapping condition under the existing category of Other Health Impairments. By doing so, ADD children would have a better chance of receiving help if needed.

As soon as the House bill was passed in May 1990, opposition to the ADD language in the bill was heard from a number of education-related groups. These groups opposed the inclusion of ADD as a special education disability. They created enough uncertainty about the issue to cause a joint House and Senate conference committee to meet to discuss the issue further and arrive at a consensus as to what should be done. To resolve the controversy, the conference committee decided to ask the Department of Education to issue a public Notice of Inquiry which would provide Congress with the widest possible range of advice on the issue.

DOE Policy Memorandum on ADD

Nearly three thousand responses to the Notice of Inquiry were submitted to the Department of Education by parents and professionals. In May 1991 the Office of Special Education and Rehabilitative Services (OSERS) provided a summary of these responses to Congress. Overall, the Department found that there was a great deal of confusion as to how ADD children were being understood and taught in schools.

With the Notice of Inquiry responses in mind, the Department of Education sought to clarify to state departments of education whether ADD children could be eligible for special education services. OSERS announced that, "Children with ADD may be considered disabled solely on the basis of this disorder within the Other Health Impaired category in situations where special education and related services are needed because of ADD." (OSERS News Update, March-April 1991, p. 2). On September 16, 1991 the U.S. Department of Education more fully explained its policy on ADD in a memorandum to chief state school officers. This memorandum, included in its entirety in Appendix A, was signed by the Assistant Secretaries of the Office of Special Education and Rehabilitative Services, the Office for Civil Rights, and the Office of Elementary and Secondary Education. The memorandum was far reaching in its content and emphasized state and local education agencies' responsibility to address the needs of children with attention deficit disorders both within general and special education. Dr. Judy Schrag, Director of Special Education Programs, received a standing ovation from parents, educators, and health care professionals at the CH.A.D.D. conference in Washington, D.C. when she announced the new ADD policy clarification.

Policy Memorandum Emphasizes Regular Classroom Accommodations

The new policy memorandum pointed out that state and local education agencies should offer protections to ADD students even if such students were found **not** to be eligible for services under Part B of IDEA. The Department encouraged such education agencies to take necessary steps to make accommodations within the classroom to meet the needs of students with ADD in the regular education setting and emphasized that education agencies must consider the provisions of Section 504 of the Rehabilitation Act of 1973 in doing so.

Section 504 is a federal law which requires public school districts to provide a free appropriate public education to every "qualified handicapped person" residing within their jurisdiction. The Office of Civil Rights (OCR) is the federal agency within the Department of Education that enforces Section 504. OCR has ruled that ADD children are "qualified handicapped persons" under Section 504 if their ability to learn or to otherwise benefit from their education is substantially limited due to ADD.

Thus, regardless of whether an ADD child meets eligibility guidelines to receive federally funded special education programs (under IDEA), Section 504 guarantees the ADD child the right to receive a free appropriate public education.

The policy memorandum emphasized the important role that teachers in regular education have in providing help to ADD students.

> Steps also should be taken to train regular education teachers and other personnel to develop their awareness about ADD and its manifestations and the adaptations that can be implemented in regular education programs to address the instructional needs of these children (p. 7).

The Department felt that through the use of appropriate adaptations and interventions in regular classes, many of which may be required by Section 504, that local education agencies will be able to effectively address the instructional needs of many children with ADD.

Policy Memorandum Clarifies That ADD Can Fall Under "Other Health Impaired" Category

With respect to special education, the memorandum indicated that children with ADD may be considered disabled solely on the basis of this disorder within the "other health impaired" category.

> The "other health impaired" category includes chronic or acute impairments that result in limited alertness, which adversely affects educational performance. Thus, children with ADD should be clasified as eligible for services under the "other health impaired" category in instances where the ADD is a chronic or acute health problem that results in limited alertness, which adversely affects educational performance (p. 3)

The policy memorandum also stated that children with ADD are also eligible for services under Part B (IDEA) if the children satisfy the criteria applicable to other disability categories. For example, children with ADD are also eligible for services under the "specific learning disability" category or Part B if they meet criteria and under the "seriously emotionally disturbed" category of Part B if they meet criteria for that category.

Furthermore, it was made clear that state and local education agencies are obligated to evaluate the possible need for special education services for children with a prior medical diagnosis of ADD and for those children who are suspected of having ADD.

ADD Centers Funded

The Department of Education's action reinforces the notion that the educational needs of children with ADD must be addressed in our nation's schools, both within regular and special education. In an effort to determine how this could best be done, Congress recently funded an ADD Resource Center at the University of Kentucky to search throughout the country for promising practices that currently exist to educate ADD children. Understanding that educators know little about attention deficit disorders, Congress also authorized funding to establish four ADD centers to collect, synthesize and distribute information about ADD to schools. Additionally, in the fiscal year 1992 House Appropriations Committee report, the committee indicated that $1,500,000 should be used for the funding of projects that develop new inservice and preservice training for special education and regular classroom teachers in order to address the needs of children with attention deficit disorders.

The pleas of parents have been heard. Thanks to new

changes in policy at the federal level, children with ADD will have a better opportunity to receive a free and appropriate public education.

Chapter 8
Teaching Children with ADD in the Regular Classroom

Giving Teachers the Tools to Help

ADD children have their greatest problems in school. Observational studies of ADD children show that they don't fit into the normal routines of the classroom. Difficulty paying attention leads to unfinished work, impulsivity results in academic errors and social disruptions, and hyperactivity causes constant fidgeting and excessive talking.

A recent study surveyed teachers' knowledge and attitudes about ADD. The vast majority of teachers surveyed viewed ADD as a significant educational problem. They felt that there should be increased input from school staff and community physicians to assist them in teaching ADD students. Teachers reported the need for information to better understand ADD students and felt they needed more training in behavioral management strategies and greater knowledge of effective classroom interventions. However, even with more training, teachers felt that large class size, numerous other teaching responsibilities, lack of planning time, and lack of teacher aides would still restrict their ability to provide help to children with ADD.

Using a Prereferral Intervention Model

If regular education classroom teachers are to successfully teach ADD students they will need assistance. Many State Education Agencies, aware of the limitations that regular education teachers have, both in terms of time constraints and preparation, are incorporating prereferral intervention programs to assist them. Broadly defined, prereferral intervention is a systematic and collaborative effort to assist regular education teachers to utilize interventions with hard-to-teach students. Prereferral intervention programs use relatively easy modifications of the classroom environment or instructional program that can be implemented by the regular classroom teacher. Despite their simplicity of use, these interventions can be very effective in producing desired changes in pupil performance. Some teachers already use several of these intervention strategies. Peer teaching, moving a student's seat, having students monitor their own behavior, contracting for better academic performance, teaching a learning strategy, etc. are familiar, informal interventions.

In a prereferral intervention model, the design and application of interventions is done through a team approach. Such teams (child study teams, child study committees, teacher assistance teams, intervention teams, etc.) are frequently made up of the regular education teacher, a school psychologist or school counselor, and special educator, but can include experts in the area of attention deficit disorders, teachers of emotionally handicapped or behaviorally impaired students, behavior management specialists, physicians, psychologists, social workers, family counselors, reading specialists, etc.. One of the members of the team is assigned the role of case manager. The case manager has the responsibility of following the student and keeping track of team decisions and the outcome of interventions and procedures used. The prereferral intervention process may last anywhere from one to several months so long as there is an active process of assessment, strategic intervention, and evaluation of results. The team assists the teacher in assessing the student's behavior and implementing systematic modification programs until the student's problems are corrected or until it is decided if more intensive intervention is necessary, e.g. referral for special education assessment.

For example, a student who is suspected of having attention deficits or who has a diagnosis of ADD may be brought to the child study team by a teacher who is looking for ways to help the child. The team might make several recommendations to the teacher. Team members could recommend accommodations that the teacher could use with the student in class. They may help the teacher design and implement a formal behavior management program for the student. A social worker or family counselor may get involved if home-based difficulties are suspected. The child may be enrolled in a social skills program if that is warranted. A case manager could be assigned to follow-up and stay in contact with the teacher throughout the year. If, after a reasonable period of time, interventions are not successful a referral for special education assessment may be necessary.

In Broward County, Florida a Superintendent's Task Force Report on Attention Deficit Disorders (1991), under the direction of Dr. Merrick R. Kalan, recommended a similar approach to providing services to ADD students. This model encouraged early identification of children suspected of having attentional problems and advocated that ADD should be addressed by the school's Child Study Team/Student Support Team. The flow chart outlines the sequence of procedures which the task force recommended be followed.

ADHD/ADD Program & Services Flow Chart

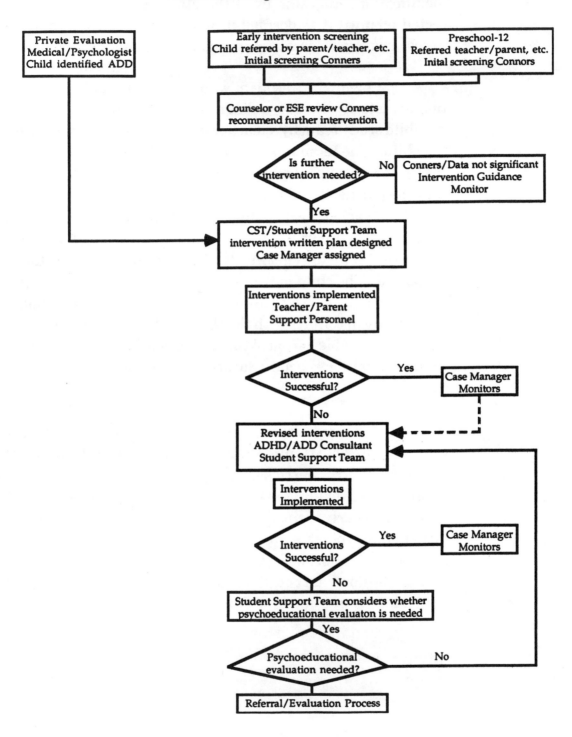

Note: From: *Superintendent's Task Force Report on Attention Deficit Disorder*. 1991. Broward County Public Schools. Student Services. Broward County, Florida. Reprinted with permission.

Similarly, the Virginia Department of Education Task Force Report (1989) entitled " Attention Deficit Hyperactivity Disorder and the Schools" suggested prereferral intervention steps to be followed in that state to assist ADD children in regular education settings. The task force recommended that schools in Virginia utilize a Child Study Committee to help regular education teachers make the necessary alterations in the regular classroom setting which would enable the ADD child to function satisfactorily. In cases wherein the Child Study Committee determines that the problems of the child are too difficult to manage within the scope of regular education, a referral for formal assessment of eligibility for special education can be made.

Prereferral intervention offers several advantages to students, parents, and teachers. If the process is successful, the students benefit by receiving intervention early, rather than having to exhibit chronic failure before the decision is made to evaluate for special education. Students also benefit from staying with peers in regular education and in not being labeled. The intervention they receive in the regular classroom is ongoing throughout the entire day rather than just a portion of the day while they are in the resource special education class. Teachers benefit by learning new problem-solving strategies which can then be applied to other students in the future. The methods they implement can be shared with their colleagues through informal networking in the preconsultation process. Teachers feel a positive sense of comraderie which comes from working on a professional team to develop effective methods of reaching students. School systems benefit from having better trained teachers who are capable of providing high quality instruction in regular education classes. Schools which emphasize a prereferral intervention model may be able to service more students quickly than will schools whose programs rely primarily on a special education model to assist high risk students.

Critics of the prereferral intervention model, however, have several legitmate concerns. They fear that such programs may lead to an eventual dismantling of special education, thereby threatening the rights of disabled children who truly need more services than can be provided in a regular classroom setting. They caution that prereferral intervention programs will require careful monitoring of results so as to determine if the child's needs can be successfully met in regular education. Those who are concerned about the use of prereferral intervention models advise that regular classroom interventions should **not** delay diagnostic assessment of the child's problems. In cases where there is suspicion of a medical, psychiatric, psychological or developmental disorder, further diagnostic assessment must be done to assure that the child has the benefit of receiving the widest possible range of treatment. For example, upon evaluation it may be discovered that the attention deficient child meets criteria for a diagnosis of attention deficit disorder for which additional treatment is recommended, e.g. medical management, parent training, etc.. Or a diagnostic evaluation may reveal that the student's inattention is related to an underlying seizure disorder or other medical condition requiring totally different treatment. Such a diagnostic evaluation should, however, be distinguished from more traditional evaluations that now generally lead to decisions regarding placement.

Forming Effective Parent-Teacher Partnerships

Getting Parents Involved

If teachers could make a wish list of what they would like to have most to help them do their job effectively, they would probably ask for smaller class sizes, more time for planning and preparation, less administrative responsibilities, and more motivated students. Topping the list, however, would be the wish to have more parents involved in their child's education, according to a 1989 article in *Instructor* magazine. Why do teachers want parents to become involved in education? Simple, it makes their job easier and it encourages the student to be more successful in school. Teachers know beyond any doubt that students whose parents are involved are more motivated to perform academically and behaviorally.

Parents of ADD students are no different than other parents who want the best education possible for their child. Like other parents, they are generally very willing to be involved in their child's education. Having experienced the same problems with their child at home as the teacher is having at school, these parents know first-hand how the teacher feels. Together, they can design learning and behavioral strategies that could be implemented in the classroom and at home. Parents can back-up teachers' learning expectations and can supervise homework and long- term projects better because of the clear communication between the school and the home. To help teachers build such a positive teacher-parent relationship, there are a few things they might need to know about parents of ADD children.

Parents of ADD Students Are Often Overwhelmed

In addition to the stresses that exist in most households these days, parents of ADD children have the additional stress of raising a child who requires a great deal of care and supervision. As difficult as an ADD child can be at school, he can be even more difficult to manage at home. Being comfortable in familiar surroundings, the child can truly let his hair down and be himself. Inattention, impulsivity, and hyperactivity can be as hard to deal with for the parent as it is for the teacher. Years of living with the unrelenting and demand nature of some ADD children, as well as their need for limits and correction, have frayed the nerves and dampened the spirits of even the most resilient of parents. Mothers, especially, are up front on the firing line and often report feelings of stress, depression, and desperation as they struggle to help their child cope.

Hanging on by the tips of their fingers, the last thing a parent in this condition wants to hear is that their child is having problems in school. Most parents of ADD children know ahead of time that the bad news is coming. They are used to hearing it. They've usually heard it from teacher after teacher since their child started school. Unfortunately, its the type of news you never really get used to, even though you've heard and lived with the same problems a dozen times before.

Parents can have many different initial reactions to the news that their child is having problems in school. Some parents, frustrated and upset, will become defensive and angry. Overwhelmed and unable to handle more problems, their frustrations may spill over to the school and the teacher, blaming them for their child's difficulties rather than accepting the fact that their son or daughter has a problem. Others may take a more receptive posture. Not knowing what to do or how to handle the child, they may dutifully follow the teacher's advice and do just about anything that offers the promise of a solution. Still others, having tried and tried to provide help for their child with little success over the years, may be discouraged and reluctant to put more energy into trying to solve their child's unending school problems.

Making The First Contact with a Parent

Deciding when to make the first contact with the student's parents is not always easy. When has a problem gotten significant enough to call home? Most teachers probably wait too long before alerting a student's parents to a problem. Parents prefer to be told about a problem early so they can do something about it rather than to hear late in the year that their child has been having problems all along. In order for parents to be involved, they must be informed.

The best rule-of-thumb to use in deciding when to call a parent is to ask yourself, would you want to be contacted if it was your child who was having these same problems? If you think you would, then contact the parents.

When you first contact the parents of an ADD child, be ready for any one of the reactions discussed in the section above. It is important that the teacher maintain a professional posture throughout the initial parent contact. Try following these steps:

- Tell the parents the reason for your call and describe the types of problems that their child is having in school.
- Express your concern for the child and discuss the procedures you have used to try to solve the student's problem.
- Allow the parents to ask questions and to express their opinion of their child's problem.
- If they relate that the child has had problems before, be very understanding.
- Find out from the parent what has been done in the past to assist the child.
- Offer some suggestions that might help, but don't preach, lecture, or come across as if you have all the answers.
- Offer your continued support, and schedule a time to speak again to plan an intervention or discuss the child further.

Some of the parents you talk to will have children who have already been diagnosed with ADD. If this is the case, your communication with the parent will probably be a lot easier. Many parents with diagnosed children are well informed about the disorder. They may have taken some parent training classes or have probably read a good deal about ADD. They may be members of an ADD support group which supplies them with current information about the disorder. Informed parents are likely to have a lot of ideas that can be helpful to you.

Providing Accommodations in the Classroom

Trying to learn more about the ADD student through the eyes of his parents can certainly give the teacher more awareness and understanding of the student's problems. Teachers who recognize ADD as a disorder and who make appropriate adjustments in their teaching style and expectations, can turn a losing year into a winning one for the student. However, for many teachers acceptance of this disorder can be difficult, perhaps, in part, due to the very nature of how ADD children look and act.

1. ADD is an invisible handicap. Children with ADD don't look any different than non-ADD kids. They generally don't have obvious speech, language, motor or mental handicaps which would make them stand out and give cause for concern. All children display some ADD-like behavior. It is sometimes difficult to determine at what point normal inattention becomes attention deficit.

2. Symptoms of ADD are not consistently present within the same child in every situation. For example, the visual impairments of a visually handicapped child affect him in all situations. The same consistency is not always true for ADD impairment. Because an ADD student may be able to attend or be still in one situation and not in another, it is easy to suspect that the child may have more volitional control than he really has. "If he can do it now, why couldn't he do it before?" This leads us to expect more of the child than the child may be able to deliver. As Dr. Russell Barkley jokingly points out in his talks on ADD, "The ADHD child succeeds once or twice and we hold it against him for the rest of his life."

Unfortunately, we don't have a very good answer to explain the inconsistency in the performance of ADD children.

However, we do know that unlike other children, those with ADD show an increased variablity of performance. It is precisely this variability which is a hallmark characteristic of the disorder itself. Understanding teachers, rather than those who seek to discredit the disorder, look for confirming signs of the presence of the disorder in the student. They recognize the variability inherent in the behavior of ADD students and see inconsistency in performance as characteristic of the child's problems, rather than as evidence that the child "could really do it if he tried." They are less likely to describe the child as lazy, unmotivated, spoiled, etc. and tend to see the child as having a problem rather than thinking of the child as being a problem. Teachers who have an understanding of ADD are flexible enough in their teaching style to make accommodations for the child's handicaps and follow recommended educational interventions for the management of the disorder.

Most ADD students can be taught successfully in regular classroom settings, provided teachers are willing to modify teaching practices to accommodate students' special needs. Small changes in how a teacher approaches the student or in what the teacher expects can often be the difference between success or failure for the student. Some general principles for making accommodations for ADD students follow.

Have Clearly Defined Rules

ADD children function best in structured environments wherein expectations are clearly set by the teacher and consistent routines have been established. Classroom rules are an important part of this structure. To be effective, rules cannot just be posted and forgotten; they should serve as a framework for guiding the student and teacher behavior throughout the year. Rules communicate the teacher's expectations regarding student behavior in the classroom. However, rules alone will not develop and maintain appropriate student behavior. They will be most effective when combined with teacher praise for desirable behavior and ignoring of undesirable behavior.

- Discuss appropriate classroom rules with students.
- Write lists of rules on the chalkboard as students offer them.
- Choose four to six rules that are the most important and phrase them positively, e.g. Cooperate with others, Raise your hand to ask permission to talk, Complete work neatly and on time, Work at your desk quietly, Be prepared each day with your work.
- Print rules on posterboard and display them in the front of the room.

Develop Routines for Repetitive Activities

In every classroom, like in every home, there are routine activities that are done daily. ADD children do better in highly structured classrooms with set procedures for carrying out activities.

- Develop structured routines to start the day off in a consistent manner.
- Design a method of handing out and collecting papers.
- Designate a specific place the teacher keeps collected papers.
- Have students keep completed work in specific locations, e.g. notebooks, folders, etc..
- Use established procedures to check homework and classroom assignments.
- Establish routines for dismissal.
- Design procedures for dealing with transitions, e.g. short breaks, introduce new lessons with interesting joke or story, etc.
- Develop strategies for discipline and for administering positive consequences.

Help the Student Stay Organized

As most teachers will readily attest, ADD students are generally not well organized. Their desks, lockers, book bags, or notebooks can be in shambles within days, if not hours, of just having been cleaned up and straightened out. Parents of ADD children also have their hands full (often with the proverbial hair from their heads that they want to pull out), when they've spent all night with their ADD child preparing tomorrow's homework, only to have it get misplaced or lost before it reaches the teacher. Teachers should place a high priority on being organized even though the ADD child may have a hard time doing so.

- Establish rules for neatness early on so that students appreciate your concern for quality work.
- Direct ADD student with organizational problems to straighten up his belongings and his work area daily. For elementary students, spot check their desks to encourage cleanliness and order.
- Check that notebooks have proper dividers for different subjects or activities and that the student uses clearly identified folders for work that is returned.
- Have the student write notes to himself for helpful reminders. Reinforce note writing strategies.
- Insist the student use a homework journal or assignment pad daily.
- Keep extra supplies on hand for the student to borrow.
- Have the student clear his desk of unnecessary material.
- Write assignments on chalkboard for the student to copy.
- Compliment student when you note improvements in neatness and organization.

Give Directions Carefully

ADD students often are poor listeners. They distract

easily and frequently miss important information said by the teacher. A common reason ADD children don't follow directions is they are often unaware that directions have been given.

- Before giving directions, get the full attention of the class. This can be done by changing the tone of your voice, flicking the lights on and off, closing the classroom door, or saying cue phrases like, "May I have your attention please?" to which the class has been conditioned to respond by listening for directions.
- Use short, simple sentences when speaking to the student. Be sure to give verbal instructions at the student's vocabulary level.
- Organize directions in sequence to avoid confusion.
- Give one instruction at a time. Avoid multiple commands.
- Give examples of what you expect the students to do.
- Check to be sure the student understands the directions. Repeat directions as many times as necessary.
- Ask students to repeat the directions back.
- Write a summary of the directions on the chalkboard for easy reference or prepare assignments written on index cards.
- To reinforce a direction to an individual student, first make eye contact, then call the child by name and give the direction.

Find the Right Place To Seat the Student

It doesn't take long to figure out who should be sitting near who in a classroom. Teachers rearrange seats constantly to find the right mix for students, especially those who are prone to be overly sociable or disruptive. Try to avoid sitting ADD students near each other, near windows, by bulletin boards, or close to areas of the room where they are subject to more distractions. The best seating is probably in close proximity to the teacher so that the student is easily accessible for teacher prompting, correction, or reinforcement, or near a good peer role model.

Keep the Classroom Stimulating

The physical structure of a classroom can have a negative or positive effect on the performance of an ADD student. Early theories that children who are distractible will perform better in sterile, distraction free learning environments led special educators to seat ADD students in isolated study carrels, free of distracting stimuli or in classrooms with minimal room decorations, etc.. Working on the "horse with blinders" theory to learning, these early educators were hopeful that with fewer distractions the ADD child would be more able to attend to work and complete tasks. Unfortunately, many of these children were just as off task in this type of setting as in more normal ones. What distractions the environment doesn't immediately provide to the child, the child will create for himself as desk chairs could easily become rockers, scraps of paper interesting objects, etc.. Much to the despair of his teacher, the ADD child manufactures distractions, perhaps in an effort to fight off boredom.

Over the past few years Dr. Russell Barkley has posed the theory that children with ADD may have an underlying deficit in motivation which may affect their attention span. He believes that ADD children are more difficult to motivate than other children and their interest in activities satiates more quickly. The fact that they can attend for long periods of time as they play Nintendo, watch television, or do something which interests them tells us that alluring stimuli can temporarily override attention deficit. Therefore, teachers need to compete for the attention of their ADD students by creating as enriching and exciting a learning environment as possible, thereby increasing the child's motivation to attend. Sydney Zentall, Ph.D. (1990) stresses the importance of using colorful worksheets to stimulate the attention of ADD students and for teachers to incorporate into their instructional program creative learning experiences which fit the student's interests.

- Design your classroom with motivation in mind. Stimulating classroom decor with colorful and interesting surroundings has more of a chance at capturing the ADD child's attention than does blank walls.
- Classrooms which have centers of interest filled with ideas to stimulate creative minds and with enthusiastic teachers to keep those minds occupied work best for ADD students.
- Use an experiential approach to get the point of your lessons across. Find out what interests the student and go from there. Use his interests as a starting point and try to build on them.

Use Computers for Learning and Motivation

Teachers may find that computer assisted learning materials are better able to hold the interest of the ADD student. Colorful graphics, interactive learning, and immediate feedback for responses act like magnets to attract attention. Teachers can use computer time as a reinforcement for good behavior at times during the school day.

Gear Assignments To Attention Span Not Just Ability

While ADD students sometimes have trouble getting started on assignments, they almost always have trouble finishing assignments. As one mother remarked:

"My child spent so much time in third grade in the nurse's office finishing his work, I don't know when he began anything new, because he had to keep finishing everything."

Closure is important to all of us and satisfaction comes

from a job well done. How good could a child feel about himself if he is always "finishing" his work and trying to catch-up to others in class?

- Make allowances for the ADD child's short attention span by shortening assignments.
- Give the child extra time to complete work if neces sary.
- Provide breaks within a long work period.
- Use prompting, self-monitoring, contracting or other behavioral strategies to help the ADD child to stay on task.

Plan Ahead for Transitions

ADD students often have trouble with transitions during the school day. Students probably make more than a dozen transitions each day. Transitions occur when:

- Students stay in their seats and change from one sub-ject to another.
- Students change their seat to go to an activity in an-other part of the classroom.
- Students complete an activity and move back to their seat.
- Students leave the classroom and go to another part of the school.
- Students come back to their classroom after being in another part of the school.

Students and teachers spend a considerable part of their day in transition. Such times are often difficult for ADD students due to problems with disorganization and impulsivity. They have trouble settling down and getting their things to-gether to proceed to a new activity. Particularly difficult for the ADD student is the move from an unstructured activity, e.g. physical education, lunch, etc. to a more structured one which requires them to have self-restraint and to work quietly. To assist students with transition the teacher should:

- Establish rules for transitions, e.g., gather the materials you need, move quietly, keep your hands and feet to yourselves, get ready for the next activity.
- Review transition rules with class until routine is established.
- Supervise students closely during transition times.
- Provide immediate and consistent feedback to students doing well.
- Set time limits for transitions, e.g., try to complete a transition within three minutes, etc.

Help the Student Set Goals

ADD students often have trouble setting goals and carrying out assignments, especially long-term projects. Book reports, science projects, term papers, etc. can present a challenge to the student and a headache to his parents. In order to set goals and finish assignments the student with ADD will very likely need your help.

- Divide large projects into bite-size parts.
- Communication with parents to let them know what is expected and when things are due.
- Use homework journals and assignment time-lines for long term projects.
- Monitor student's work carefully so he doesn't fall behind and get discouraged.
- Reinforce progress as work gets completed.

Provide Frequent Praise

By the time most ADD students have completed two or three grades in school, they have often had a stream of negative experiences with teachers. ADD students usually have a hard time winning teacher approval and developing a positive relationship. As every teacher knows, the building of a positive teacher-student relationship is essential both to facilitate learning and to encourage the development of positive self-esteem in the student. Such a relationship, like any other positive, meaningful interaction must contain ingredients of caring, understanding, respect, and encouragement. In addition to bolstering shaky self-esteem, a teacher's positive regard will encourage students to put more effort into their work both to satisfy their teacher and themselves.

The first few days and weeks of school can be important as a tone-setter for the remainder of the school year. Many, although not all, ADD children are fairly well behaved in new situations and will generally show a honeymoon effect in school during the first few weeks. Teachers could take advantage of this postive display of behavior.

- Attend to the student's pro-learning behavior, recognizing efforts at achievement, and praising attempts as well as successes.
- Ignore minor negative behaviors and quickly attend to incompatible positive behaviors (ignore blurting out, praise hand-raising).
- Maintain close proximity to the child throughout the day by preferential seating close to the teacher or by the teacher walking near the student's desk.
- Spend one or two minutes each day to have a brief talk with the child.
- Keep a mental note of what kind of attention the child likes. When does his face brighten with pride? What words work to encourage? Does he respond to nonverbal reinforcers, e.g. a smile, a wink, or a nod? Is he most proud when recognized publicly by verbal acknowledgements of his efforts or is he more motivated by the promise of tangible rewards?

Use Teacher Attention To Motivate

Teacher attention is an extremely powerful force in shaping behavior. Attention motivates students to perform and the teacher is in a position to give positive attention to students contingent on their behavior. Most often teachers will use attention to manage student behavior while students are involved in seatwork activities. However, attention can be used to manage other activities such as those during instructional lessons, transition times, or unstructured class activities. In providing attention to students, teachers should consider the following procedures:

- Move about the room looking for opportunities to attend to positive behavior with praise.
- Scan the classroom frequently. Scanning lets children know the teacher is watching.
- Spot check the work of children who are good at looking busy but who may not be working.
- Praise the ADD student frequently when you notice that he is complying with class rules.

Use Prudent Reprimands

Teacher reprimands for misbehavior are frequently used for classroom control. Prudent reprimands provide immediate negative feedback to the student and are delivered unemotionally, briefly, and when they are backed up with a mild punishment such as loss of privilege, time-out, or loss of points, if a token system is used. Less successful in changing student behavior are teacher reprimands which are delayed, long-winded, and delivered in an emotionally charged style with empty threats of consequences.

Give the Student with ADD Responsibility

Giving the ADD student responsibilties which assist the teacher in managing the classroom can help the child feel like an important contributor to the class. Assigning him leadership positions on teams, giving him jobs which at he can be successful, and, showing the other students that you respect the ADD student by trusting him to do a job well can promote acceptance from others and builds confidence within the child.

Treat the Student with ADD as a Whole Child, Not Just a Label

When students are diagnosed as having a disorder there is a tendency to see them as they have been labeled rather than to view them as children. One can make arguments in either direction about the pros and cons of labeling children. Advocates for labeling would assert that labels drive services. Opponents point out that labeling of disabled children may make them even more "dis-labeled" in the eyes of those trying to help them. Clearly, we must appreciate the advantages and disadvantages of using labels to categorize students and we must always be cognizant that regardless of a common label, every ADD child is different. Each has his or her own strengths and weaknesses and should be seen as uniquely individual.

Having recently read a manuscript of an article by Constance Weaver, Professor of English at Western Michigan University, I was reminded that for the ADD child to succeed in school we must appreciate the child as an individual. Weaver advocates a "whole language" approach to educating ADD children. She explains that in using such an approach teachers should be sensitive to the unique interests and abilities of the child and should shape the curriculum to the child rather than make the child fit into a preconceived curriculum that might not meet the child's needs and interests. She emphasizes that teachers should try to alleviate the student's problem area by working around weaknesses and capitalizing on strengths. Teachers should provide opportunities for choice in what students would like to read, research, or write about. Creative thinking (usually something ADD children are pretty good at) should be encouraged and fostered along with peer collaboration and group problem-solving, team projects, and learning through discussion and conversation.

Learning about the child's interests outside of the classroom can be a key to motivating the child in school. Whole language teaching involves the student's parents in the learning process and through close parent-teacher interaction the teacher can gain a broader perspective of the child who can then be viewed as a whole person, not just a student, and certainly more than just a label.

What makes the student with ADD exceptional is not his disability, but his ability. Teachers, through accommodating the student's needs by modifying the environment alone, will have only done part of the job. To do the rest, they must focus beyond the surface inattention, impulsivity, or hyperactivity and see the child's strengths that lie deeper within.

Chapter 9
Classroom Interventions

While the accommodations described in the previous chapter can be helpful for many ADD students, often additional interventions will be needed to enhance academic performance and student behavior. This chapter is designed to provide teachers with the step-by-step information they will need to be able to implement a variety of helpful interventions in their classrooms. These interventions should be effective in assisting teachers to solve the common problems that students with ADD present in school. We have tried to provide a sufficient variety of interventions in the knowledge that not every ADD student will respond successfully to the same approach. Teachers will, hopefully, have enough variety to choose from so they can implement those interventions which fit their teaching style best.

Some of the strategies to be reviewed in this chapter are behavioral interventions. Behavioral interventions are commonly used by teachers to modify student behavior. The goals of behavioral interventions are generally to increase appropriate or adaptive behavior, and to decrease inappropriate or maladaptive behavior. The success of behavioral interventions for ADD students has been well documented in reducing rates of disruptive, off-task behavior and in improving compliance, organization, attention, and work production. Behavior modification programs are particularly helpful with ADD students because they motivate, provide structure, and establish clearly defined goals and objectives for students to reach. Many ADD students, not sufficiently motivated by the typical rewards in school which naturally motivate most other students, require additional incentives to complete work, pay attention, and stay organized.

Teachers familiar with general behavioral principles tend to like using behavior modification programs in their classrooms. Generally, such interventions are relatively easy to implement and provide fairly quick results. Although more recent advances in behavioral technology, which involve the use of self-monitoring procedures and cognitive-behavioral interventions are less familiar to teachers, these methods are gaining acceptance by teachers as helpful classroom tools.

Several non-behavioral strategies are also discussed, including the utilization of students as peer teachers and the strategic use of volunteers in the classroom. No teacher can be an expert in everything needed to run an efficient and effective classroom. Expecially when individual differences in students are so varied. ADD, being unfamiliar to many teachers, will require members of a school's faculty to collaborate with one another in order to share knowledge and expertise about the disorder and to formulate creative and practical ideas to help ADD students. The benefits of using a prereferral consultation model are outlined in this chapter. Teachers are strongly encouraged to use such a model so they can share with one another or learn from consultants about effective classroom strategies.

Throughout this chapter the reader will find a number of student worksheets. Copies of these worksheets are contained at the back of the handbook and can be reproduced for classroom use. These worksheets were designed for self-monitoring and recording behavior, contracting with the students, setting up classroom token economy systems as well as home and school-based contingency programs. All classroom teachers have used similar forms to assist their students in charting their behavior or to motivate student performance.

The following interventions will be reviewed:

- Behavioral Contracting
- Token Economy Systems
- Home and School-Based Contingency Programs
- Behavioral Principles
- Self-Monitoring
- Time-Out
- Modeling
- Peer Teaching
- Prereferral Strategies
- Using Volunteers

The reader is referred to the ADAPT Program by Harvey C. Parker, Ph.D. for additional forms and worksheets useful in the design and implementation of accommodations and behavioral interventions for students in elementary through middle school. Teachers can use ADAPT forms found in the ADAPT Teacher Planbook to assess the need for specific accommodations and interventions and can monitor student progress after an accommodation plan is implemented. In addition, many of the worksheets discussed in this chapter are also found in the ADAPT Student Planbook. Those already using ADAPT forms will benefit from reviewing the behavioral interventions which are discussed in this chapter. The ADAPT forms are available through the ADD WareHouse (800-ADD-WARE).

Behavioral Contracting

A behavioral contract is an agreement drawn up between two or more parties, in this case a teacher, a parent, and a student, wherein the student agrees to behave in a specified manner in exchange for some specific reciprocal behavior from the teacher or parent. The purpose of the contract is to restructure the environment to provide a consistent set of expectations and consequences to the student, based upon certain pre-defined performance criteria.

Behavioral contracts, whether written or oral, should clearly delineate the expectations of all parties, should contain well-defined methods of assessing student performance, and should specify precise rewards and/or penalties to be provided based on student performance. Written behavioral contracts tend to be more official than oral contracts and should contain the signatures of all parties, the date when the contract was entered into, and the signature of a witnessing party.

Behavioral contracts have been used successfully for many years to motivate students to perform. Contracts are often successful because they provide a "win-win" approach to helping the student and take into consideration the personal goals of each party.

The use of behavioral contracts with students with ADD may require certain modifications which may not normally be needed with non-ADD students:

1. Young students, in general, may lack adequate language development to understand the essential meaning of a contract and the implication that this is an agreement, promise, or "deal" which is meant to be kept by both the teacher and the student. A young ADD student, in particular, may have such a lack of impulse control that contracting is ineffective, since the student is just unable to manifest enough self-control even for very short peri-

ods of time to fulfill his end of the agreement. This is especially true of very hyperactive young children in preschool through first or second grade.

2. Contracting with ADD children, in general, may require the teacher or parent to emphasize immediacy of reinforcement. Non-ADD youngsters are more likely able to wait a day or longer to "cash-in" on their positive performance as per the terms of their behavioral contracts. Many ADD students will probably need shorter periods of time and more opportunities to receive reinforcement than will their non-ADD counterparts. Every ADD student will respond differently with respect to length of time between reinforcement, as some will require reinforcement at the end of each period, some at the end of the morning or afternoon, and some will be able to wait until the end of the day or week before "cashing-in."

How To Use Behavioral Contracting with ADD Students

1. Explain what a behavior contract is. For young children the contract can be described as a "game" which gives the student an opportunity to win things from the teacher. For older children, explain that contracts are used throughout society in business, in social relationships, and between countries. Equate the idea of a contract to the notion of a promise or an agreement between two people who give their word to exchange one thing for another.

2. Explain that contracts can be used in school to help motivate students to improve their performance.

3. For younger children select one or two "target" behaviors on which you would like the student to focus. Demonstrate the behavior so that the child clearly understands

what you mean. For instance, if you are asking the child to pay attention to you when you are talking, you might sit at the desk, show the child that paying attention means to look at the person talking, listen to that person, and do what they say to do. Or, if your goal is to increase work production, then you should tell the child exactly how this will be measured, e.g. by counting problems completed.

For older students, discuss with the student general behaviors that he exhibits which need improving. Specify these behaviors as "target" behaviors as specifically as possible. Encourage student input in defining the "target" behaviors.

4. Write down one or two target behaviors for younger students while older students may be able to work on four or more such target behaviors: e.g. raises hand before asking a question or giving an answer, copies homework assignments from board each day in an assignment journal, pays attention for 15 minutes at the start of every math lesson, etc..

5. Specify how each target behavior will be measured and when, e.g. Whenever I see you raise your hand before asking a question or giving an answer I will mark it down; When you get 5 marks I will let you know; I will time you during each math lesson to see if you were paying attention for fifteen minutes. At the end of the fifteen minutes I will let you know how you did.

6. With student input, decide on an appropriate reward (or penalty) to be given for performing (or not performing) the target behavior(s). Specify when the reward (or penalty) is to be given. Remember, ADD students may need more frequent rewards than non-ADD students. Make a menu of such rewards or change the reward regularly to maintain motivation. Researchers have

found that ADD children may require higher levels of reinforcement to maintain motivation toward a goal.

7. Write down the specifics of the contract and have it signed by the student. Make a copy for both the teacher and student.

8. Review the contract daily. When target behaviors are demonstrated by the student use social praise with consistent administration of pre-determined reinforcers when performance levels have met or exceeded criteria.

Following Class Rules
Contract

The following class rules will be followed:

_____

_____

_____

If _____
Student's Name

follows these rules

_____
Reward

If _____
Student's Name

does not follow these rules

_____
Consequence

Date_____

Getting To My Goal
Contract

Today my goal is to:

_____

_____

_____

If _____
Student's Name

reaches the goal

_____
Reward

If _____
Student's Name

does not reach the goal

_____
Consequence

Date_____

Contract

I _____, a student at_____
　　　　name of student　　　　　　　　　　　　　　　　　name of school

do hereby declare that I promise to _____

_____.

I _____, a teacher at _____
　　　　name of teacher　　　　　　　　　　　　　　　　　name of school

do hereby declare that in exchange for _____ fulfilling his
　　　　　　　　　　　　　　　　　　　　　　　name of student

promise as stated above, I will _____

_____

In WITNESS WHEREOF, we have subscribed our names this _____ day
　　　　　　　　　　　　　　　　　　　　　　　　　　　　　　　day

of _____, 19_____.
　　　　month　　　　　　year

_____
signature of teacher

_____
signature of student

_____
signature of witness

Source: The ADD Hyperactivity Handbook for Schools by Harvey C. Parker, Ph.D. This form may be reproduced for classroom use.

Token Economy Systems

Token economy systems are a form of behavioral contracting which uses tokens as an immediate reward for certain behavior or task performance. Tokens generally have no intrinsic value other than their worth when exchanged for valued objects, activities or privileges. Teachers are oftentimes unable to provide more tangible reinforcers "on the spot" and therefore utilize token systems to motivate students to reach certain behavioral or performance criteria. Token systems have an additional advantage over simple behavioral contracts in that they offer the promise of a hierarchal reward system and teach the student to delay gratification.

Token systems are generally much more effective with ADD students than simply providing social praise or positive attention for appropriate performance. Behavioral interventions that can offer a tangible reward or the promise of one, through the accrual of tokens or points, are usually very effective with ADD students.

How To Use Token Economy Systems with ADD Students

1. Explain the concept of a token economy system to the student. Tell the student that he will receive or lose tokens based upon his performance throughout the school day.

2. Select an appropriate token. Commonly used tokens may be points on a card or chart (for older students age eight and up) or poker chips, fake money, stamps, etc. (for students below eight). Make sure the student could not reproduce the token on his own. For example if you are using points on a card use a pen to tally points, etc..

3. Discuss with the student the specific goals that you had

in mind for the student to reach. Decide which school behavior is important for the student to demonstrate in order to reach these goals. List two to five behaviors targeted for change on a daily or weekly chart. Make sure the target behaviors are positively phrased and described in a way which is observable and measurable. Do not list negative, general statements, e.g. is less stubborn (should be "complies immediately with teacher's instructions, "calls out in class less (should be "asks permission before speaking").

4. Assign a token value for each behavior. Tokens serve to motivate the student to perform targeted behaviors. Simple behaviors, or those which are frequently demonstrated by the student, should have a smaller token value than behaviors which are more complicated or infrequently demonstrated by the student. Decide with the student what the target behaviors will be worth and the method by which tokens will be administered. Remember, ADD students, especially younger ones, may require frequent reinforcement through administration of tokens shortly after the target behavior has been performed.

5. Fines can be a part of the token system as well. Select one negative behavior which is particularly problematic and remove tokens when that behavior is displayed. While it is better to have a positively oriented token program than a negatively oriented one, the judicious use of fines can be effective in discouraging inappropriate behavior.

6. Determine rewards for which the tokens can be exchanged. A large variety of rewards should be listed so as to encourage student motivation. Rewards may be activities which the student likes, free time, the opportunity to not do a homework assignment, food, objects, etc.. Determine ahead of time activities which the student prefers and offer these as possible rewards. Include

both "inexpensive" and "expensive" rewards and have one or two which are highly valued by the student and which may be earned by saving tokens over time.

7. Decide when tokens will be given and when they might be exchanged for rewards. Again, younger ADD students or ADD students with serious performance problems, may need tokens delivered immediately upon demonstrating a behavior, while others may be able to wait for the period to end or for the end of the morning or day to receive tokens. Similarly, some ADD students may need to "cash in" tokens for rewards from their list more frequently than others.

   Generally speaking, when starting a new program, try to reward new target behaviors frequently by administering tokens often and by offering the student frequent opportunities to cash-in the tokens for rewards. Some students may want to save up their tokens for a larger, more special predetermined privilege to be awarded at the end of the week.

8. Construct a daily or weekly chart on which the target behaviors will be listed along with their respective token value. Also list the rewards, the value of each reward, and when the reward may be received by the student.

9. Using the daily or weekly chart, discuss with the student his performance on a daily basis. Praise success and encourage better performance in weak areas. Make suggestions to the student on ways he can better succeed. Offer to use verbal or non-verbal prompts to remind the student to perform certain behaviors. Maintain a positive, encouraging attitude.

   Dr. Micahel Gordon invented the Attention Training System (ATS) to be used along with a classroom token economy to help motivate students to pay attention. The ATS is a small electronic counter which is placed on the student's desk. The ATS automatically awards the child a point every sixty seconds. If the student wanders off task, the teacher uses a remote control to deduct a point and activate a small warning light on the student's module. The ATS delivers unobtrusive, but effective feedback and functions during regular classroom activites. Each teacher module can control four student modules. Points earned on the ATS may be exchanged for rewards or free time activities within the token economy system.

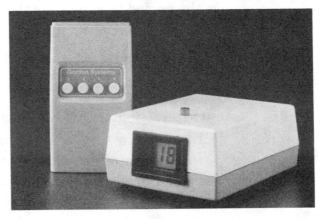

The Attention Training System by Michael Gordon, Ph.D.

Although some teachers initially express concern that an electronic device such as the ATS may cause a distraction in the classroom, most classes adapt to the novelty of the ATS in a few days and teachers find it to be a very helpful way to promote attention-to-task. The Attention Training System is available through Gordon Systems, Inc. P.O. Box 746 DeWitt, NY 13214 or through the ADD WareHouse, (800) ADD-WARE.

SCHOOL-BASED TOKEN PROGRAM

Name _____   Week of _____

PERIOD OR SUBJECT

TARGET BEHAVIORS TO EARN POINTS	POINT VALUES	POINTS EARNED DAILY				
	+					
	+					
	+					
	+					
TOTAL NUMBER POINTS EARNED						

Menu of rewards or activities to choose from:

_____ = _____ Points

_____ = _____ Points

_____ = _____ Points

Name _____   Date _____

PERIOD OR SUBJECT

TARGET BEHAVIORS TO EARN POINTS	POINT VALUE	POINTS EARNED DAILY				
Completed classwork	Yes/No					
Completed homework	Yes/No					
Any assignments due?	Yes/No					
Any recent grades?	Yes/No					
Arrived to class on time?	Yes/No					
Parent's Initials [ ] Teacher's Initials						

Write any comments below and initial:

Source: The ADD Hyperactivity Handbook for Schools by Harvey C. Parker, Ph.D. This form may be reproduced for classroom use.

SCHOOL-BASED TOKEN PROGRAM

Name _____   Week of _____

TARGET BEHAVIORS TO EARN POINTS	POINT VALUES	POINTS EARNED DAILY				
		MON	TUE	WED	THU	FRI
	+					
	+					
	+					
	+					
TARGET BEHAVIORS TO LOSE POINTS		POINTS LOST DAILY				
	-					
	-					
	-					
POINTS EARNED THIS DAY						
BALANCE FROM YESTERDAY						
NEW BALANCE FOR TODAY						
POINTS SPENT TODAY						
TOTAL POINTS LEFT						

Menu of rewards or activities to choose from:

_____ = _____ Points

_____ = _____ Points

_____ = _____ Points

Home and School-Based Contingency Programs

Home and school-based contingency programs involve the collaboration between school and home in the assessment of student behavior by the teacher, and the administration of rewards and consequences at home, based upon the teacher's assessment. Home and school-based contingency programs are effective supplements to classroom behavioral systems such as a classroom token economy program or behavioral contract.

Home and school-based contingency programs have been successfully used with ADD students and are popular with teachers. Dr. Russell Barkley proposed a home and school-based program which employs a daily report card on which several behaviors are identified according to the student's needs. Teachers can rate the student's behavior at different points during the day. The student brings the card home each day for parental review and for administration of predetermined rewards and consequences.

Unlike a school-based token economy system or behavioral contract, home and school-based contingency programs have the advantage of incorporating the student's parents into the behavioral program that is being used in school. Parents of ADD students, used to working with teachers, quickly adapt to the home-based contingency program and often appreciate having daily feedback as to their child's school performance. Daily reporting generally facilitates better parent-teacher communication and encourages the development of home-school partnerships. Parents don't have to wait for parent-teacher conferences or report cards to learn about their child's progress.

While home and school-based contingency programs are effective for a good many ADD students, there are some problems which can develop when they are implemented.

First, some ADD students cannot delay gratification long enough to receive reinforcements later that day when they return home. This is particularly true when working with young ADD students in the primary grades who may need a more immediate reinforcement schedule. Such students may require a supplementary token economy program in school for the delivery of rewards coupled with home-based rewards and consequences to strengthen the immediacy of the program.

Second, some students will be irresponsible in bringing cards home or returning them to school on a daily basis. Students can be trained to use their cards daily. Teachers should establish routines for scoring of cards in school and parents should have consistent routines for daily review of the card at home. Mild consequences for not bringing the card to or from school may sometimes need to be implemented to encourage reluctant or forgetful students.

Third, parental compliance in reviewing the daily card and in delivery of contingencies is generally out of the teacher's control. Poor parental compliance will inevitably cause the system to fail.

How To Use the Goal Card Program: A Home and School-Based Contingency Program for ADD Students

The Goal Card Program, useful for children in grades one through eight, is a home and school-based contingency program which targets five behaviors commonly found to be problematic for ADD children in the classroom. There are two forms of the program: a single rating card on which the child is evaluated once per day each day for the entire week and a multiple rating card on which the child is evaluated several times per day either by subject, activity, period, or teacher.

Most children in elementary school will be able to use a single rating Goal Card because they will be evaluated by one teacher one time per day. Those elementary school students who require more frequent daily ratings, due to high rates of inappropriate behavior, or because they are evaluated by more than two teachers each day, will need a multiple rating card. Middle school students, who usually have several teachers in one day, will need to use the multiple rating card.

Regardless of whether the child is evaluated one or more times a day the target behaviors can remain the same and may include:

- Paid Attention
- Completed Work
- Completed Homework
- Was Well Behaved
- Desk and Notebook Neat

The student is rated on a five point scale (1=Poor, 2=Improved, 3=Fair, 4=Good, 5=Excellent). When a category of behavior does not apply for the student for that day, e.g. no homework assigned, the teacher marks N/A and the student is automatically awarded 5 points.

STEP 1: Explaining the Program to the Child

The Goal Card Program may be introduced to the child by his parents alone, together with his teacher, or with the assistance of a health care professional. The program should be described in a positive manner as a method by which to help the child achieve more success in school.

1. The child is instructed to give the Goal Card to his teacher(s) each day for scoring.

2. The teacher(s) scores the card, initials it and returns it to

the student to bring home to his parents for review.

3. Each evening the parents review the total points earned for the day. If the child is using the single rating Goal Card, it is to be brought to school each day for the rest of the week to be completed by the teacher. If a mulitiple rating Goal Card is used, then the child should use the other side of the card or be given a new card to bring to school for use the following day.

4. Encouragement is offered to the child by the parents in the form of verbal praise and tangible rewards for his successes, while loss of privileges is applied for point totals below a prescribed amount each day (see below). It is important that a combination of rewards and consequences be utilized since ADD children are noted to have a high reinforcement tolerance. That is, they seem to require larger reinforcers and stronger consequences than non-ADD children.

5. Explain to the child that if he forgets, loses, or destroys the Goal Card he is given zero points for the day and appropriate consequences should follow.

If we are to expect complete cooperation from the child then both parents and teachers need to demonstrate a strong involvement with the program through daily evaluation by the teacher and nightly review by the parents.

STEP 2: Setting Up Rewards and Consequences

When using the Goal Card Program be careful to set your reinforcement and punishment cut-off scores at a realistic level so that the child can be successful on the card provided that he is making a reasonable effort in school. Although individual differences need to be considered, we have found that a Goal Card score of 17 points or more per day is an effective cut-off score for starting the program.

As the child improves in performance, the cut-off score can be raised a little at a time in accordance with the child's progress. If the child receives less than the cut-off number of points on any given day then a mild punishment (e.g. removal of a privilege, earlier bed time, etc.) should be provided, however, for points at or above the amount expected, a reward should be forthcoming.

Constructing a List of Rewards

The child and parents should construct a list of rewards which the child would like to receive for bringing home a good Goal Card. Some sample rewards are:

- Additional time for television in the evening after homework
- Staying up later than usual
- Time on video game
- A trip to the store for ice-cream, etc.
- Playing a game with mom or dad
- Going to a friend's house after school
- Earning money to buy something or to add to savings
- Exchanging points for tokens to save up for a larger reward at some future time

Constructing Negative Consequences

The child and parents should construct a list of negative consequences one of which could be imposed upon the child for failure to earn a specified number of points on the Goal Card. Negative consequences should be applied judiciously given consideration for the ADD student's inherent difficulties. Some examples are:

- Early bedtime for not reaching a set number of points

• Missing dessert
• Reduction in length of playtime or television time
• Removal of video game for the day

STEP 3: Using the Program—The Parent Record Form

During the first three days of the program, baseline data should be collected. This is the breaking-in phase wherein points earned by the student will count toward rewards, but not toward loss of privileges. As with any new procedure, it is likely that either the child or teacher will occasionally forget to have the Goal Card completed. Such mistakes should be overlooked during this breaking-in phase.

After this brief period it is essential that the teacher score the Goal Card daily. The teacher should ask the child for the card even when the child forgets to bring it up for scoring and should reinforce the child for remembering on his own to hand in the card for scoring. If the child repeatedly does not bring the card to the teacher for scoring the teacher should explain the importance of daily review of the card to the child. A mild consequence may be applied if the child continues to forget the card.

Generally the best time to score the card for elementary school students who are on a single rating system is at the end of the day. Middle school students, of course, should obtain scores after each period. Ignore any arguing or negotiating on the part of the student regarding points earned. Simply encourage the child to try harder the next day.

Parents should be certain to review the Goal Card on a nightly basis. It is not wise to review the card immediately upon seeing the child that afternoon or evening. Set some time aside before dinner to review the card thoroughly and dispense appropriate rewards or remove privileges if necessary. After reviewing the card parents should complete the Parent Record Form which is a monthly calendar to record points earned each day for that month. This will serve as a permanent record and can be used for students who are earning points for long term rewards.

STEP 4: Self-Evaluation Training

The self-evaluation phase of the Goal Card Program is important in that it offers the child the opportunity to evaluate his own performance in school and creates greater self-aware-ness of behavior. After the child has been successful on the program for at least one month, the teacher should ask the child to complete his own Goal Card each day and to compare his ratings with that of the teacher's for the day. When child and teacher ratings for a particular behavior are substantially different, the teacher should explain why the child received the teacher rating.

Continue with the self-evaluation phase if the child's performance continues to be positive.

STEP 5: Phasing Out the Program

Initially, the delivery of rewards and the prudent use of negative consequences drives the Goal Card Program and provides the initial motivation to the child to succeed. When the program is working well and the child consistently brings home good marks on the Goal Card, he gains a sense of pride about his performance. The joy of a job well done becomes an even more powerful incentive to the child than extrinsic rewards or the fear of negative consequences. When such a result is achieved the parents and teacher should discuss phasing out the program so as not to build reliance on the Goal Card.

Begin the phasing out procedures as soon as the student's behavior is consistently positive for a six week period. Partial phasing out has already been instituted by the child's self-evaluating behavior (Step 4). Additional phasing out of the program can be accomplished by using the card less frequently (every other day or every other week). Teachers need to continue to positively reinforce the child for demonstration of appropriate target behaviors, even well after the program is discontinued.

Single Rating Goal Card

Child's Name _____   Grade _____

Teacher: _____   School _____

Week of _____

Goal Card	MON.	TUES.	WED.	THURS.	FRI.
1. Paid attention in class					
2. Completed work in class					
3. Completed homework					
4. Was well behaved					
5. Desk & notebook neat					
Totals					
Teacher's Initials					

Teacher's Comments   Parent's Comments

_____
_____
_____
_____
_____
_____
_____
_____
_____
_____

N/A — Not applicable
O — Losing, forgetting or destroying card

1 — Poor
2 — Needs Improvement
3 — Fair

4 — Good
5 — Excellent

Source: The ADD Hyperactivity Handbook for Schools by Harvey C. Parker, Ph.D. This form may be reproduced for classroom use.

Multiple Rating Goal Card

Child's Name_____   Grade _____

Teacher: _____   School _____

Date _____   Teacher's Comments   Parent's Comments

Goal Card

1. Paid attention in class					
2. Completed work in class					
3. Completed homework					
4. Was well behaved					
5. Desk & notebook neat					
Totals					
Teacher's Initials					

N/A — Not applicable   1 — Poor   4 — Good
O — Losing, forgetting or destroy-   2 — Needs Improvement   5 — Excellent
　ing card   3 — Fair

Parent Goal Card Record Form

Parents' Goal Card Record Form

Month _____

Name _____

Rewards & Consequences | Points

1. _____

2. _____

3. _____

Sunday	Monday	Tuesday	Wednesday	Thursday	Friday	Saturday
☐ Points	☐ Points	☐ Points	☐ Points	☐ Points	☐ Points	☐ Points
☐ Points	☐ Points	☐ Points	☐ Points	☐ Points	☐ Points	☐ Points
☐ Points	☐ Points	☐ Points	☐ Points	☐ Points	☐ Points	☐ Points
☐ Points	☐ Points	☐ Points	☐ Points	☐ Points	☐ Points	☐ Points
☐ Points	☐ Points	☐ Points	☐ Points	☐ Points	☐ Points	☐ Points

Source: The ADD Hyperactivity Handbook for Schools by Harvey C. Parker, Ph.D. This form may be reproduced for classroom use.

Behavioral Principles

Teachers have applied the principles of behavior modification in classrooms for many years. Behavior modfication is based on the assumption that teachers can increase, decrease or eliminate specific behaviors of their students by manipulating responses which follow those behaviors. Three types of responses can affect behavior: positive reinforcement, negative reinforcement, and punishment or response-cost.

Positive reinforcement involves the administration of a pleasurable or rewarding response to the student, following the demonstration of a specific behavior. Positive reinforcers increase the likelihood of a behavior re-occurring. By using positive reinforcement to strengthen an appropriate behavior we can simultaneously weaken another, incompatible, inappropriate behavior. For example, a teacher will strengthen in-seat behavior by praising a student for sitting at his desk, while at the same time weakening out-of-seat behavior, since the two behaviors are incompatible.

Negative reinforcement involves the removal of an aversive or uncomfortable event following the demonstration of a specific behavior. Negative reinforcers also increase the likelihood of a behavior re-occurring.

Punishment, or response-cost, involves the presentation of an aversive or uncomfortable consequence to the student or the removal of the student from a positive situation following the demonstration of a specific behavior. Punishment, or response cost, decreases the likelihood of a behavior re-occurring.

Applying principles of positive reinforcement, negative reinforcement, and punishment properly requires the teacher to evaluate what is rewarding and what is not rewarding to the individual student. Students differ greatly in their response to consequences. For example, social praise may be rewarding to some students, but embarrassing to others, just as punishments may vary in their effectiveness from student to student. Determining how rewarding or punishing a consequence is for a student can be accomplished by questioning the student or by applying such consequences and observing the effects on the student's behavior.

How To Use Behavioral Principles for ADD Students

1. Select a specific behavior which you want to increase.

2. Record each time the behavior occurs over a given period of time. For example; how often the student starts a task within two minutes after the task is given, how often the student blurts out without asking for permission to speak, and how long the student stays on task during an independent math assignment.

3. Analyze the events which are currently preceding and following the behavior. These are called antecedents and consequences. They are usually the events which precipitate and maintain a behavior.

Determining the antecedent events gives the teacher a clue as to what might precipitate a targeted behavior. In certain circumstances, removing antecedents alone may eliminate a behavior. For instance, the off task behavior of a student may be the result of the student looking out the window. Changing the student's seat away from the window will remove the antecedent. In other circumstances, by providing an antecedent you may increase the likelihood of the student displaying a behavior. For instance, walking by a student immediately after giving an instruction to complete a task may prompt the student to get to work.

Furthermore, determining the consequences which follow a targeted behavior gives the teacher an idea as to what might maintain the behavior. For example, a student's blurting out may be followed by pleasantly perceived laughter from other students, thereby reinforcing the student's behavior. Asking other students to ignore such behavior or punishing it when it occurs may alter the consequences enough to reduce the behavior.

4. If your goal is to improve the frequency of a targeted behavior then select a reinforcer which you think the student might like. Oftentimes good reinforcers can be determined by asking the student what they would like or by watching to see their preferred interests. Built-in reinforcers are common to the classroom environment. For instance, attention and praise, awarding of jobs, offerings of free time, reduction in amount of work required, good notes sent home, being first to do a valued activity, etc.. Decide on how much of a reinforcer is needed to motivate the student. If behavior does not improve think about increasing the size of the reinforcement, for instance, 15 minutes of free time instead of 10 minutes, or see if another reinforcer would be more attractive to the student. A reinforcer may need to be changed after a while as it may lose appeal for the student.

5. Initially, when teaching a new behavior, it is important to present positive reinforcements immediately and continuously. That is, reinforce right after you see the behavior and everytime the behavior occurs. At first the child may not demonstrate the target behavior you are looking for. In that case you would have to reinforce behaviors that approximate the target behavior. This is called shaping behavior. For instance, in the case of a student who doesn't complete independent assignments, he might never obtain a reinforcement for completed

work. However, he could be reinforced for doing a certain amount and then reinforced again for doing more, and so on until his behavior was shaped to complete entire assignments.

6. If positive reinforcement is not effective in improving a behavior, even after several different reinforcers have been tried, then the teacher might need to use negative reinforcement or punishment to change behavior. It is usually best, however, to give the positive reinforcement program a good chance to work before applying negative methods.

Negative reinforcement allows the child to avoid an aversive consequence by behaving in a specific way. For instance, "If you do your math work now, you will not have to do it for homework." or "Be quiet or you will lose recess." In using negative reinforcement tell the student what they can do to avoid the aversive consequence. If they don't do what they are supposed to, provide the consequence in a firm, business-like way without emotion, lectures, or long-winded explanations to the student.

Punishment involves the removal of the student from having a positive experience or the application of an aversive consequence. The aversive consequence or punishment is presented after the inappropriate behavior is demonstrated with the expectation that the behavior will decrease after it is punished. When using punishment it is important to make sure that the consequence delivered to the student is indeed aversive. For instance, teacher attention, even negative attention, may be reinforcing to a student rather. Getting in trouble may be amusing to the student, it may create popularity with other students, and it may get the student out of being in class or out of having to do unpleasant work.

While an aversive consequence may seem aversive to the teacher it may not be negative to the student and, therefore, will not carry the weight of a punishment and will not result in a decline in inappropriate behavior. The teacher needs to find the right punishment for the behavior and for the child. Overpunishing or delivering punishments in an emotionally harsh manner discourages, angers, and demoralizes students, and can produce more negative than positive effects. Punishment, when used, should be administered sparingly and judiciously.

Sample Compliments:

Great job!
You made it look easy.
Good thinking!
FANTASTIC!
I knew you could do it.
That's terrific.
That's good.
You figured that one out!
Keep at it.
I knew you could do it.
Right on!
Wow, you are good.
Keep up the good work.
GREAT!
Right on target.
You must be proud of yourself.
That's right.
Nice try.
You did very well today.
PERFECT!
I'm impressed with you.
UNBELIEVABLE!

Way to go!
Now you're cookin'!
Keep up the good work!
I like your style.
You really catch on quick.
I'm proud of you.
OUTSTANDING!
Much better.
Good for you.
A fine job.
Couldn't be better.
Good listening.
Well, aren't you something.
SENSATIONAL!
Looking great.
SUPERB!
Good answer.
You got it right!
You don't miss anything.
That was great.
You keep improving.
OUT OF SIGHT!

Self-Monitoring

Self-monitoring is a method of teaching students self-control over their behavior. Self-monitoring requires that the student act as an observer for his or her own behavior and record their observations. In doing so students usually achieve better self-control.

Researchers have demonstrated that self-monitoring procedures can be used successfully in classrooms for students varying in ages and abilities and in both regular and special education settings. The bulk of classroom use of self-monitoring procedures has focused on increasing rates of positive behavior, for instance, attention-to-task, academic productivity, and academic accuracy.

When learning self-monitoring, students have to perform a routine in which they stop what they are doing, evaluate their behavior, and record whether a specific target behavior has occurred or is occurring. Most self-monitoring procedures have been targeted at improving attention to task and employ cueing of the student when to initiate the self-monitoring routine. Popular cueing techniques involve tape-recorded tones presented at irregular intervals (mean intertone interval of 45 seconds). Each tone serves to prompt the student to evaluate whether they were performing the target behavior, for instance, paying attention to their work, and to self-record their performance on a data sheet. In using this procedure teachers frequently ask if it would be more effective to provide students with auditory cues through earphones so that they would not be audible to other students in the classroom. There is some limited evidence suggesting that when other students who are not the targets of the self-monitoring intervention hear the cues, their behavior improves as well.

How To Use Self-Monitoring To Improve Attention-To-Task

1. Explain to the student that you would like to help him learn to pay attention better. Explain to younger students that paying attention to work means that they should keep their eyes on their work, think about what they are doing, and follow instructions to complete the assignment. Teachers should demonstrate examples of off-task behavior such as daydreaming, drawing or doodling at the desk, talking to a nearby student, etc.

2. The teacher should have a signalling tape which will provide an audible tone to the student and cue the student to self-monitor. A self-recording form is provided on which the student could mark whether or not he was paying attention when he heard the audible tone. You can make your own signalling tape by recording a tone at irregular intervals (mean interval approximately 45 seconds) or by purchasing commercially available signalling tapes. *The Listen, Look and Think Program* (Specialty Press, Inc.) is available through the ADD WareHouse (800-ADD-WARE) and contains a continuous-play self-recording tape, instruction booklet, and self-evaluation forms for students to record and assess their performance.

3. Demonstrate the signalling tape and recording forms to a group of students who have trouble paying attention. In this way it will be less embarrassing for any one student to use the procedure. Eventually, as the self-monitoring procedure becomes more of an established routine in the classroom, it may be used more with individual students when needed.

4. Decide with the student(s) when it would be best for the student(s) to self-monitor attentiveness. Usually self-monitoring is done when independent seat work is required. Students will vary in their attentiveness to a task depending on the characteristics of the task. Some students will be more interested in one subject over

another and may benefit from using a self-monitoring procedure only on low-interest tasks or on tasks on which they find it difficult to keep their minds set.

5. Set up the signalling tape and give each student using the procedure a self-recording form which includes a self-evaluation section. Review the procedures for self-recording and self-evaluation. Do not be concerned whether the student records their attention-to-task correctly or not. Research indicates that even when students' assessments of their on-task behavior are found to be exaggerated in comparison with independent observational data, improvement in attention is still noted.

6. After some period of noticeable improvement in attention-to-task with the self-monitoring procedure, the teacher can begin to withdraw elements of the procedure either by withdrawing the audible tone first, or by withdrawing the self-recording form first. It will be important, however, for the teacher to continue to positively reinforce on-task behavior in some manner. Attention-to-task usually continues without these aids, but if the positive effects begin to lessen, the teacher can provide "booster" training sessions by re-introducing the self-monitoring procedures periodically.

Was I Paying Attention?

Name _____   **Date** _____

Subject_____

Listen to the beep tape as you do your work. Whenever you hear a beep, stop working for a moment and ask yourself, "Was I paying attention?" Mark your answer (√) below and go back to work. Answer the questions on the bottom when you finish.

Was I Paying Attention?

Yes	No

Was I Paying Attention?

Yes	No

Did I follow the directions?	Yes	No
Did I pay attention?	Yes	No
Did I finish my work?	Yes	No
Did I check my answers?	Yes	No

How To Use Self-Monitoring To Improve Attention, Self-Control, and Organization

1. Explain to the student the importance of paying attention, maintaining self-control, and keeping organized.

2. Review the "I Can Do It" self-monitoring record form and instruct the student to check himself at the end of each morning and afternoon (or adapt for specific subjects) whether he was paying attention, controlling his behavior, and keeping his things in order.

3. Discuss with the student, activities the student would like to earn, based upon his performance on the "I Can Do It" record form.

4. The teacher should rate the child each morning and afternoon as well on a separate "I Can Do It" recording form and should ask the student to compare his ratings to those of the teachers. The student should try to match the teacher's twice daily ratings.

5. The student should be allowed to participate in a preselected activity, based upon the number of check marks he tallied for the morning and/or afternoon.

6. Some students will have difficulty waiting until the end of the morning or afternoon to rate their behavior. In such cases the student may need a modified version of the "I Can Do It" form which would allow for more frequent self-monitoring.

I Can Do It!

Name _____   Date _____

Put a √ if you did this.

	Morning	Afternoon
I CAN PAY ATTENTION		
I paid attention to the teacher		
I followed directions		
I finished all my work		
I CAN CONTROL MY BEHAVIOR		
I raised my hand		
I asked permission before getting up		
I cooperated with others		
I CAN KEEP MY THINGS IN ORDER		
My desk was neat		
My work was put away in its place		
My writing was neat		
ADD UP YOUR CHECK MARKS HERE	#	#
Activities I have earned		
_____	_____	_____
_____	_____	_____

How To Use Self-Monitoring To Improve Handwriting

1. Explain to the student that you would like him to pay more attention to his handwriting. For younger students, explain that paying attention to handwriting means that they should keep their eyes on their work, think about what they are doing, and try to write as neatly as they can. Teachers should model behaviors that have been associated with poor handwriting such as poor pencil grip, awkward posture, poor paper orientation relative to body position, and rushing through work.

2. The teacher should ask the student to write four samples of a short paragraph of three or four lines showing their "best" penmanship, " good" penmanship, "fair" penmanship and "poor" penmanship on four separate large index cards. These writing samples should then be labeled as Best, Good, Fair, and Poor.

   Remember, students with fine-motor handicaps will not be able to write as neatly. When making up penmanship samples, accept what they can do and rate their sample productions as Best, Good, Fair, and Poor relative to their ability. Such students may need additional help for handwriting problems. Discontinue if this self-monitoring procedure becomes too taxing or frustrating for them. Consider a referral to a specialist who can help the student further with handwriting difficulties.

3. Immediately after giving a writing assignment the teacher should review the rules of good handwriting with the student. These rules are on the handwriting recording form (next page) in the form of questions to cue appropriate behavior. For example:

- Is my pencil sharp?
- Am I holding the pencil correctly?
- Am I sitting properly?
- Is my paper where it should be?
- Am I paying attention to neatness ?
- Am I taking my time when I write?

4. After finishing the assignment the student should fill out the handwriting recording form by circling the correct answer to each of the five questions. The student then should compare his handwriting to the writing samples he created earlier and rate the neatness of his current work.

Writing Reminders

Name _____ **Date** _____

Subject_____

Answer these questions before you begin to write.

Is my pencil sharp?	Yes	No
Am I holding the pencil correctly?	Yes	No
Am I sitting properly?	Yes	No
Is my paper where it should be?	Yes	No
Am I paying attention to neatness?	Yes	No
Am I taking my time when I write?	Yes	No

How To Use Self-Monitoring and Self-Timing To Improve Productivity

1. Have student break assignment into three sections.

2. Train student to estimate the amount of time which he will need to complete each section.

3. Advise student to be cautious and to avoid careless errors that could result from rushing through assignments. This is particularly important for those children who have attention deficits and who tend to do their work too quickly.

4. Provide student with a timing device, e.g. clock or alarm which will signal when estimated time is up.

5. Ask student to keep track whether he reached his goals in completing sections of work within the estimated time frame.

Self-Monitoring Form:

	Reading	Math	Language	Science	Social Studies
Mon.					
Tue.					
Wed.					
Thu.					
Fri.					

I will put a tally mark in the box every time I finish my work before the time is up.

Name_____ Date Started_____

How To Use Self-Monitoring To Improve Social Skills in the Classroom

1. Train students in the use of appropriate social interaction skills through didactic teaching procedures and through role-playing. There are a number of social skills training programs on the market for this purpose (refer to Chapter 6 for details).

2. With the student, select a specific social skill for the student to practice for the day. Model the skill for the student and ask him to identify when others in the class exhibit that particular skill.

3. Use the social skills recording form on which the student could self-monitor his performance of the skill periodically throughout the day.

Sample social skills:

Giving others a turn
Cooperating with others
Respecting the rights of others
Doing someone a favor
Starting a conversation
Leading a group
Expressing your ideas or feelings
Saying you're sorry
Ignoring someone's behavior
Being polite
Introducing yourself
Handling failure
Rewarding yourself
Asking for help
Saying thank you
Giving a compliment
Listening

Getting Along With Others

Name_____   Date _____

Choose a skill from those below or select one of your own ideas.

Skill to be practiced today:

_____

Practice in: Classroom   Lunchroom   Schoolyard
(Circle)

Sample Social Skills

1. Giving others a turn

2. Cooperating with others

3. Expressing your ideas or feelings

4. Doing someone a favor

5. Starting a conversation

6. Leading a group

7. Respecting the rights of others

8. Saying you're sorry

9. Ignoring someone's behavior

10. Being polite

How To Use Self-Monitoring To Transfer Self-Control Learning from a Resource Classroom To a Regular Classroom

1. The resource room teacher should teach appropriate target behaviors in a resource setting by using a token economy system and awarding points for demonstration of appropriate behaviors that are targeted for change.

2. The resource room teacher instructs the student to evaluate his own behavior by awarding himself points and compares his self-evaluations with the resource teacher's evaluations at the end of each period in the resource room.

3. Students are awarded points for demonstrating appropriate behavior and can earn additional points for matching the teacher's ratings of their behavior with their own ratings. Self-evaluations of behavior are recorded on a separate evaluation card.

4. The resource room teacher's ratings of the student's behavior are gradually faded out and the student is asked to evaluate his own behavior on the self-evaluation card with no external teacher evaluation.

5. Generalization to the regular education class is accomplished by having the student carry with him to the mainstream class the self-evaluation card on which he has been recording his points. Regular classroom teachers then instruct the student to engage in the same self-evaluating routine that he has learned in the resource setting.

How To Use Self-Monitoring To Improve Hand-Raising Behavior

1. Review with student the rules regarding the appropriate use of hand-raising to ask permission to talk.

2. Explain the problems that result in the classroom when a student calls out an answer or speaks out of turn, e.g. disrupts other students, does not give a turn to others, etc.

3. Model appropriate hand-raising behavior. Encourage student who has difficulty waiting for recognition to repeat what he wants to say silently to himself while his hand is raised, e.g. student should say to himself over and over while waiting, "The answer is...", or "I want to ask the teacher if ...".

4. When training this new behavior, the teacher should make an effort to call on the student immediately after the student raises his hand. Accompany this with positive reinforcement, e.g. "Thank you for raising your hand."

5. Remind student to mark a circle on his self-monitoring record form whenever he raises his hand before talking.

Raise Your Hand Before Talking

Name _____   **Date**_____

Fill in a circle everytime you raise your hand before talking.

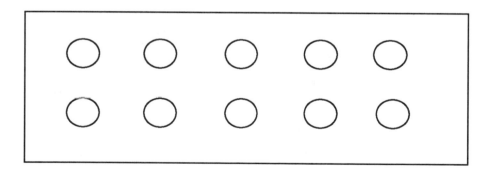

Source: The ADD Hyperactivity Handbook for Schools by Harvey C. Parker, Ph.D. This form may be reproduced for classroom use.

How To Use Self-Monitoring To Improve Proofreading Skills

1. Review with the student the importance of proofreading written work.

2. Go over the important elements of proofreading. Explain that the following items should be checked:
   • Heading
   • Margins
   • Proper spacing between words
   • Neatness of handwriting
   • Starting sentences with capitals
   • Using punctuation correctly
   • Cross out mistakes with only one line
   • Accurate spelling

3. Explain how to use the Proofreading Checklist record form.

Proofreading Checklist

Name _____   Date _____

Assignment _____   Class _____

Check your work to see if you have done the following:

	Yes	No
Heading on paper?		
Margins correct?		
Proper spacing between words?		
Handwriting neat?		
Sentences start with capital letters?		
Sentences end with correct punctuation?		
Crossed out mistakes with only one line?		
Spelling is correct?		

__ I proofread my paper. __ Someone else proofread my paper.

Time-Out

Time-out is a mild punishment technique whereby the student is asked to leave a reinforcing setting after committing an inappropriate action. Time-out has been used by teachers for years. Sending children to the hallway, asking them to sit by themselves in the room, or withdrawing attention from them in the classroom are all examples of time-out. Based upon the fact that inappropriate behaviors are weakened by punishment, time-out offers the teacher a sensible way to respond to the student.

How To Use Time-Out with ADD Students

1. Determine a place in the classroom that could be used as a time-out place. The time-out place could be a specific desk away from the other students, a place in the room which is marked off by strips of tape, etc.. If a separate room is being used make sure it is well lit, ventilated, free of any material which could hurt the student, and that the student is observable by the teacher.

2. Review the classroom rules with students, explaining as well, what time-out means and when it will be applied.

3. Use a consistent method to warn the student whose behavior is inappropriate that they may be sent to time out if they choose to continue. Be brief; do not lecture, scold, or repetitively remind the student to behave. One warning, administered calmly and tactfully, is best.

4. If the student continues to display the inappropriate behavior tell him he must go to time-out. Again, deliver the time-out instruction in a firm, calm and uncritical manner. Do not give long-winded explanations or debate with the student about your reasons for directing him to time-out. It is essential, however, that the teacher follow through in administering the time-out if the student's

inappropriate behavior persists after being given a warning.

Lack of consistent follow-through by the teacher and/or excessive warnings administered without action taken, will weaken the teacher's credibility and will render the time out procedure ineffective.

5. Usually time-out is brief, from one to ten minutes, with younger children requiring less time. Tell the student how long his time-out is. Begin timing when all inappropriate behavior stops. Tell the student that he cannot be released from time-out unless he is behaving appropriately during time out.

6. Time-out is time out from reinforcement so all potential reinforcers should be removed from the student while he is in time-out. When in time-out the student should be ignored by the teacher and by classmates.

7. If a separate room has been used for time-out the teacher should keep a record of when the student was sent to time out, for how long, and for what reason.

8. After the student is released from time-out look for signs of appropriate behavior and reinforce it consistently. Remember, punishment only suppresses negative behaviors; it doesn't strengthen positive behaviors.

9. Do not use time-out as a way of keeping disruptive students segregated from the rest of the class. Teachers are sometimes justly criticized for seating such students away from others so as to minimize disruptions in the classroom. However, prolonged segregation in this manner could result in damage to a student's self-esteem.

Modeling

Modeling is a method of learning through observation and imitation. The student is encouraged to watch someone who exhibits a specific skill with the intention of their eventually being able to emulate that same skill. The student may be asked to just observe the model, observe and rehearse the modeled behavior, or to observe and recite to themselves a description of the modeled behavior, and then rehearse the behavior.

How To Use Modeling with Students

1. Choose a behavior which you would like the student to emulate.

2. Describe the elements of the behavior which you would like the child to emulate and provide coaching for the child so they understand how to perform the behavior you are expecting. For example, if your goal is to teach attending behavior you might review with the student the important elements of attending, namely: maintaining eye contact, focusing concentration, subvocalizing, etc..

   If the goal were related to acquisition of a social skill, such as making plans with another child, the teacher would review the important elements of doing so, namely: acting friendly, smiling, engaging in a conversation, and asking the other child to do something together with you. It might help to write the elements of a behavior down so that they are clear to the child.

3. The teacher should then serve as the model for the behavior and should recite aloud the elements of the behavior as she is performing them. She should invite the student to watch her, recite along with her the

elements of what she is doing, and then ask the student to rehearse the behavior himself. The teacher should practice this process with the student several times per day over a number of days.

4. Throughout the day the teacher should cue the student to practice the newly learned behavior. The student should be encouraged to subvocalize the elements of the behavior as they have been written down for him.

5. The teacher may point out other students in the class who also demonstrate the targeted behavior and should ask the student to observe them when they are thus behaving.

6. The teacher should provide incentives to the student for successful modeling and should verbally praise the student for approximate successes so as to encourage skill building.

Peer Teaching

Peer teaching is a technique wherein one student works with another student under the supervision of a teacher. The peer teacher may be assigned to assist in teaching an academic skill or social skill, to be a study partner, be a companion during lunch, a behavior manager, or to serve as a sounding board for another student.

Peer teaching can benefit both the student who receives the instruction and the provider of such intruction. Not only can bright, achieving students serve as peer teachers, but those students who are not excelling well and whose self-esteem is lacking may benefit by serving as peer teachers.

How To Use Peer Teaching with Students

The Student with ADD as a Peer Teacher

1. The teacher decides that the student with ADD would benefit from being a peer teacher. Such teaching would likely utilize the ADD student as either an academic tutor or a behavior manager. As an academic tutor the ADD student will instruct another student in an academic skill during a prescribed time period under the supervision of the teacher.

   As a behavior manager, the ADD student might explain a behavior management program to another student, may keep track of behaviors, may dispense reinforcement, etc. during a prescribed period of time. The teacher determines the strengths of the ADD student and finds another student, either in the same grade or younger, who might benefit from his assistance.

2. The teacher must select a tutoring place either in the classroom or in a nearby room.

3. The teacher should notify the parents of both students so that neither set of parents will be surprised if their child reports that they are helping or receiving help from another student.

4. Peer teachers should be taught basic teaching skills such as giving praise to correct responses, listening patiently, querying as whether their student needs additional explanation or practice, and avoidance of criticism. Teachers should role play situations so that the peer teacher can "get the feel" of tutoring another student.

5. The teacher should periodically question both the peer teacher and student about the peer teaching process to get continuous feedback and make adjustments accordingly. Personalities may conflict, academic skills may be hard to explain, behavioral programs may meet with limited success, etc. The supervising teacher needs to be alert to potential problems so that solutions can be applied early in the process, thereby reducing any wasted time or frustration to the parties involved.

The Student with ADD as a Recipient of Peer Teaching

1. The teacher decides what the goals of having a peer teacher would be for the ADD student. As discussed above, the goal could be one of academic skill improvement or behavioral improvement. The selection of the peer teacher is extremely important in that it should be someone who will be sensitive and understanding of the ADD student's difficulties and one who will encourage a positive attitude and build up self-esteem.

2. The teacher must select a tutoring place either in the classrom or in a nearby room.

3. The teacher should notify the parents of both students so

that neither set of parents will be surprised if their child reports that they are helping or receiving help from another student.

4. Peer teachers should be taught basic teaching skills such as giving praise to correct responses, listening patiently, querying as whether their student needs additional explanation or practice, and avoidance of criticism. Teachers should role-play situations so that the peer teacher can "get the feel" of tutoring another student. In addition, the teacher should carefully explain to the peer teacher some of the difficulties that the particular ADD student may have in school such as in attending to work, completing work, rushing, etc..

5. The teacher should periodically question both the peer teacher and student about the peer teaching process to get continuous feedback and make adjustments accordingly. Personalities may conflict, academic skills may be hard to explain, behavioral programs may meet with limited success, etc. The supervising teacher needs to be alert to potential problems so that solutions can be applied early in the process.

Prereferral Strategies

Prereferral consultation refers to a process whereby regular and special educators meet and collaborate to plan interventions for at-risk, or hard-to-teach students in regular academic settings. In this model the special educator serves as a resource for the regular classroom teacher. Various people within the district who have areas of expertise in teaching difficult students may serve as prereferral consultants to the regular education teacher.

How To Use Prereferral Consultation

Dr. Bob Algozzine (1990) lists several stages to be followed in using a prereferral intervention model.

Stage One: Informal Preconsultation

Informal preconsultation refers to the process by which a teacher collects problem-solving ideas from a variety of sources to help a student. Preconsultation is initiated when the regular classroom teacher runs across a problem which she cannot solve. Often initial help is sought from peers as teachers discuss strategies informally with one another. Frequently a teacher will seek assistance from the student's prior teacher and will try to find out what was helpful to the student in the past. Or teachers at the same grade level who each have the student for a class may confer with one another as to what strategies each finds to be effective for the student. Informal consultation with other teachers can offer many ideas which will lead to implementing effective strategies.

If this informal preconsultation with other teachers is not helpful, the teacher may ask for the assistance of a school administrator. The administrator and teacher may arrive at other ideas or may decide to request the assistance of a consultant who has expertise of the kind that may be helpful in solving the student's problem.

Stage Two: Collaborative Problem-Solving

Collaborative problem-solving refers to the process by which consultants are asked to collaborate with the regular teacher to find ways to solve the student's problem. Regular meetings may be held between the consultant and teacher for several weeks, months, or throughout the school year. The focus of these meetings will be to identify strategies that could be implemented in the classroom to assist the student. To do so, the collaborative problem-solving process will likely take several steps:

1. Identification and analysis of the student's problem through informal procedures such as: assessment checklists, classroom observations, review of cumulative records, discussion with previous teachers, etc..

2. Setting goals for what the student should accomplish as a result of the problem solving process.

3. Review of previous interventions that have been applied and determination as to why they may not have been successful, or, if they were successful for a short time, why success was not maintained.

4. Brainstorming of potential new interventions which may assist the student.

5. Selection of a most-likely-to-succeed intervention plan which will be clearly described and determination of how the intervention plan will be monitored and its effectiveness measured.

6. Determination of how long the intervention plan should be tried before planning another collaborative problem-solving meeting to discuss the results.

Stage Three: Implementation and Evaluation

During this stage the regular education teacher will implement the intervention plan and the data-gathering process by which to judge results. At future meetings with the consultant the teacher will review the plan's effectiveness to determine whether alternative strategies are needed or, if the plan is working well, how long it should be in effect and how best to increase maintenance and generalization of the desired outcome.

Using Volunteers

Volunteers have been used in the classroom for many years. Class mothers have become a fixture in American schools. Active parent-teacher organizations promote parental involvement in the child's education. Community-based senior citizen programs actively promote the elderly's involvement in the education of the young and cite the many advantages to both young and old which result from such a helping relationship. Businesses are becoming partners in education all across the country.

Volunteer assistants are a valuable resource in the classroom. Teachers who know how to use volunteers as members of their instructional team benefit from the extra pair of hands available to grade papers, help students who need extra attention, work with children who have special problems, and handle paperwork which ordinarily takes a great deal of instructional time away from the teacher.

Classroom volunteers come with a wide assortment of skills. Some may be retired teachers who have years of experience to offer, but most volunteers will be business people, professionals, housewives, or senior citizens who have never stepped into a classroom other than as students themselves. What they lack in experience, however, may be more than made up for in energy, enthusiasm, and a desire to help.

How To Use volunteers

1. When approached by someone who wants to volunteer in the classroom the teacher should set up an appointment to meet with the person and get to know them better. During that time the teacher should become familiar with the volunteer's background, the reasons why they chose to volunteer, and how they would like to be of assistance. Many volunteers like working directly with

students, others have a special talent they wish to share, and others prefer to help out with classroom management such as grading papers, keeping classroom records, etc.. After this initial meeting the teacher will decide if the volunteer candidate is suitable for the classroom and how they may be of help.

2. The teacher and volunteer should agree on a specific schedule when the volunteer will be at school. Phone numbers should be exchanged in case of a last minute change of plans either in the volunteer's schedule or in the teacher's planning for the day.

3. Chosen volunteers should be treated in a professional manner. The teacher will need to make time to introduce the volunteer to other members of the school's staff, and to enable the volunteer to tour the school, and become familiar with certain relevant school policies. Confidentiality of student information should be stressed.

4. Volunteers need to be trained and supervised. Both they and the teacher need to have a clear understanding of what tasks they will be undertaking, the best methods of accomplishing them, and what results are expected. Teachers should check the volunteer's work every so often and offer constructive feedback.

Chapter 10
Solutions for Common
Problems of Students with ADD

While no two ADD students are alike, they do have common problems which may be solved by implementing specific behavioral strategies. The following section of the handbook looks at a number of common behavior problems of ADD students. Following a brief description of the problem, explanations are offered as to the possible reasons why the problem behavior is maintained by the student. Often, the behavior of ADD students can be explained as symptomatic of their disorder. Steps for the teacher to follow in solving the problem are suggested.

The following problems are discussed:

1. Talking excessively
2. Calling out in class
3. Forgetting materials
4. Being off task during independent work
5. Poor listening skills and not following oral directions
6. Handing in late or uncompleted assignments
7. Turning in sloppy work
8. Failing to complete homework assignments

Talking Excessively

Description of the Behavior

Jeffrey talks constantly at school. His chattering prevents him from doing his work to speak nothing of the disruption to the entire class. Whenever Mr. Charles reprimands Jeffrey for talking, one of two things happens. Jeffrey either becomes embarrassed and stops talking for a minute or two only to start up again, or he looks at Mr. Charles with an insulted expression and defends himself by denying he was talking to anyone.

What Maintains the Behavior?

Excessive talking is a common problem in every classroom and it is particularly common in hyperactive boys and girls. ADD girls, especially, may exhibit their hyperactivity in conversation while boys find it more socially acceptable to fidget and be restless. Talking in school is very reinforcing. It is probably more fun to carry on a conversation than it is to do schoolwork. Some children enjoy talking because it draws the teacher's attention to them, albeit in a negative way. Talking is also a way students can escape from doing their assigned work or from listening to lessons. Students who are frustrated with their work because they don't understand assignments or because the work is too difficult, may stop trying and talk to others.

Solutions

1. The teacher needs to establish rules in the classroom as to when talking to others is acceptable or not. Some students are not able to distinguish when talking is appropriate, especially if the teacher maintains a cooperative work environment where students work together to complete projects.

2. Discuss with the talkative student why talking is inappropriate at certain times. Explain that excessive talking disturbs others and interferes with the student's ability to complete work.

3. At the beginning of a lesson give the student a signal when it is time to be quiet. Signals may include an index finger up against your lips, red and green papers posted to indicate times when it is OK to start conversations and appropriate to end them, or a statement to the entire class that this is time for listening, not talking.

4. Establish a consequence for unacceptable talking and apply the consequence consistently to all students who break the no talking rule. Suggested consequences are name on the board, time-out in a section of the classroom for five minutes, loss of time from recess (e.g. five minutes for each infraction of the no talking rule).

5. If you notice a student talking, first try to reinforce a nearby student for working quietly.

6. If the student continues to talk, issue a warning to stop.

7. If the student stops and then continues, act right away by providing one of the consequences in step 4. However, remember to use negative consequences judiciously with ADD students. Always emphasize the use of positive approaches first for changing behavior.

Calling Out in Class

Description of the Behavior

Mrs. Wallace can't seem to get Reggie to stop calling out in class. Instead of raising his hand and waiting his turn, Reggie just blurts out his answers. Not only is he frequently wrong, but his behavior is annoying to other members of the class who have tried to wait patiently to be called on. Reggie's calling out behavior has become quite disruptive in other ways. Whenever he notices somebody doing something they're not supposed to, Reggie is right there, blurting out what happened. He can't seem to control himself, but it is hard on Mrs. Wallace to conduct her class with so many interruptions.

What Maintains the Behavior?

Children call out for a variety of reasons. Some are so impulsive that whenever they get excited or frustrated, everyone has to know about it. For these children, overarousal is difficult to suppress and they act out verbally or physically. ADD children are particularly prone to overreact to excitement or disappointment. During transition times from unstructured to structured activities, impulsive children will have a difficult time settling down.

After a while, some children who are used to calling out just forget to raise their hand. They have become so accustomed to calling out that it has become a habit which needs to be broken.

Solutions

1. During transition from one activity to another, let students know what is expected of them. Emphasize the use of hand raising to ask permission to talk.

2. Ignore students who call out without raising their hand and asking permission to talk.

3. Verbally praise students who raise their hands before talking.

4. Quickly call on students who have raised their hands.

5. Positively acknowledge hand raising behavior by stating: "Jim, you've raised your hand, what is the answer?"

6. Use the hand raising self-monitoring program described in the previous chapter.

Forgetting Materials

Description of the Behavior

"Johnny can't seem to get it together," reports Mrs. MacIntyre in describing an ADD student in her class. Despite the fact that he is now in sixth grade, he continues to come to class unprepared. Being in middle school seems to have worsened his problems as Johnny is unable to organize himself enough to be able to keep track of all his books and assignments and to remember to bring the right materials to each class.

What Maintains the Behavior?

Chances are that Johnny doesn't purposely forget to bring the correct materials to class. Disorganization is characteristic of many ADD children. Their impulsive, hurried style frequently causes them to be unprepared and forgetful.

Solutions

1. Teachers will often need the help of a student's parents to improve a child's organizational skills.

2. Despite the student's inherent organizational problems, the teacher and parents should make the student accountable for bringing the proper materials to class and home by the use of charts, reminder notes, etc..

3. The teacher should discuss with the student exactly what materials are required.

4. Students with lockers should be asked to return to their locker to get required materials. Elementary school students should borrow appropriate materials. Students who forget books or assignments should be asked to call up friends in class to obtain missing material.

5. Assist students by posting signs around the room to remind them to take everything they need home and bring everything they need to back to school.

>   "Do you have everything you need?"
>   "Where are you going?"
>   "What do you need?"

Ask the student's parents to post signs by the front door of the student's house to remind him to take everything to school in the morning.

6. Request that the student's parents review with him each night and morning the materials he will need for school. For elementary and young middle school students, the parents might check book bags or notebooks to ensure that all work and books are brought to school.

7. Penalizing ADD students who are chronically unprepared by lowering grades or requiring them to make up missing work may be helpful. However, if the teacher notices that such aversive consequences do not produce results, they should be discontinued in favor of more positive approaches.

Off-Task During Independent Work

Description of the Behavior

Mr. Fredericks has two students in his class who he just can't seem to get motivated. David is constantly talking to other classmates, playing with one thing or another, and forever has to be reminded to stop doing this or that and to get back to doing his work. Jeremy is quiet and detached from other kids. He, too, has trouble paying attention, but he seems to be off in his own world. He sits dreamily at his desk, stares off into the distance and seems startled when the teacher calls on him.

What Maintains the Behavior?

Inattention is a cardinal characteristic of ADD. While hyperactive ADD children are busy doing something else rather than their work, non-hyperactive ADD children are usually lost in their own thoughts. In either case, attentiveness and motivation to stay on-task may be lacking and the child may have lost interest in the work to be accomplished. Boredom with the task is a common cause of inattention. ADD children tend to become bored more easily than their non-ADD peers. Work that is too difficult for the child to complete may cause the child to give up easily. Unfortunately ADD children tend not to persist in the face of frustration and may stop working sooner than others.

Solutions

1. Recognizing that an inattentive student may need more reminders to pay attention, the teacher should seat the student in close proximity to her to make it easy to provide such reminders.

2. When students are doing quiet seat work, scan the room frequently paying particular attention to the inattentive

students to determine if they are staying on task. Provide positive attention to students who are working, thereby indirectly reminding those off-task to pay more attention.

3. For chronically inattentive students, talk to them alone about the problem and explain the importance of their finishing assigned work. Make certain that their assignment is checked at the end of the lesson.

4. Help the student divide the assigned work into three parts. Encourage the student to work for 10 or 15 minutes on the first part and show you how he did. Proceed onto parts two and three in the same manner. Breaking assignments into smaller parts makes the work seem easier, and more frequent teacher feedback encourages persistence.

5. Train students who are "stuck" on problems to raise their hand and ask for help, or to go on to other parts of their work and come back to the difficult problems later.

Poor Listening Skills, Not Following Directions

Description of the Behavior

Janet never seems to pay attention during class lessons. Her mind is always on something else. Mrs. Charles knows that as soon as this math lesson is over and she gives an assignment to the class to practice the new skill she taught, Janet will not know what she is supposed to do and will need help completing the work.

What Maintains the Behavior?

ADD children often miss important information given by the teacher. Some may be able to get by at times without having direct instruction on new material, but most will eventually be affected in school as inattention interferes with learning. ADD students without hyperactivity will often exhibit "dreamy, inattentive" behavior. These students will frequently be slow in geting work done and will chronically miss handing in assignments. They seem to develop an indifference about their failure to turn in school work which often frustrates their teachers.

Solutions

1. Try to involve the ADD child in the lesson. When motivating the class at the start of a lesson or when giving directions, include the inattentive student by name (along with naming other students who are listening) to get his attention. For example: "Jim, Julie, and Jack, I know you'll will like what we're going to do next!"

2. Try to direct parts of the lesson to the inattentive student by making the lesson relevant to the student's personal interests or life experiences.

3. During the lesson, make frequent eye contact with the inattentive student. Ask the student questions more often than you might other students, to keep the connection between you and the student active.

4. Start important statements, such as those just before you give directions to an assignment, with phrases like:
   "Listen up now, please!"
   "May I have your attention? This is important."
   The class gets used to these statements as cues to pay special attention. Before proceeding, pause and make sure you have everybody's attention.

5. Supplement oral directions with written instructions on the chalkboard.

6. Assign a peer teacher to assist the inattentive student in getting started on an assignment and have the two work together to compare results at the end of the period.

7. Provide frequent positive reinforcement to students who are attending. Repeat phrases like:
   "I'm happy to see you are all paying attention."
   "Thanks for listening so well."

   While the use of phrases like these may seem uncomfortable at first, they will go a long way toward encouraging proper attending behavior.

Handing in Late or Incomplete Assignments

Description of the Behavior

Jack consistently hands in assignments late and his work is frequently incomplete. He tends to make a million and one excuses for not having his work ready on time and generally he will need firm reminders and warnings before an assignment will finally get turned in. This behavior continues despite repeated warnings from his teacher.

What Maintains the Behavior?

Students hand in late or incomplete assignments for a variety of reasons. Poor time management and procrastination are probably the major causes of lateness. Students interested in other activities put off doing their work until it is too late to complete or, at least, too late to complete accurately. Some students have a great deal of trouble structuring their time at home. The student's family may not put a great deal of emphasis on homework. Parents may not inquire about school-work enough or monitor the student's homework sufficiently to provide the structure that the student needs. In some cases, teachers may not make the student accountable for assigned work. If the teacher does not collect and/or check to see that assignments are completed, the child may take a chance on not doing the work, anticipating that the teacher will not check anyway.

Solutions

1. The teacher should consistently check all work that is assigned.

2. Established deadlines for when work is due should be clearly posted. Monitor the ADD student's progress on long-term projects and provide frequent positive rein-

forcement and encouragement along the way.

3. Students should be made aware ahead of time as to the consequences for work that is handed in late. For example, parents may be contacted, a grade may be lowered, or the assignment may not be accepted at all after a certain date.

4. Teachers should check off work at the beginning of the period on the assigned due date.

5. ADD students who chronically hand in late assignments should not be given a second chance too often. Parents should be contacted and conferenced. A home-school report system could be implemented so that parents could structure the environment at home to promote student accountability.

6. Teacher should maintain accurate records of late assignments.

Turning In Sloppy Work

Description of the Behavior

Mrs. Clark knows that Joanne could do neater work. Joanne's papers are sloppily written, with no heading, no respect for margins, little regard for spelling, and mistakes are heavily crossed out.

What Maintains the Behavior?

Students turn in sloppy work for a variety of reasons. They may not take pride in their performance or may expect too little from themselves. Such students often want to get the work finished as quickly as possible regardless of whether or not they are done correctly. Some students have developed poor work habits. Past teachers may have accepted substandard papers. Except in situations wherein a student has a handicapping condition which would interfere with their ability to write neatly or spell correctly, most students could correct sloppy work if motivated to do so.

Solutions

1. Teachers should establish clear guidelines for neatness.

    a. Proper heading should be on all work.
    b. Papers should not be crumpled.
    c. Ink should not be smeared.
    d. Writing should be done in one style, not part cursive and part printing.
    e. Mistakes should be erased if done in pencil and crossed out once if done in ink.
    f. Letters should be sized and spaced evenly.
    g. Handwriting should be slanted in one, consistent direction.
    h. Handwriting should stay on the lines and within

proper margins.

   i. Mispellings should be corrected.

   j. Proper captalization and puncutuation should be used.

2. Teachers should generously reinforce ADD student's attempts at neatness.

3. Teachers should return papers that are not done neatly and should expect them to be done over (unless the student has a fine-motor impairment which accounts for poor performance in this area. In such cases, consider additional training in the use of computer keyboarding skills.).

4. Use a self-monitoring procedure to encourage neatness. Find four samples of the student's work which vary from neat to sloppy. Ask the student to rate the four samples (Best, Good, Fair, and Poor) and put ratings on the top of each paper . Laminate these samples and have the student keep them in a notebook for reference. Encourage the student to use the neatest sample as an example of how all future work should be done. Have the student compare the neatness of any new work to the quality of the work of each of the four examples (see self-monitoring ideas in previous chapter).

5. Provide encouragement to students whose neatness is improving.

6. For elementary students, display examples of neat work to other members of the class.

Failing To Hand in Homework

Description of the Behavior

Ian does not hand in homework. He always makes excuses for missing work, claiming that he lost it, he forgot it, he left it home, he didn't know he was supposed to do it, and on and on.

What Maintains the Behavior?

Most students who have homework problems lack motivation. Some students resist writing down assignments and, therefore, don't keep track of what they are supposed to do. Others simply avoid doing homework because it's more fun to do other things at home. ADD students may exhibit the same lack of motivation, but they also have additional problems which cause homework difficulties.

ADD students tend to be very disorganized and often have trouble keeping track of homework assignments, especially long-term projects. They often forget to bring home proper books or worksheets. Having several assignments to do can become overwhelming for seriously impaired ADD students. They often don't know where to start and will need a parent to help them break assignments up and get them going. Frequently having not paid close attention in class, they will be lost in how to do certain assignments that may have been reviewed by the teacher earlier that day. Parents will have to go over lessons again and explain the work. Low frustration tolerance and short attention spans, especially late in the day or early evening, combine with fatigue to make homework a nightmare for both the child and parents alike. In many instances, after all is said and done and the homework is finally completed, many ADD students will forget where they put it and won't be able to locate it in their book bag or notebook when the teacher asks for it the next day.

Some ADD students learn to avoid these problems by lying about homework or by selectively "forgetting" to write certain assignments down in their homework journal. Some students will become so discouraged with homework that they will take all night to do even the simplest of problems, having no motivation to do their work faster. Some parents, tired after a day of work and exhausted from years of battling with homework, will have given up and relaxed their rules at home. In light of the ADD child's problems with organization, attention span, and low frustration tolerance, it is easy to see why homework problems are commonly found in this group of students.

Solutions

1. Teacher may choose to shorten homework assignments.

2. Establish clear deadlines for when homework is due.

3. Determine if the child understands the work. To ensure understanding, have the student do some of the work in class before assigning it for homework.

4. Help the child set up a homework journal in which he should record daily assignments and due dates. Review the journal with the child at the end of each day. Remind the child to bring home the proper materials to complete the homework. Some ADD students may need an extra set of books at home.

6. Help the parent set up homework routines at home and establish a communication system between teacher and parent to explain any problems the student may be having with homework.

7. Make the student accountable for homework when it is due in school. Check the student's homework and record if assignments are late or missing.

Chapter 11
Teaching Children with ADD in Special Education

Many ADD students will do fine in regular education classrooms with teachers who understand them and who apply the accommodations and interventions discussed in the previous chapters. However, some ADD children will need more intensive help and may require special education services.

Such special education services may be provided in various forms, depending on the amount of assistance the student requires. Some ADD children will benefit from a "pull-in" program wherein a behavioral consultant, trained in understanding children with ADD, provides supplementary services to the student within the regular classroom. The consultant may meet with the regular classroom teacher to construct and implement strategies to help the student, or the consultant may work directly with the student to train specific behaviors.

Other ADD children may require a "pull-out" or resource program wherein they leave the classroom for part of the day and receive extra help from a special education teacher who has been trained to teach children with attention deficit disorders.

In extreme cases, usually for ADD children with severe difficulties related to inattention, impulsivity, or hyperactivity, and for those who have co-existing problems such as specific learning disabilities or emotional disturbance, a self-contained classroom may be required. In such cases the use of behavioral interventions would be ongoing throughout the school day as the child goes through the instructional curriculum geared to his educational needs.

The PGARD Group, in collaboration with CH.A.D.D. and ADDA parent support groups, noted in their response to the Department of Education's Notice of Inquiry, that of the 2 million ADD children in our nation's schools, approximately 1 million would need special education services. They estimated that 70% of that group are probably already receiving services under other disability categories such as specific learning disability or emotional disturbance. Many of these students, however, are not receiving appropriate services to treat their attention deficit disorder. In addition, 30% (or 300,000) of ADD children who do not have co-existing disorders, but whose attention deficits are so severe that they are in need of special education services, have been excluded from special education altogether.

Of the 1 million ADD students who are in need of special education, the PGARD Group estimated that 35% could be served either by supplementary services delivered in the regular classroom or by part-time resource services in a special education classroom. Less than 15% would need self-contained special education classrooms.

Individualized Instruction

At the heart of the whole process of special education programming is the provision of an individualized educational program (IEP) for the student who, as a result of his disability, is unable to fully benefit from customary methods of instruction. The IEP should be based on a recent, comprehensive evaluation of the child and the parents should be fully apprised of the contents of the evaluation prior to the construction of the IEP. The IEP is *individualized* in that it meets the child's unique identified educational needs rather than those of the group; that it focuses on *educational* issues and that it describes the *program* of services the child will receive. The IEP must be reviewed at least once a year, but can be reviewed more often at the parents' request.

The IEP, by law, should be a comprehensive plan of action for the school to follow in delivering services to the student. Basically the IEP should tell the reader where the student is now in terms of certain specified skills, where the student is expected to be in the future, how the student will acquire the skills, how long it should take, and how one will measure whether the program was successful.

Writing An IEP

Once a determination has been made that the student needs special education and/or related services, a series of meetings must be held to write an IEP. In order to best develop an IEP all people who know the student well, must collaborate in designing an appropriate plan and must monitor its implementation and results. Parents of the student play an important role in this process along with teachers, school administrators, guidance personnel, etc.. At a minimum, the law stipulates that the following people should have input into the student's IEP: a person with authority to commit the school's resources, the classroom teacher, a parent, and possibly the student as well (determined by the parent). At the initial IEP meeting there should be someone present who is knowledgeable about the student's disability. Parents play an important role in the IEP process. IEP planning meetings must be held with parents and school officials at a mutually agreeable time and place.

Student's Current Educational Performance

This part of the IEP is designed to provide information about the student's current educational performace and addresses strengths and weaknesses. It is likely that a variety of resources will be utilized to obtain information about current performance. Teacher evaluations, assessments from appropriate professionals such as psychologists, speech and language pathologists, medical doctors, physical therapists, etc., opinions of outside consultants, review of a student's cumulative folder, direct observation of the student and other procedures all may have an important role to play in determining a student's current level of functioning. Descriptions about current levels of functioning should be done in as objective and quantifiable manner as possible paying attention to both academic and nonacademic skills which require improvement.

Setting Annual Goals and Short-Term Objectives

The IEP team is responsible for setting realistic annual goals and short-term objectives for the student. The annual goals are essentially the IEP team's prediction of what the student should be able to accomplish within a year utilizing the instructional procedures outlined in the IEP. Each goal, in turn, is divided into short-term objectives which represent the steps that the student will take in reaching annual goals. By tracking a student's success as work is done on short-term objectives, parents, teachers, and students can keep track of progress on annual goals.

The IEP team is responsible for writing annual goals and objectives for those areas of educational performance which require special education services. Identifying which annual goals are important to include in the IEP, and which are not, can be a difficult process and the team will rely heavily on reports from the classroom teachers, parents, and any recent, comprehensive educational or psychological assessments done to measure the student's current level of functioning. The number of annual goals in the IEP will likely depend on the severity of the student's disability and how wide-ranging an effect it has on performance.

The annual goals and short-term objectives set by the IEP team will serve as the special education teacher's blueprint of what the instructional curriculum should be for the student that year. As with any blueprint, detail and specificity are important. If the goals of the IEP team are to be met they must be spelled out clearly, with an objective description of what is expected, when it is to be achieved, and the degree of student competence sought. Therefore, annual goals must:

- Describe specifically the skills to be learned.
- Describe the conditions under which the skills are expected to be demonstrated and when.
- Specify the expected level of performance of the learned skills.

Annual goals should be broken down into component parts, namely, short-term objectives. By specifying discrete objectives in the form of performance criteria, the teacher's instructional blueprint becomes even clearer and will more likely result in fulfilling the requirements of the IEP. Each annual goal should have at least two short-term objectives arranged in order of instructional sequence.

Theoretical and Practical Issues Affect IEP Construction

The decision as to which annual goals and objectives to focus on in the IEP and how they should be achieved may not be easy to make. For theoretical and practical reasons different members of the IEP team may want to focus on different goals and objectives and may come up with different ways of attaining them.

For example, we could focus on the predicament that educators face when programming for students with learning disabilities or emotional disturbances. In these cases, experts differ about what we should teach learning disabled students, e.g. which instructional goals and objectives are important and what procedures should be used to reach them. Some believe it is important to focus on remediation of psychological processes, others feel language development is important to stress, others focus on literacy skills, while others will emphasize instruction in learning strategies and vocational subjects. Proponents of teaching psychological processes will tend to write instructional objectives that will be aimed at improving auditory and visual perception. Advocates who stress language deficits as a primary cause of learning disabilities, might write instructional objectives emphasizing expressive and receptive processes in oral or written language, improving syntactic structures, and other language-based teaching approaches. Still others, whose emphasis is on literacy skills and content, would want instructional objectives for listening, speaking, reading, handwriting, written composition, mathematics computation, and mathematical problem solving included in the IEP.

Experts also differ about how children with serious emotional disturbance should be taught and which instructional objectives should be emphasized. Approaches to the treatment of emotional disorders are varied and can include different theoretical orientations, e.g. psychodyamic, humanistic, behaviorial, eclectic, etc..

Experts in the area of attention deficit disorders may also disagree as to which instructional objectives are important for a student to reach. Certainly there are many from which to choose. Attention training, social skills training, cognitive training, behavior modification, affective development, organizational skill building, study habit training, self-esteem improvement, self-control training, etc. are just a few of the areas for which to write instructional objectives. What is correct for each child will not only depend upon the child's individual needs, but in all likelihood will depend, as well, on the theoretical biases of those who design the plans.

Equally difficult to decide upon will be the methods by which instructional objectives should be met. Should medication be instituted? Is behavior modification more approripate for the child than cognitive training? Should we attempt to teach social skills, and, if so, which program should be used?

Sample Goals and Objectives

Name. Tim Randall
School: Any Elementary School
Date of Birth: 3/06/80
Any Street
Chronological Age: 10 years 10 months
Any City, Any State 00000
Grade in School: 5.5
Times Retained: 0

Related Services: Physical Education (Regular)
Psychological Services
Psychological Counseling-Individual and Group
Parent Counseling
School Health Services (Supervision of medication; consult with pediatrician)
Occupational Therapy

Present Levels: Teacher observation suggests that Tim needs support in the areas of interpersonal, self-related and task-related behaviors.

Strategies/Materials: Individual and group instruction and interactions with staff will be utilized in application of the diagnostic/prescriptive process; specific material includes:

1. Harcourt Brace, BOOKMARK Reading Program
2. Walker, Social Skills Training Curriculum
3. Self-Esteem: A Classroom Affair Volume 2 More Ways to Help Children Like Themselves
4. Scott, Foresman and Co., Language Arts Program
5. Gordon, Attention Training System
6. Bash & Camp, Think Aloud Classroom Program: Means-End Problems Solving
7. Bash & Camp, Think Aloud Classroom Program: Using Verbal Labeling to Organize Information for Improved Memory.
8. Bash & Camp, Think Aloud Classroom Program: Predicting What Might Happen Next
9. Bash & Camp, Think Aloud Classroom Program: The Nature of Authority
10. Bash & Camp, Think Aloud Classroom Program: Identifying Emotions
11. Classroom Token Economy System
12. Parker, Listen, Look and Think Program: for self-recording of attention.
13. Pencil Grip

Annual Goal: Tim will improve reading comprehension skills.

Short-Term Objectives:
1. Tim will draw conclusion from a story in a fifth grade reader 80% of the time.
2. Tim will recognize the same idea stated in different words 80% of the time.
3. Tim will predict outcomes 80% of the time.
4. Tim will state sequence of events in a story with 80% accuracy.

Annual Goal: Tim will incorporate principles of language arts into written expression.

Short-Term Objectives:
1. Given 6 sentences, each containing two underlined parts, Tim will indicate whether each part is correctly or incorrectly punctuated and/or capitalized with a criterion of 10 out of 12.
2. Given a short paragraph, Tim will indicate an understanding of the concept that a paragraph is a group of sentences about one idea by: indicating which sentence in the given paragraph does not belong in the paragraph and by making up an additional sentence which would belong in the paragraph.
3. Given a number of dictionary entries, Tim will recognize the various parts and will illustrate an understanding of them by answering related questions.
4. Given 5 groups of words Tim will state whether or not each word group is a complete sentence with a criterion of 4 out of 5.

Annual Goal: Tim will improve interpersonal behaviors.

Short-Term Objectives:
1. When teased or called a name, Tim will respond by:
   a. ignoring b. changing the subject c. using some other constructive means appropriate to the situation 80% of the time.
2. Given an appropriate informal situation, Tim will initiate a conversation with peers by approaching a peer and being the first one to speak in a conversation 80% of the time.

Annual Goal: Tim will improve self-related behaviors.

Short-Term Objectives:
1. When asked, Tim will be able to give an adequate verbal description of feelings or mood, e.g. one that is consistent

with exhibited behavior, 80% of the time.
2. When asked about self, Tim will make positive statements 80% of the time.

Annual Goal: Tim will improve task related behaviors.

Short-Term Objectives:
1. During a period of time when nothing is scheduled for Tim and work is completed, Tim will find ways of using free time which the teacher defines as acceptable or constructive 80% of the time.
2. When presented with potentially distracting actions or verbalizations from peers while doing a seat assignment, Tim will ignore the distractions by not responding and continuing with the work 80% of the time.
3. When required, Tim will willingly read aloud in a small group of three or four students without signs of excessive nervousness or fear 80% of the time.
4. Before handing in work to the teacher, Tim will look over the work to check for errors 80% of the time.
5. When working on a seat assignment, Tim will remain on task for 80% of the time.

Annual Goal: Tim will improve in auditory short-term memory.

Short-Term Objectives:
1. Tim will complete 2 and 3 step directions of increasing complexity with 90% accuracy.
2. Tim will be given complex verbal directions (i.e. underline the third word from the end) and will correctly perform the requested actions with 90% accuracy.
3. Tim will increase use of visual imagery to facilitate increased auditory comprehension and auditory memory for short paragraphs with 90% accuracy.

Annual Goal: Tim will increase his appropriate in-seat behavior.

Short-Term Objectives:

1. Tim will refrain from tipping his chair for 15 minutes at a time.
2. Tim will refrain from touching others as they walk by 80% of the time.
3. Tim will refrain from tapping objects such as a pencil, paper clip, eraser, ruler, etc. for 15 minutes at a time. This will gradually increase as Tim develops competence or reaches maximum level of ability.

Annual Goal: Tim will wait until called upon before verbally responding.

Short-Term Objectives:

1. Tim will gain permission from the teacher, by raising his hand when he needs to talk with a peer 80% of the time.
2. Tim will contribute his opinion or answer question after being recognized 80% of the time.
3. Tim will refrain from making sounds which are inappropriate for the situation 80% of the time.

Annual Goal: Tim will improve in following oral and written directions independently.

Short-Term Objectives:

1. Tim will follow written directions in correct sequential order 80% of the time.
2. Tim will follow oral directions in correct sequential order 80% of the time.

Annual Goal: Tim will improve in not bothering other students who are working.

Short-Term Objectives:

1. Tim will refrain from bothering other students who are trying to work, listen, etc 80% of the time.

Annual Goal: Tim will control excessive impulsivity.

Short-Term Objectives:
1. Tim will wait quietly for assistance from an instructor 80% of the time.
2. Tim will await his turn when engaged in activities with peers on 5 out of 7 trials.
3. Tim will attempt a task without asking for assistance 80% of the time.
4. Tim will listen to directions before beginning a task 80% of the time.
5. Tim will read directions before beginning a task 80% of the time.

Annual Goal: Tim will improve compliance to authority.

Short-Term Objectives:
1. Tim will follow through with teacher directives within 2 minutes of being instructed. This will gradually decrease.
2. Tim will follow teacher directives when given 2 cues. This will gradually decrease in number.
3. Tim will stop an activity when told to do so by the teacher 80% of the time.

Annual Goal: Tim will maintain a moderate tone of voice during group activities.

Short-Term Objectives:
1. Tim will temporarily remove himself from an activity when he begins to become overexcited 50% of the time.
2. Tim will use a tone of voice appropriate to the situation 80% of the time.
3. Tim will stop an activity when told to do so by the teacher 80% of the time.

Annual Goal: Tim will improve graphomotor skills in handwriting activities.

Short-Term Objectives:
1. Tim will show better pencil grip and position paper on desk more appropriately when writing.
2. Tim will form letters correctly and adhere to lines and space alloted on page.
3. Tim will use better planning in his layout of text on a page and utilize proper headings on papers.

Two Model Programs for Students with ADD

Currently there are only a handful of public education programs designed to assist students with ADD in a special education setting. The first program to be discussed is located at the University of California, Irvine and has been operating for several years. The UCI-OCDE program is a joint project between the university and the Orange County Department of Education. The second program to be discussed is a newly funded program for kindergarten students and is based in Massachusetts. Preliminary data obtained thus far from this program looks promising as well.

The UCI-OCDE Program

The University of California, Irvine and the Orange County Department of Education provide a cooperative school-based treatment program for children with a diagnosis of attention deficit disorder or oppositional defiant disorder. Dr. James Swanson is the director and developer of the UCI-OCDE program which is housed on the university campus. The program serves ADD children from kindergarten through fifth grade. The curriculum and services provide both an educational and clinical component to the children attending the school.

Children in the UCI-OCDE program work on a very

structured token economy level system which is closely supervised by the classroom teacher. There is a low student:teacher ratio of approximately 7:1. Students can earn points at the rate of 32 points per hour for positive behavior and academic performance in five areas: getting started (2 points), staying on task (4 points), interacting with peers and teacher (4 points), completing work (4 points), and stopping and cleaning up (2 points). The children are evaluated every half-hour by the teacher and begin with 16 points at the start of each thirty minute interval, with points deducted for inappropriate behavior. Children earn their way to one of three levels. At level one, they are given direct feedback of the number of points earned. Children at level two report their estimates of points earned and try to match theirs with the teacher's evaluation of how many points they earned during a specified time period. Children at level three continue to receive points for maintaining positive behavior.

In the clinical component, social skills training and cognitive behavior therapy are provided daily in a group setting. This training involves teaching children social skills and problem-solving using direct instruction, role playing, and in vivo practice, while the children participate in games and group activities. The children's performance is carefully monitored by teachers throughout the session and they learn to self-evaluate and reward their own performance. Their social behavior is also monitored and evaluated by their classroom teacher throughout the day resulting in increased maintenance and generalization of prosocial behavior. As their behavior improves, they receive less feedback and their reinforcement schedule is gradually decreased. At the end of the school day, each child has the opportunity to exchange the points they earned in class and during social skills training for privileges.

Other components of the UCI-OCDE program include a six to eight week parent training course to teach parents the basic principles of behavior modification. Parents become familiar with the token economy system under which their children function at school, and can apply similar principles of behavior management at home. The clinical component of the program involves the use of double-blind laboratory assessment to determine medication effectiveness, using computerized tests of cognitive ability.

After leaving this intensive full-day program, the children return to a transition school at which they will receive additional close supervision and monitoring of social behavior in the classroom by a representative of the UCI-OCDE program before returning to their home school.

Barkley-Worcester, MA Program

Drawing upon the UCI-OCDE program, Dr. Russell Barkley, in collaboration with the Worcester, MA Public Schools, designed a prevention/treatment program for kindergarten children with attentional problems and oppositional behavior. Co-investigator, Dr. Terri Shelton and educational consultant, Cheryl Crosswaite, M.Ed., provided a description of this new program for the CH.A.D.D.ER newsletter (1992). The program focuses on behavioral interventions, social skills training, and academic curriculum.

The behavioral interventions segment of the program was designed with the belief that children with attentional difficulties will need a great deal of immediate and consistent feedback about their behavior. To provide this, the program uses a highly structured point system through which students are given a high rate of positive verbal reinforcement throughout the day. Children earn at least 10 "big deal" stickers each day for good attitude, paying attention, and working well with others, etc.. Teachers and aides are reminded to comment positively on the student's behavior at frequent intervals.

To keep track of a child's success, behavior is evaluated every 30 minutes and the child is ranked into one of three groups: "Red" being the best, and meaning that the child followed the rules and didn't exhibit any misbehavior; "Yellow" if the child was noncompliant or interrupted; and "Blue" if the child was repeatedly noncompliant and exhibited any aggression. Each student's status is posted on a board in the classroom. At the end of the morning and at the end of the day, the student can engage in activities which correspond to their color grouping. Negative behavior such as noncompliance (e.g. not listening, not finishing work, etc.), interrupting, and aggression (e.g. calling names, fighting, pestering) are managed through a response cost program with the child moved to a lower color group and asked to perform an unpleasant task (e.g. a simple writing assignment).

Social skills are taught and practiced in the classroom for 30 minutes a day. Role playing, using puppets to demonstrate social skills, and "stop and think" problem-solving is modeled. Social skills are actively encouraged and reinforced in the classroom and parents are notified what skills are being taught so they can observe such behavior at home and reinforce appropriately.

Keeping in mind the variability of skills in children with developmental problems, the academic curriculum is designed to fit the child at his individual level. Emphasis is put on training children to stop, read directions, and check their work. Small group and one-to-one instruction is provided with larger group instruction being given in increasing amounts to prepare the children for entry into a regular first grade program

Chapter 12
Helping Parents
Find the Right Help

Every parent would like to raise their child to be a happy, healthy and productive member of society. Even when their kids are on the right track toward reaching that goal, it is hard for parents to relax and not worry about what could go wrong. Fortunately, most children do okay. They usually start off on an even footing with everyone else and with a decent education, proper support from their families, and a little persistence and effort, they make it through their child and adolescent years ready to handle adult responsibilities.

Some children, however, have trouble right from the start. Parents of children with hidden handicaps such as learning disabilities, emotional problems, or attention deficit disorder often sense a problem with their child at a young age, but can't quite put their finger on what is wrong. They wait for the child to develop and hope that problems will improve with time. Sometimes they get lucky and mother nature does the trick. The child matures and the problems are taken care of. For other children, however, problems get worse and become even more pronounced when the child enters school.

Teachers play an extremely important role in helping parents identify problems in their child's development. Being familiar with normative behavior and the characteristics of similar aged children, teachers have a good basis of comparison.

In many instances the teacher is the first person to document a problem with the child. While some parents become defensive when told by the teacher that their child has a problem, most are relieved to find that someone else notices what they may have sensed for years. Although often frightened by the thought of something being wrong, most parents are eager to look for answers and to seek help.

Finding the right person to help the parent can be difficult. In the case where a child is suspected to have learning and/or attentional problems, parents should be advised that when selecting a physician, psychologist, or educational specialist to evaluate and treat their child, they should find someone in their community who has had training in the assessment and treatment of children with learning and behavioral problems, and preferably in working with ADD children. Once such a person is found, the next step to receiving the right kind of help is to get a comprehensive assessment of the child. As indicated in chapter 4, ADD assessments usually involve getting information from a variety of sources. Often the child's medical doctor, teachers, and parents will be involved in the evaluation process. Clinical or school psychologists will frequently be called upon to administer tests of intellectual functioning, information processing, achievement, and emotionality. A medical examination may rule out any medical problems which could contribute to the child's difficulties. Teachers and parents will complete rating scales designed to objectively measure the child's behavior in school and at home. When it is finished, a comprehensive evaluation should result in accurate diagnosis and should provide parents with a greater understanding of the nature and severity of their child's problems.

If the assessment reveals that the child has an attention deficit disorder, parents should be given material to read so they could become more familiar with how to help their child. Parent education becomes an integral part of the treatment process. Typical questions parents ask upon hearing the ADD diagnosis center around causes, outcomes, and concerns about what the future will hold for their child. Those parents whose children are advised to take medication, for example, can easily become anxious about the process of giving their child medicine and often need time to become educated, to digest the concept, and to become comfortable with it before taking that step. To assist in the process of parent education, we have included a listing of suggested readings for parents and ADD fact sheets that teachers can give to parents. These are located in the Appendix.

Through education about the disorder, parents of ADD children learn to make adjustments for their child's welfare. Given the special needs that ADD children have for structure and consistency in the home, many parents have to face the fact that they may have to make considerable changes in the way their households operate. Parents whose ADD children require a great deal of supervision in school will often rearrange priorities to make time to assist their child with school work. For some, this may mean setting aside more time, while others may have to pay for tutors or special private schools. Medical expenses and bills for counseling can strain the family's budget. Helping siblings understand the special needs of their ADD brother or sister, as well as educating grandparents, cousins, and other relatives about ADD, can be an important step in building family teamwork to help the ADD child succeed.

Teachers, knowing well the challenges that the ADD child poses in the classroom, should be able to relate to the difficulties that parents face at home. Parents appreciate teachers who are willing to listen compassionately and who offer assistance to their child without any hint of judgement or disapproval. Unfortunately, some teachers are quick to judge the child and incriminate the parent without fully understanding what attention deficit disorder is all about. Such teachers still believe that ADD comes from improper parenting, abuse, or neglect. They think the solution to the child's problems will come in the form of tighter rules and harsher discipline. They blame the parent for allowing the child to get out of control.

Teachers who think this way usually do more harm than good. Parents of ADD children did not cause their child to have ADD as a result of their parenting methods. In general, these parents are no different than parents of non-ADD children. Do they make mistakes? Sure they do, but no more than any one else.

Proven and Unproven/Disproven Therapies

Teachers may be asked to provide some direction to parents who are looking for sources of help. There are a number of therapies which have been used to treat children and adolescents with attention deficit disorders. Unfortunately, they are not all helpful. Therapies can be divided into two groups; those which have been proven to be effective treatments and those which are unproven or have been disproven as effective.

Proven Therapies for ADD

Generally, therapies which have been shown to be effective in the treatment of ADD include:

- Parent counseling and education about ADD
- Parent training in child and adolescent management
- Parent support groups
- Self-monitoring training
- Self-control training in natural settings
- Social skills training
- Family communication training
- Pharmacological therapies
- Teacher training for classroom management
- Classroom accommodations and interventions

Many of these treatments were discussed in previous chapters. Not all of them will be used for every ADD child. Use of any one or more specific therapies will depend upon the unique needs of the child.

Unproven or Disproven Therapies for ADD

A number of therapies have not been proven to be effective in the treatment of ADD or have been disproven as effective. A brief description follows of some of the more common therapies which are sometimes provided to ADD children, but which have not been scientifically proven to be effective for the treatment of this disorder.

Dietary Management (Elimination Diets)

Those who advocate the use of elimination diets for the treatment of learning and attentional disorders applaud the results they have seen with the use of such dietary restrictions. The most popular elimination diet, the Feingold Diet (also called the K-P diet) is based on Dr. Benjamin Feingold's work with hyperactive children. Dr. Feingold estimated that in 40% to 50% of cases, food additives cause hyperactivity. The diet seeks to eliminate artificial colors and flavors and a number of food preservatives along with naturally occurring chemicals known as salicylates. Although some parents report very positive results when they adjust their child's diet to meet Feingold's specifications these results have not been able to stand up to scientific scrutiny in double-blind research studies. Robert Hunt, M.D. (1990), in a recent review of diet studies, reports that despite considerable testimonial evidence from parents that dietary modification has decreased hyperactivity in their children, well-controlled studies have failed to demonstrate a strong positive relationship between diet and hyperactivity. Paul Wender, M.D. reviewed many of the Feingold diet studies and found that of 240 children evaluated only 1% showed any consistent, positive behavioral change through dietary modification.

Despite the lack of research support for the efficacy of dietary management in the treatment of ADD, many teachers continue to hold on to the misconception that dietary factors strongly influence student behavior. "What did Johnny eat for breakfast this morning? He was very hyper all day." is a question too frequently asked by teachers to parents of ADD children. Dietary management remains a controversial and a still unproven therapy for ADD.

Megavitamin/Orthomolecular (Supplement Diets)

Orthomolecular therapy is based on the premise that certain disorders result from a deficiency of specific chemical substances in the brain which can be resupplied through the ingestion of large quantities of vitamins, usually vitamins C, B_3, and B_6. Initially having gained popularity several years ago as a treatment for severe mental disorders, for which it has also been disproven as an effective treatment, interest in orthomolecular therapy as a treatment for learning and behavior disorders surfaced. To date there is no conclusive evidence that this approach is an effective treatment for ADD.

Sensory Integration Therapy

Based upon the research of Dr. A. Jean Ayres, some occupational therapists will use sensory integration therapy to help ADD children by reducing the child's tactile defensiveness or sensitivity to touch. In sensory integration therapy, the child is exposed to physical stimulation in carefully selected and controlled doses. The therapist adjusts the amount of tactile stimulation over time as a way of conditioning the child to tolerate such stimulation more easily. To do this the therapist may stimulate touch sensations by using cloths or brushes rubbed against the skin. Graded stimulation is believed to enhance the capacity of the brain for intersensory integration. Although sensory integration therapy may have some limited benefit for children suffering from developmental disabilities such as pervasive developmental disorder (autism) or mental retardation, as a treatment for attention deficit disorder its effectiveness has not been proven.

Chiropractic Manipulation

Chiropractors believe that a number of diseases, some mental illnesses, behavior and learning disorders included, are caused by misaligned vertebrae which disrupt normal nerve function. They attempt to restore normal functioning through spinal manipulation. While widely accepted as an effective treatment for a number of disorders of the joints and muscles, the efficacy of chiropractic manipulation in the treatment of attention deficit disorder has not been proven.

Optometric Training

Some optometrists believe that problems with visual perception can have serious implications for learning, and especially for reading. Through sensory-motor-perceptual training techniques, optometrists who do such training suggest that visual perceptual problems can be corrected, thereby rendering the child more accessible for learning. Several professional associations including the American Academy of Pediatrics, the American Academy of Ophthamology and Otolaryngology, and the American Association of Ophthamology issued a joint statement which was critical of a sensory-motor-perceptual training approach to treating learning disabilities (Silver, 1984).

Cerebellar-Vestibular Dysfunction

Initially, Dr. Harold Levinson's approach to treating learning disabilities and hyperactivity by correcting vestibular dysfunction gained popularity when it was first presented in his 1981 book on the subject. Dr. Levinson advocated that some forms of learning problems are caused by dysfunction of the body's balance system, the vestibular system. He suggested that this dysfunction could be corrected by using medications such as those used for motion sickness. Dr. Levinson's successes using this method are described in his book, but the information is purely anecdotal in nature and his theories have not been scientifically proven.

Play therapy

Play therapy is a nondirective type of psychotherapy which is used with children who display certain types of emotional difficulties. While play therapy may be of some benefit in the treatment of some of the secondary emotional problems which are sometimes found in children suffering from attention deficit disorder, there is no scientific evidence that such therapy is effective in reducing rates of inattention, impulsivity, or hyperactivity in children.

Relaxation Therapy/Biofeedback Training

Relaxation therapy was initially developed as a treatment for stress-related disorders. In relaxation therapy, the person is given instructions on how to relax, either through use of; guided imagery, progressive muscle tensing and relaxing, or through autogenic training. Certain types of biofeedback training can assist people in learning the relaxation response by providing feedback regarding the body's physiologic state. Different types of physiologic feedback are helpful for different conditions. Temperature feedback has been shown to be effective for migraine sufferers, for example, while muscle potential may be useful feedback in the treatment of stress-related problems. Recently, electroencephalographic (EEG brain waves) feedback has been publicized (Adduci, 1991) as an effective treatment for ADD children. The premise behind such treatment is that children can be taught to control their level of neurological arousal, thereby, learning to better control behavior and attention. Unfortunately, to date there have been no controlled scientific studies which provide conclusive evidence as to the effectiveness of this treatment (Barkley, 1992 Unpublished manuscript). The use of EEG biofeedback remains an unproven treatment for ADD.

Parent Support Groups

Support groups can be immensely beneficial to parents. By meeting other parents who share similar problems in raising their children with ADD, parents develop a sense of comraderie with one another and find support. Usually groups of parents meet on a monthly or twice-monthly basis. Guest speakers lead discussions on various topics and provide expert information on medical managment, child rearing issues, educational interventions, self-esteem building, family dynamics, etc.. Most groups leave time for both formal and informal "rap" sessions among the parents, giving parents the opportunity to share experiences and to learn from one another. Teachers are encouraged to attend and parents welcome the opportunity to share ADD information with them.

Support groups have become a valuable resource for parents who are looking for information and help. Parents network to help each other find professionals in the community who are most knowledgeable about the disorder and to locate schools which work well with ADD students. As advocates, parent groups can influence local school districts to provide inservice training for teachers and can encourage local libraries to have ADD information available to the community. Local and regional conferences, sponsored by parent support groups, provide a source of continuing education for professionals from all related disciplines, as well as the opportunity for parents to learn side-by-side with educators and health care professionals.

CH.A.D.D., Children with Attention Deficit Disorders, is a national support group for parents of ADD children and for educators and health care professionals who have an interest in ADD children. With nearly 300 chapters nationally, and international affiliates in progress, CH.A.D.D. provides information and services to thousands of members throughout the United States. CH.A.D.D. members receive monthly newsletters on attention deficit disorders which contain valuable tips for raising and teaching ADD children, ADD fact sheets, and a guide for educators. Conferences held annually attract ADD researchers, educators, clinicians, and parents who can offer practical information to other parents and professionals. For more information about CH.A.D.D. and to locate the CH.A.D.D. chapter nearest you, contact:

> CH.A.D.D.
> National Headquarters
> 499 Northwest 70th Avenue, Suite 101
> Plantation, Florida 33317
> (954) 587-3700 • (800) 233-4050
> Internet: www.chadd.org/

ADDA, the Attention Deficit Disorder Association, is a national organization which has been active in addressing the needs of adults with attention deficit disorders. Through its annual conference on adult issues, ADDA has succeeded in bringing important information to the forefront. For more information about ADDA, contact:

> Attention Deficit Disorder Association
> P.O. Box 972
> Mentor, Ohio 44061
> (800) 487-2282

LDAA, the Learning Disabilities Association of America, is a national support group for parents of children with learning disabilities. In existence for over 25 years, LDA is well known for the support and information it provides to parents of learning disabled children world over. For more information about LDA, contact:

> Learning Disabilities Association of America
> 4156 Library Road
> Pittsburgh, PA 15234
> (412) 341-1515

Chapter 13
Helping Children with ADD Understand Themselves Better

In the past few years a number of books have been written for children to help them understand what attention deficit disorder is all about. Parents and teachers are often uncertain about how to explain such problems to children. Young children may not understand why they have more trouble keeping still and paying attention than others do, and most teenagers with ADD will minimize any attentional problems or deny them altogether.

Approaching children in the proper manner is a sensitive task. The following books and video will be helpful in assisting teachers who would like to acquaint their ADD students about the disorder. These materials can be ordered directly from their publishers (see References) or from the ADD WareHouse, (800) ADD-WARE.

Shelly, The Hyperactive Turtle by Deborah Moss

Shelly moves like a rocket and is unable to sit still for even the shortest periods of time. Because he and the other turtles are unable to understand why he is so wiggly and squirmy, Shelly begins to feel out-of-place. But after a vist to the doctor, Shelly learns what "hyperactive" means and gets the right kind of help.

Otto Leans About His Medication by Mathew Galvin, M.D.

Dr. Galvin wrote a wonderful book explaining attention deficit disorder in story format. It is intended to be read to and by the child. Otto, a fidgety young car that has trouble paying attention in school, visits a special mechanic who prescribes a medicine to control his hyperactive behavior.

Eagle Eyes: A Child's View of Attention Deficit Disorder by Jeanne Gehret, M.A.

Clumsy and impulsive on a nature walk, Ben drives away the birds he admires. Over time, however, he learns to focus his attention like an eagle on the things that really count. By the end of this sympathetic story, Ben successfully helps his father when an emergency arises. *Eagle Eyes* helps readers of all ages understand ADD and gives practical suggestions for organization, social cues and self-calming. Expressive illustrations with a nature theme enhance this tale for reluctant readers.

Learning To Slow Down and Pay Attention by Kathleen Nadeau, Ph.D. and Ellen Dixon, Ph.D.

Written for children to read, and illustrated with delightful cartoons and activity pages to engage the child's interest, *Learning To Slow Down and Pay Attention* helps children to identify problems and explains how their parents, their doctor and their teacher can help. In an easy-to-understand language the book describes how an ADD child can learn to pay better attention in class, manage feelings, get more organized, and learn to problem solve.

Jumpin' Johnny Get Back To Work! A Child's Guide to ADHD/Hyperactivity by Michael Gordon, Ph.D.

This entertaining and informative book will help children understand the essential concepts involved in the evaluation and treatment of ADHD. *Jumpin' Johnny* tells what it's like to be inattentive and impulsive, and how his family and school work with him to make life easier. Children find this book to be amusing, educational and accurate in its depiction of the challenges that confront them daily. Dr. Gordon's humor and extensive clinical experience with ADHD children shine through every page of this charming but realistic story.

Making the Grade: An Adolescent's Struggle with ADD by Roberta N. Parker   **Facts About ADD: Commonly Asked Questions** by Harvey C. Parker, Ph.D.

Making the Grade is the heartwarming story of seventh grader Jim Jerome's struggle to succeed in school. Eager to make a good showing in junior high, Jim soon finds his problems with self-control and inattention threaten his chances of success scholastically and athletically. With the help of his parents, teachers and concerned health care professionals, Jim learns about ADD and ways to help himself.

Although a fictional account of how ADD can affect pre-teen and young teenage students, *Making the Grade* is, nonetheless, a very relatable story for eleven to fourteen year old adolescents who have attention deficit disorder.

Following the story is a section entitled *Facts About ADD: Commonly Asked Questions* which offers more direct information to young readers. Dr. Parker explains the symptoms, causes, treatments and outcomes of ADD in a frank and postive way.

Putting On the Brakes by Patricia O. Quinn, M.D. and Judith Stern, M.A.

An honest, accessible overview of attention deficit hyperactivity disorder for children ages 8 to 12. Written for children to read, *Putting On The Brakes* focuses on the feelings and emotions of children with ADD and suggests specific techniques for gaining control of the situation, becoming better organized, and functioning better at school, home, and with friends. Children with ADD will find the acknowledgement and explanation of their problems a relief, and the coping strategies a great help. The book addresses such topics as the physiology and symptoms of ADD, medication used in treatment, and various types of family and community support that are available.

Keeping A Head In School: A Student's Book About Learning Abilities and Learning Disorders by Mel Levine, M.D.

This book, written especially for students by Dr. Mel Levine, a pediatrician and well known authority on learning problems, demystifies learning disorders for young people affected by them. *Keeping A Head In School*, helps nine to fifteen year old students with learning disorders gain a better understanding of their personal strengths and weaknesses. They see that learning styles vary greatly and find specific ways to approach work and manage the struggles that may beset them in school. Dr. Levine's helpful book is intended to convince students that the struggle is worth the effort and will ultimately be rewarding.

My Brother's A World-Class Pain: A Sibling's Guide to ADHD by Michael Gordon, Ph.D.

This is the first book written for the oft-forgotten group of those affected by ADD: the brothers and sisters of ADD children. While they frequently bear the brunt of the ADD child's impulsiveness and distractibility, siblings usually are not afforded opportunities to understand the nature of the problem and to have their own feelings and thoughts addressed. This story about an older sister's efforts to deal with her active and impulsive brother sends the clear message to siblings of the ADD child that they can play an important role in a family's quest for change.

Eukee the Jumpy Jumpy Elephant by Cliff Corman, M.D. and Esther Trevino, M.F.C.C.

Eukee moves through the jungle like a tornado, unable to pay attention like the other elephants. He begins to feel sad, but gets help after a visit to the doctor who explains why Eukee is so jumpy and hyperactive. With love, support and help, Eukee learns ways to help himself and gains renewed self-confidence. Ideal for ages 3-8.

It's Just Attention Disorder: A Video Guide for Kids by Sam Goldstein, Ph.D. and Michael Goldstein, M.D.

Accurate diagnosis for ADD has become a reality and now the next step becomes treatment. To be helped, ADD children and adolescents must want help. *It's Just Attention Disorder* was created to help parents, teachers, and counselors assist the ADD child and adolescent to become an active participant in the treatment process. Filmed in an "MTV" format, this video will hold the attention of even the most inattentive. It has been designed to acquaint the ADD child and adolescent with basic information concerning the nature and treatment of ADD. Included with the video are a User's Manual and Study Guide.

For more information about what resources are available to help ADD children directly, contact a local support group in your area. Many of these groups run programs for ADD children which enhance self-awareness and greater understanding of attention deficit disorder. CH.A.D.D. maintains chapters in every state and will gladly help you locate a support group in your community. Call (954) 587-3700 for more information.

Appendix A
United States Department of
Education ADD Memorandum

Appendix A: United States Department of Education ADD Memorandum

UNITED STATES DEPARTMENT OF EDUCATION
OFFICE OF SPECIAL EDUCATION AND REHABILITATIVE SERVICES

THE ASSISTANT SECRETARY

MEMORANDUM

SEP 1 6 1991

DATE   :

TO   :   Chief State School Officers

FROM   :   Robert R. Davila
              Assistant Secretary
              Office of Special Education
                and Rehabilitative Services

              Michael L. Williams
              Assistant Secretary
              Office for Civil Rights

              John T. MacDonald
              Assistant Secretary
              Office of Elementary
                and Secondary Education

SUBJECT   :   Clarification of Policy to Address the Needs of
              Children with Attention Deficit Disorders within
              General and/or Special Education

I.   Introduction

There is a growing awareness in the education community that attention deficit disorder (ADD) and attention deficit hyperactive disorder (ADHD) can result in significant learning problems for children with those conditions. While estimates of the prevalence of ADD vary widely, we believe that three to five percent of school-aged children may have significant educational problems related to this disorder. Because ADD has broad implications for education as a whole, the Department believes it should clarify State and local responsibility under Federal law for addressing the needs of children with ADD in the schools. Ensuring that these students are able to reach their fullest potential is an inherent part of the National education goals and AMERICA 2000. The National goals, and the strategy for achieving them, are based on the assumptions that: (1) all children can learn and benefit from their education; and (2) the educational community must work to improve the learning opportunities for all children.

---

[1] While we recognize that the disorders ADD and ADHD vary, the term ADD is being used to encompass children with both disorders.

MARYLAND AVE. S.W. WASHINGTON D.C.

Page 2 — Chief State School Officers

This memorandum clarifies the circumstances under which children with ADD are eligible for special education services under Part B of the Individuals with Disabilities Education Act (Part B), as well as the Part B requirements for evaluation of such children's unique educational needs. This memorandum will also clarify the responsibility of State and local educational agencies (SEAs and LEAs) to provide special education and related services to eligible children with ADD under Part B. Finally, this memorandum clarifies the responsibilities of LEAs to provide regular or special education and related aids and services to those children with ADD who are not eligible under Part B, but who fall within the definition of "handicapped person" under Section 504 of the Rehabilitation Act of 1973. Because of the overall educational responsibility to provide services for these children, it is important that general and special education coordinatetheir efforts.

II.   Eligibility for Special Education and Related Services under Part B

Last year during the reauthorization of the Education of the Handicapped Act (now the Individuals with Disabilities Education Act), Congress gave serious consideration to including ADD in the definition of "children with disabilities" in the statute. The Department took the position that ADD does not need to be added as a separate disability category in the statutory definition since children with ADD who require special education and related services can meet the eligibility criteria for services under Part B. This continues to be the Department's position.

No change with respect to ADD was made by Congress in the statutory definition of "children with disabilities;" however, language was included in Section 102(a) of the Education of the Handicapped Act Amendments of 1990 that required the Secretary to issue a Notice of Inquiry (NOI) soliciting public comment on special education for children with ADD under Part B. In response to the NOI (published November 29, 1990 in the Federal Register), the Department received over 2000 written comments, which have been transmitted to the Congress. Our review of these written comments indicates that there is confusion in the field regarding the extent to which children with ADD may be served in special education programs conducted under Part B.

A.   Description of Part B

Part B requires SEAs and LEAs to make a free appropriate public education (FAPE) available to all eligible children with disabilities and to ensure that the rights and protections of Part B are extended to those children and their parents 20 U.S.C. 1412(2); 34 CFR SS300.121 and 300.2. Under Part B, FAPE, among other elements, includes the provision of special education and related services, at no cost to parents, in conformity with an individualized education program (IEP). 34 CFR §300.4.

Page 3 — Chief State School Officers

In order to be eligible under Part B, a child must be evaluated in accordance with 34 CFR §§300.530-300.534 as having one or more specified physical or mental impairments, and must be found to require special education and related services by reason of one or more of these impairments.[2] 20 U.S.C. 1401 (a) (1); 34 CFR §300.5. SEAs and LEAs must ensure that children with ADD who are determined eligible for services under Part B receive special education and related services designed to meet their unique needs, including special education and related services needs arising from the ADD. A full continuum of placement alternatives, including the regular classroom, must be available for providing special education and related services required in the IEP.

B.   Eligibility for Part B services under the "Other Health Impaired" Category

The list of chronic or acute health problems included within the definition of "other health impaired" in the Part B regulations is not exhaustive. The term "other health impaired" includes chronic or acute impairments that result in limited alertness, which adversely affects educational performanc. Thus, children with ADD should be classified as eligible for services under the "other health impaired" category in instances where the ADD is a chronic or acute health problem that results in limited alertness. which adversely affects educational performance. In other words, children with ADD, where the ADD is a chronic or acute health problem resulting in limited alertness, may be considered disabled under Part B solely on the basis of this disorder within the "other health impaired" category in situations where special education and related services are needed because of the ADD.

C.   Eligibility for Part B services under Other Disability Categories

Children with ADD are also eligible for services under Part B if the children satisfy the criteria applicable to other disability categories. For example, children with ADD are also eligible for services under the "specific learning disability" category of Part B if they meet the criteria stated in §§300.5(b) (9) and 300.541 or under the "seriously emotionally disturbed" category of Part B if they meet the criteria stated i §300.5(b) (8).

---

[2]The Part B regulations define 11 specified disabilities. 34 CFR §300.5(b) (1)-(11). The Education of the Handicapped Act Amendments of 1990 amended the Individuals with Disabilities Education Act (formerly the Education of the Handicapped Act) to specify that autism and traumatic brain injury are separate disability categories. See section 602(a) (1) of the Act, to be codified at 20 U.S.C. 1401(a) (1).

III.   Evaluations under Part B

A.   Requirements

SEAs and LEAs have an affirmative obligation to evaluate a child who is suspected of having a disability to determine the child's need for special education and related services. Under Part B, SEA's and LEAs are required to have procedures for locating, identifying and evaluating all children who have a disability or are suspected of having a disability and are in need of special education and related services. 34 CFR §§300.128 and 300.220. This responsibility, known as "child find," is applicable to all children from birth through 21, regardless of the severity of their disability.

Consistent with this responsibility and the obligation to make FAPE available to all eligible children with disabilities, SEAs and LEAs must ensure that evaluations of children who are suspected of needing special education and related services are conducted without undue delay. 20 U.S.C. 1412(2). Because of its responsibility resulting from the FAPE and child find requirements of Part B, an LEA may not refuse to evaluate the possible need for special education and related services of a child with a prior medical diagnosis of ADD solely by reason of that medical diagnosis. However, a medical diagnosis of ADD alone is not sufficient to render a child eligible for services under Part B.

Under Part B, before any action is taken with respect to the initial placement of a child with a disability in a program providing special education and related services, "a full and individual evaluation of the child's educational needs must be conducted in accordance with requirements of §300.532." 34 CFR §300.531. Section 300.532(a) requires that a child's evaluation must be conducted by a multidisciplinary team, including at least one teacher or other specialist with knowledge in the area of suspected disability.

B.   Disagreements over Evaluations

Any proposal or refusal of an agency to initiate or change the identification, evaluation, or educational placement of the child, or the provision of FAPE to the child is subject to the written prior notice requirements of 34 CFR §§300.504-300.505.[3] If a parent disagrees with the LEA's refusal to evaluate a child or the LEA's evaluation and determination that a child does not have a disability for which the child is eligible for services under Part B, the parent may request a due process hearing pursuant to 34 CFR §§300.506-300.513 of the Part B regulations.

Appendix A: United States Department of Education ADD Memorandum

IV. <u>Obligations Under Section 504 of SEAs and LEAs to Children with ADD Found Not To Require Special Education and Related Services under Part B</u>

Even if a child with ADD is found not to be eligible for services under Part B, the requirements of Section 504 of the Rehabilitation Act of 1973 (Section 504) and its implementing regulation at 34 CFR Part 104 may be applicable. Section 504 prohibits discrimination on the basis of handicap by recipients of Federal funds. Since Section 504 is a civil rights law, rather than a funding law, its requirements are framed in different terms than those of Part B. While the Section 504 regulation was written with an eye to consistency with Part B, it is more general, and there are some differences arising from the differing natures of the two laws. For instance, the protections of Section 504 extend to some children who do not fall within the disability categories specified in Part B.

A. <u>Definition</u>

Section 504 requires every recipient that operates a public elementary or secondary education program to address the needs of children who are considered "handicapped persons" under Section 504 as adequately as the needs of nonhandicapped persons are met. "Handicapped person" is defined in the Section 504 regulation as any person who has a physical or mental impairment which substantially limits a major life activity (e.g., learning). 34 CFR §104.3(j). Thus, depending on the severity of their condition, children with ADD may fit within that definition.

------

[3]Section 300.505 of the Part B regulations sets out the elements that must be contained in the prior written notice to parents:

> (1) A full explanation of all of the procedural safeguards available to the parents under Subpart E;
> (2) A description of the action proposed or refused by the agency, an explanation of why the agency proposes or refuses to take the action, and a description of any options the agency considered and the reasons why those options were rejected;
> (3) A description of each evaluation procedure, test, record, or report the agency uses as a basis for the proposal or refusal; and
> (4) A description of any other factors which are relevant to the agency's proposal or refusal.

34 CFR §300.505(a) (1)-(4).

Page 6 — Chief State School Officers

B.   Programs and Services Under Section 504

Under Section 504, an LEA must provide a free appropriate public education to each qualified handicapped child. A free appropriate public education, under Section 504, consists of regular or special education and related aids and services that are designed to meet the individual student's needs and based on adherence to the regulator requirements on educational setting, evaluation, placement, and procedural safeguards. 34 CFR §§104.33, 104.34, 104.35, and 104.36. A student may be handicapped within the meaning of Section 504, and therefore entitled to regular or special education and related aids and services under the Section 504 regulation, even though the student may not be eligible for special education and related services under Part B.

Under Section 504, if parents believe that their child is handicapped by ADD, the LEA must evaluate the child to determine whether he or she is handicapped as defined by Section 504. If an LEA determines that a child is not handicapped under Section 504, the parent has the right to contest that determination. If the child is determined to be handicapped under Section 504, the LEA must make an individualized determination of the child's educational needs for regular or special education or related aids and services. 34 CFR §104.35. For children determined to be handicapped under Section 504, implementation of an individualized education program developed in accordance with Part B, although not required, is one means of meeting the free appropriate public education requirements of Section 504.[4] The child's education must be provided in the regular education classroom unless it is demonstrated that education in the regular environment with the use of supplementary aids and services cannot be achieved satisfactorily. 34 CFR §104.34.

Should it be determined that the child with ADD is handicapped for purposes of Section 504 and needs only adjustments in the regular classroom, rather than special education, those adjustments are required by Section 504. A range of strategies is available to meet the educational needs of children with ADD. Regular classroom teachers are important in identifying the appropriate educational adaptions and interventions for many children with ADD.

---

[4]Many LEAs use the same process for determining the needs of students under Section 504 that they use for implementing Part B.

Page 7 — Chief State School Officers

SEAs and LEAs should take the necessary steps to promote coordination between special and regular education programs. Steps also should be taken to train regular education teachers and other personnel to develop their awareness about ADD and its manifestations and the adaptations that can be implemented in regular education programs to address the instructional needs of these children. Examples of adaptations in regular education programs could include the following:

> providing a structured learning environment; repeating and simplifying instructions about in-class and homework assignments; supplementing verbal instructions with visual instructions; using behavioral management techniques; adjusting class schedules; modifying test delivery; using tape recorders, computer-aided instrction, and other audiovisual equipment; selecting modified textbooks or workbooks; and tailoring homework assignments.

Other provisions range from consultation to special resources and may include reducing class size; use of one-on-one tutorials; classroom aides and note takers; involvement of a "services coordinator" to oversee implementation of special programs and services, and possible modification of nonacademic times such as lunchroom, recess, and physical education.

Through the use of appropriate adaptations and interventions in regular classes, many of which may be required by Section 504, the Department believes that LEAs will be able to effectively address the instructional needs of many children with ADD.

C.   Procedural Safeguards Under Section 504

Procedural safeguards under the Section 504 regulation are stated more generally than in Part B. The Section 504 regulation requires the LEA to make available a system of procedural safeguards that permits parents to challenge actions regarding the identification, evaluation, or educational placement of their handicapped child whom they believe needs special education or related services. 34 CFR §104.36. The Section 504 regulation requires that the system of procedural safeguards include notice, an opportunity for the parents or guardian to examine relevant records, an impartial hearing with opportunity for participation by the parents or guardian and representation by counsel, and a review procedure. Compliance with procedural safeguards of Part B is one means of fulfilling the Section 504 requirements.[5] However, in an impartial due process hearing raising issues under the Section 504 regulation, the impartial hearing officer must make a determination based upon that regulation.

---

[5] Again, many LEAs and some SEAs are conserving time and resources by using the same due process procedures for resolving disputes under both laws.

Page 8 — Chief State School Officers

V.   Conclusion

Congress and the Department have recognized the need to provide information and assistance to teachers, administrators, parents and other interested persons regarding the identification, evaluation, and instructional needs of children with ADD. The Department has formed a work group to explore strategies across principal offices to address this issue. The work group also plans to identify some ways that the Department can work with the education associations to cooperatively consider the programs and services needed by children with ADD across special and regular education.

In fiscal year 1991, the Congress appropriated funds for the Department to synthesize and disseminate current knowledge related to ADD. Four centers will be established in Fall, 1991 to analyze and synthesize the current research literature on ADD relating to identification, assessment, and interventions. Research syntheses will be prepared in formats suitable for educators, parents and researchers. Existing clearinghouses and networks, as well as Federal, State and local organizations will be utilized to disseminate these research syntheses to parents, educators and administrators, and other interested persons.

In addition, the Federal Resource Center will work with SEAs and the six regional resource centers authorized under the Individuals with Disabilities Education Act to identfy effective identification and assesment procedures, as well as intervention strategies being implemented across the country for children with ADD. A document describing current practice will be developed and disseminated to parents, educators and administrators, and other interested persons through the regional resource centers, network, as well as by parent training centers, other parent and consumer organizations, and professional organizations. Also, the Office for Civil Rights' ten regional offices stand ready to provide technical assistance to parents and educators.

It is our hope that the above information will be of assistance to your State as you plan for the needs of children with ADD who require special education and related services under Part B, as well as for the needs of the broader group of children with ADD who do not qualify for special education and related services under Part B, but for whom special education or adaptations in regular education programs are needed. If you have any questions, please contact Jean Peelen, Office for Civil Rights; (Phone: 202/732-1635), Judy Schrag, Office of Special Education Programs (Phone: 202/732-1007); or Dan Bonner, Office of Elementary and Secondary Education (Phone: 202/401-0984).

Appendix B
ADD Fact Sheet for Parents

Children With Attention Deficit Disorders
ADD Fact Sheet

Prevalence and Characteristics of ADD

Current interest in Attention Deficit Disorders (ADD*) is soaring. Magazine articles, newspaper reports, network newscasts, and television talk show hosts have found this to be a timely topic. Scientific journals report thousands of studies of ADD children and youth and ADD support groups continue to grow at an astounding rate as parents seek to learn more about this disorder in an effort to help their youngsters succeed at home and at school. Children with ADD are characterized by symptoms of inattention, impulsivity, and sometimes, hyperactivity which have an onset before age seven and which persist for at least six months. These children comprise approximately 3-5% of the school age population with boys significantly outnumbering girls.

In order to receive a diagnosis of ADD a child must exhibit at least eight of the following characteristics for a duration of at least six months with onset before age seven:

Characteristics of ADD

1. often fidgets with hands or feet or squirm in seat (in adolescence may be limited to subjective feelings of restlessness)
2. has difficulty remaining seated when required to do so
3. is easily distracted by extraneous stimuli
4. has difficulty awaiting turns in games or group situations
5. often blurts out answers to questions before they have been completed
6. has difficulty following through on instructions from others (not due to oppositional behavior or failure of comprehension)
7. has difficulty sustaining attention in tasks or play activities
8. often shifts from one uncompleted activity to another
9. has difficulty playing quietly
10. often talks excessively
11. often interrupts or intrudes on others, e.g. butts into other children's games
12. often does not seem to listen to what is being said to him or her
13. often loses things necessary for tasks or activities at school or at home (e.g. toys, pencils, books)
14. often engages in physically dangerous activities without considering possible consequences (not for the purpose of thrill-seeking) e.g. runs into street without looking

A second diagnosis, Undifferentiated Attention Deficit Disorder, refers to those children who exhibit disturbances in which the primary characteristic is significant inattentiveness without signs of hyperactivity. Recent studies of this group of ADD children without hyperactivity indicates that they tend to show more signs of anxiety and learning problems, qualitatively different inattention, and may have different outcomes than the hyperactive group.

Causes of ADD

There are still many unanswered questions as to the cause of ADD. Over the years the presence of ADD has been weakly associated with a variety of conditions including: prenatal and/or perinatal trauma, maturational delay, environmentally caused toxicity such as fetal alcohol syndrome or lead toxicity, and food allergies. History of such conditions may be found in some individuals with ADD, however, in most cases there is no history of any of the above.

Recently, researchers have turned their attention to altered brain biochemistry as a cause of ADD and presume differences in biochemistry may be the cause of poor regulation of attention, impulsivity and motor activity. A recent landmark study by Dr. Alan Zametkin and researchers at NIMH have traced ADD for the first time to a specific metabolic abnormality in the brain. A great deal more research has to be done to reach more definitive answers.

Identification of ADD

The identification and diagnosis of children with ADD requires a combination of clinical judgement and objective assessment. Since there is a high rate of co-existence of ADD with other psychiatric disorders of childhood and adolescence any comprehensive assessment should include an evaluation of the individual's medical, psychological, educational and behavioral functioning. The more domains assessed the greater certainty there can be of a comprehensive, valid and reliable diagnosis. The taking of a detailed history, including medical, family, psychological, developmental social and educational factors is essential in order to establish a pattern of chronicity and pervasiveness of symptoms. Augmenting the history are the standardized parent and teacher behavioral rating scales which are essential to quantifiably assess the normality of the individual with respect to adaptive functioning in a variety of settings such as home and school Psyucholeducational assessment investigating intellectual functioning and cognitive processes including reasoning skills, use of language, perception, attention, memory, and visual-motor functioning as well as academic achievement should often be performed.

Treatment of ADD

Most experts agree that a multi-modality approach to treatment of the disorder aimed at assisting the child medically, psychologically, educationally and behavior is often needed. This requires the coordinated efforts of a team of health care professionals, educators and parents who work together to identify treatment goals, design and implement interventions and evaluate the results of their efforts.

Medications used to treat ADD are no longer limited to psychostimulants such as methylphenidate (Ritalin), dextroamphetamine (Dexedrine) and pemoline (Cylert) which have been shown to have dramatically positive effects on attention, overactivity, visual motor skills and even agresssion in 70% or more ADD children. In the past several years the

A.D.D. FACT SHEET, Prepared by Harvey C. Parker, Ph.D. 1991

tricyclic antidepressant medications, imipramine (Tofranil), and norpramine (Desipramine), have been studied and used clinically to treat the disorder with other types of antidepressants: fluxetine, chlorimipramine and buproprion much less frequently prescribed. Clonidine (Catapress), antihypertensive, and carbamazepine (Tegretol), an anticonvulsant, have been shown to be effective for some children as well.

Ideally, treatment should also include consideration of the individual's psychological adjustment targeting problems involving self-esteem, anxiety and difficulties with family and peer interaction. Frequently family therapy is useful along with behavioral and cognitive interventions to improve behavior, attention span, and social skills. Educational interventions such as accommodations made within the regulate education classroom, compensatory educational instruction or placement in special education may be required depending upon the particular child's needs.

Outcome of ADD

ADD is an extremely stable condition with approximately eighty percent of young children diagnosed ADD also meeting criteria for an ADD diagnosis when reevaluated in adolescence. Unfortualtey, ADD does not often occur in isolation from other psychiatric disorders and many ADD children have co-existing oppositional and conduct disorders with a smaller number (probably less than 25%) having a learning disability. Studies indicate that ADD students have a far greater likelihood of grade retention, school drop out, academic underachievement and social and emotional adjustment difficulties.

Most experts agree, however that the risk for poor outcome of ADD children and adolescents can be reduced through early identification and treatment. By recognizing the disorder early and taking the appropriate steps to assist the ADD child and family many of the negatives commonly experienced by the child can be avoided or minimized so as to protect self-esteem and avoid a chronic pattern of frustration, discouragement and failure.

While the hard facts about attentional deficits give us good reason to be concerned about ADD children, the voice of advocating parents coupled with the commitment of educated health care professionals and educators provide us with hope for the future well-being of this population of deserving youth.

Important Points To Remember

1. ADD children make up 3 - 5% of the population. A thorough evaluation can help determine whether attentional deficits are due to ADD or to other factors.

2. Once identified, ADD children are best treated with a *multi-modal* approach. Best results are obtained when medication, behavioral management programs, educational interventions, parent training, and counseling, when needed, are used together to help the ADD child. Parents of ADD children and adolescents play the key role of coordinating these services.

3. Teachers play an essential role in helping the ADD child feel comfortable within the classroom despite their difficulties. Adjustments in classroom procedures and work demands, sensitivity to self-esteem issues, and frequent parent-teacher contact can help a great deal.

4. ADD may be a life-long disorder requiring life-long assistance. Families, and the children themselves, need continued support and understanding.

Suggested Reading For Parents

Barkley, Russell. *Attention Deficit Hyperactivity Disorder. Guilford Press, 1990.*

Fowler, Mary. *Maybe You Know My Kid.* Birch Lane Press, 1990.

Goldstein, Sam & Goldstein Michael. *Why Won't My Child Pay Attention?* Neurology, Learning and Behavior Center, 1989.

Gordon, Michael. *ADHD/Hyperactivity: A Consumer's Guide.* GSI Publications, 1990.

Ingersoll, Barbara. *Your Hyperactive Child.* Doubleday, 1988.

Parker, Harvey C. *The ADD Hyperactivity Workbook for Parents, Teachers & Kids.* Impact Publications, 1988.

Phelan, Thomas W. *1-2-3 Magic!* Child Management, 1990 (Video and Book)

Phelan, Thomas W. *ADHD Video Parts I & II.* Child Management, 1991 (Video and Book)

Wender, Paul *The Hyperactive Child, Adolescent and Adult.* Oxford Press, 1987.

Books for Children

Gehret, Jeanne. *Eagle Eyes,* Verbal Images Press, 1991.

Gordon, Michael. *Jumpin' Johnny Get Back To Work!,* GSI Publications, 1991.

Moss, Deborah. *Shelly The Hyperactive Turtle,* Wood bine Press, 1989.

Nadeau, Kathleen & Dixon, Ellen. *Learning to Slow Down and Pay Attention,* Chesapeake Psychological Services, 1991.

For Further Information About ADD contact:

CH.A.D.D.
Children With Attention Deficit Disorders
499 Northwest 70th Avenue, Suite 308
Plantation, Florida 33317
(305) 587-3700

CH.A.D.D. is a non-profit parent-based organization providing support to families of children with attention deficit disorders and information to professionals. CH.A.D.D. maintains over two hundred and twenty-five chapters nationwide to provide services for children and adolescents with ADD. To locate a chapters nearest you call our national headquarters.

* The terms ADD and ADHD are used synonymously in this paper.

Appendix C
Medication Fact Sheet
for Parents and Teachers

Medical Management of Children with Attention Deficit Disorders
Commonly Asked Questions

by

Children with Attention Deficit Disorders (CH.A.D.D.)
American Academy of Child and Adolescent Psychiatry (AACAP)

Harvey C. Parker, Ph.D.
CH.A.D.D., Executive Director

George Storm, M.D.
CH.A.D.D., Professional Advisory Board

Committee of Community Psychiatry and Consultation to Agencies of AACAP
Theodore A. Petti, M.D., M.P.H., Chairperson
Virginia Q. Anthony, AACAP, Executive Director

This article may be reproduced and distributed without written permission.

1. What is an Attention Deficit Disorder?

Attention deficit disorder (ADD), also known as attention deficit hyperactivity disorder (ADHD), is a treatable disorder which affects approximately three to five per cent of the population. Inattentiveness, impulsivity, and oftentimes, hyperactivity, are common characteristics of the disorder. Boys with ADD tend to outnumber girls by three to one, although ADD in girls is underidentified.

Some common symptoms of ADD are:
1. Excessively fidgets or squirms
2. Difficulty remaining seated
3. Easily distracted
4. Difficulty awaiting turn in games
5. Blurts out answers to questions
6. Difficulty following instructions
7. Difficulty sustaining attention

8. Shifts from one activity to another
9. Difficulty playing quietly
10. Often talks excessively
11. Often interrupts
12. Often doesn't listen to what is said
13. Often loses things
14. Often engages in dangerous activities

However, you don't have to be hyperactive to have an attention deficit disorder. In fact, up to 30% of children with ADD are not hyperactive at all, but still have a lot of trouble focusing attention.

2. How can we tell if a child has ADD?

Many factors can cause children to have problems paying attention besides an attention deficit disorder. Family problems, stress, discouragement, drugs, physical illness, and learning difficulties can all cause problems that look like ADD, but really aren't. To accurately identify whether a child has ADD, a comprehensive evaluation needs to be performed by professionals who are familiar with characteristics of the disorder.

STRESS
DISCOURAGEMENT
PHYSICAL ILLNESS
LEARNING DIFFICULTIES
FAMILY PROBLEMS

The process of evaluating whether a child has ADD usually involves a variety of professionals which can include the family physician, pediatrician, child and adolescent psychiatrist or psychologist, neurologist, family counselor and teacher. Psychiatric interview, psychological and educational testing, and/or a neurological examination can provide information leading to a proper diagnosis and treatment planning. An accurate evaluation is necessary before proper treatment can begin. Complex cases in which the diagnosis is unclear or is complicated by other medical and psychiatric conditions should be seen by a physician.

Parents and teachers, being the primary sources of information about the child's ability to attend and focus at home and in school, play an integral part in the evaluation process.

3. What kinds of services and programs help children with ADD and their families?

Help for the ADD child and the family is best provided through *multi-modal* treatment delivered by a team of professionals who look after the medical, emotional, behavioral, and educational needs of the child. Parents play an essential role as coordinators of services and programs designed to help their child. Such services and programs may include:

- Medication to help improve attention, and reduce impulsivity and hyperactivity, as well as to treat other emotional or adjustment problems which sometimes accompany ADD.

- Training parents to understand ADD and to be more effective behavior managers as well as advocates for their child.

- Counseling or training ADD children in methods of self-control, attention focusing, learning strategies, organizational skills, or social skill development.

- Psychotherapy to help the demoralized or even depressed ADD child.

- Other interventions at home and at school designed to enhance self-esteem and foster acceptance, approval, and a sense of belonging.

4. What medications are prescribed for ADD children?

Medications can dramatically improve attention span and reduce hyperactive and impulsive behavior. Psychostimulants have been used to treat attentional deficits in children since the 1940's. Antidepressants, while used less frequently to treat ADD, have been shown to be quite effective for the management of this disorder in some children.

5. How do psychostimulants such as Dexedrine (dextroamphetamine), Ritalin (methylphenidate) and Cylert (pemoline) help?

Seventy to eighty per cent of ADD children respond in a positive manner to psychostimulant medication. Exactly how these medicines work is not known. However, benefits for children can be quite significant and are most apparent when concentration is required. In classroom settings, on-task behavior and completion of assigned tasks is increased, socialization with peers and teacher is improved, and disruptive behaviors (talking out, demanding attention, getting out of seat, noncompliance with requests, breaking rules) are reduced.

The specific dose of medicine must be determined for each child. Generally, the higher the dose, the greater the effect and side effects. To ensure proper dosage, regular monitoring at different levels should be done. Since there are no clear guidelines as to how long a child should take medication, periodic trials off medication should be done to determine continued need. Behavioral rating scales, testing on continuous performance tasks, and the child's self-reports provide helpful, but not infallible measures of progress.

Despite myths to the contrary, a positive response to stimulants is often found in adolescents with ADD, therefore, medication need not be discontinued as the child reaches adolescence if it is still needed.

6. What are common side effects of psychostimulant medications?

Reduction in appetite, loss of weight, and problems in falling asleep are the most common adverse effects. Children treated with stimulants may become irritable and more sensitive to criticism or rejection. Sadness and a tendency to cry are occasionally seen.

The unmasking or worsening of a tic disorder is an infrequent effect of stimulants. In some cases this involves Tourette's Disorder. Generally, except in Tourette's, the tics decrease or disappear with the discontinuation of the stimulant. Caution must be employed in medicating adolescents with stimulants if there are coexisting disorders, e.g. depression, substance abuse, conduct, tic or mood disorders. Likewise, caution should be employed when a family history of a tic disorder exists.

Some side effects, e.g. decreased spontaneity, are felt to be dose-related and can be alleviated by reduction of dosage or switching to another stimulant. Similarly, slowing of height and weight gain of children on stimulants has been documented, with a return to normal for both occurring upon discontinuation of the medication. Other less common side effects have been described but they may occur as frequently with a placebo as with active medication. Pemoline may cause impaired liver functioning in 3% of children, and this may not be completely reversed when this medication is discontinued.

Over-medication has been reported to cause impairment in cognitive functioning and alertness. Some children on higher doses of stimulants will experience what has been described as a "rebound" effect, consisting of changes in mood, irritability and increases of the symptoms associated with their disorder. This occurs with variable degrees of severity during the late afternoon or evening, when the level of medicine in the blood falls. Thus, an additional low dose of medicine in the late afternoon or a decrease of the noontime dose might be required.

7. When are tricyclic antidepressants such as Tofranil (imipramine), Norpramin (desipramine) and Elavil (amytriptyline) used to treat ADD children?

This group of medications is generally considered when contraindications to stimulants exist, when stimulants have not been effective or have resulted in unacceptable side effects, or when the antidepressant property is more critical to treatment than the decrease of inattentiveness. They are used much less frequenlty than the stimulants, seem to have a different mechanism of action, and may be somewhat less effective than the psychostimulants in treating ADD. Long-term use of the tricyclics has not been well studied. Children with ADD who are also experiencing anxiety or depression may do best with an initial trial of a tricyclic antidepressant followed, if needed, with a stimulant for the more classic ADD symptoms.

8. What are the side effects of tricyclic antidepressant medications?

Side effects include constipation and dry mouth. Symptomatic treatment with stool softeners and sugar free gum or candy are usually effective in alleviating the discomfort. Confusion, elevated blood pressure, possible precipitation of manic-like behavior and inducement of seizures are uncommon side effects. The latter three occur in vulnerable individuals who can generally be identified during the assessment phase.

9. What about ADD children who do not respond well to medication?

Some ADD children or adolescents will not respond satisfactorily to either the psychostimulant or tricyclic antidepressant medications. Non-responders may have severe symptoms of ADD, may have other problems in addition to ADD, or may not be able to tolerate certain medications due to adverse side effects as noted above. In such cases consultation with a child and adolescent psychiatrist may be helpful.

10. How often should medications be dispensed at school to an ADD child?

Since the duration for effective action for Ritalin and Dexedrine, the most commonly used psychostimulants, is only about four hours, a second dose during school is often required. Taking a second dose of medication at noon-time enables the ADD child to focus attention effectively, utilize appropriate school behavior and maintain academic productivity. However, the noon-time dose can sometimes be eliminated for children whose afternoon academic schedule does not require high levels of attentiveness. Some psychostimulants, i.e. SR Ritalin (sustained release form) and Cylert, work for longer periods of time (eight to ten hours) and may help avoid the need for a noon-time dose. Antidepressant medications used to treat ADD are usually taken in the morning, afternoon hours after school, or in the evening.

In many cases the physician may recommend that medication be continued at non-school times such as weekday afternoons, weekends or school vacations. During such non-school times lower doses of medication than those taken for school may be sufficient. It is important to remember that ADD is more than a school problem — it is a problem which often interferes in the learning of constructive social, peer, and sports activities.

11. How should medication be dispensed at school?

Most important, regardless of who dispenses medication, since an ADD child may already feel "different" from others, care should be taken to provide discreet reminders to the child when it is time to take medication. It is quite important that school personnel treat the administration of medication in a sensitive manner, thereby safeguarding the privacy of the child or adolescent and avoiding any unnecessary embarrassment. Success in doing this will increase the student's compliance in taking medication.

The location for dispensing medication at school may vary depending upon the school's resources. In those schools with a full-time nurse, the infirmary would be the first choice. In those schools in which a nurse is not always available, other properly trained school personnel may take the responsibility of supervising and dispensing medication.

12. How should the effectiveness of medication and other treatments for the ADD child be monitored?

Important information needed to judge the effectiveness of medication usually comes from reports by the child's parents and teachers and should include information about the child's behavior and attentiveness, academic performance, social and emotional adjustment and any medication side-effects.

Reporting from these sources may be informal through telephone, or more objective via the completion of scales designed for this purpose.

The commonly used teacher rating scales are:
• Conners Teacher Rating Scales
• ADD-H Comprehensive Teacher Rating Scale
• Child Behavior Checklist
• ADHD Rating Scale
• Child Attention Problems (CAP) Rating Scale
• School Situations Questionnaire

Academic performance should be monitored by comparing classroom grades prior to and after treatment.

It is important to monitor changes in peer relationships, family functioning, social skills, a capacity to enjoy leisure time, and self-esteem.

The parents, school nurse or other school personnel responsible for dispensing or overseeing the medication trial should have regular contact by phone with the prescribing physician. Physician office visits of sufficient frequency to monitor treatment are critical in the overall care of children with ADD.

13. What is the role of the teacher in the care of children with ADD?

Teaching an ADD child can test the limits of any educator's time and patience. As any parent of an ADD child will tell you, being on the front lines helping these children to manage on a daily basis can be both challenging and exhausting. It helps if teachers know what to expect and if they receive in-service training on how to teach

and manage ADD students in their classroom.

Here are some ideas that teachers told us have helped:
• Build upon the child's strengths by offering a great deal of encouragement and praise for the child's efforts, no matter how small.
• Learn to use behavior modification programs that motivate students to focus attention, behave better, and complete work.
• Talk with the child's parents and find helpful strategies that have worked with the child in the past.
• If the child is taking medication, communicate frequently with the physician (and parents) so that proper adjustments can be made with respect to type or dose of medication. Behavior rating scales are good for this purpose.
• Modify the classroom structure to accommodate the child's span of attention, i.e. shorter assignments, preferential seating in the classroom, appealing curriculum material, animated presentation of lessons, and frequent positive reinforcement.
• Determine whether the child can be helped through special educational resources within the school.
• Consult with other school personnel such as the guidance counselor, school psychologist, or school nurse to get their ideas as well.

14. What are common myths associated with ADD medications?

Myth: Medication should be stopped when a child reaches teen years.
Fact: Research clearly shows that there is continued benefit to medication for those teens who meet criteria for diagnosis of ADD.
Myth: Children build up a tolerance to medication.
Fact: Although the dose of medication may need adjusting from time to time there is no evidence that children build up a tolerance to medication.
Myth: Taking medication for ADD leads to greater likelihood of later drug addiction.
Fact: There is no evidence to indicate that ADD medication leads to an increased likelihood of later drug addiction.

Myth: Positive response to medication is confirmation of a diagnosis of ADD.
Fact: The fact that a child shows improvement of attention span or a reduction of activity while taking ADD medication does not substantiate the diagnosis of ADD. Even some normal children will show a marked improvement in attentiveness when they take ADD medications.
Myth: Medication stunts growth.
Fact: ADD medications may cause an initial and mild slowing of growth, but over time the growth suppression effect is minimal if non-existent in most cases.
Myth: Taking ADD medications as a child makes you more reliant on drugs as an adult.
Fact: There is no evidence of increased medication taking when medicated ADD children become adults, nor is there evidence that ADD children become addicted to their medications.
Myth: ADD children who take medication attribute their success only to medication.
Fact: When self-esteem is encouraged, a child taking medication attributes his success not only to the medication but to himself as well.

Summary of Important Points

1. ADD children make up 3-5% of the population, but many children who have trouble paying attention may have problems other than ADD. A thorough evaluation can help determine whether attentional deficits are due to ADD or to other conditions.

2. Once identified, ADD children are best treated with a *multi-modal* approach. Best results are obtained when behavioral management programs, educational interventions, parent training, counseling, and medication, when needed, are used together to help the ADD child. Parents of children and adolescents with ADD play the key role of coordinating these services.

3. Each ADD child responds in his or her own unique way to medication depending upon the child's physical make-up, severity of ADD symptoms, and other possible problems accompanying the ADD. Responses to medication need to be monitored and reported to the child's physician.

4. Teachers play an essential role in helping the ADD child feel comfortable within the classroom procedures and work demands, sensitivity to self-esteem issues, and frequent parent-teacher contact can help a great deal.

5. ADD may be a life-long disorder requiring life-long assistance. Families, and the children themselves, need our continued support and understanding.

6. Successful treatment of the medical aspects of ADD is dependent upon ongoing collaboration between the prescribing physician, teacher, therapist and parents.

Appendix D
ADD Guide For Teachers

ATTENTION DEFICIT DISORDERS:

A GUIDE FOR TEACHERS

Prepared for distribution by the Education Committee of
CH.A.D.D.
Children With Attention Deficit Disorders
"Parents Supporting Parents"

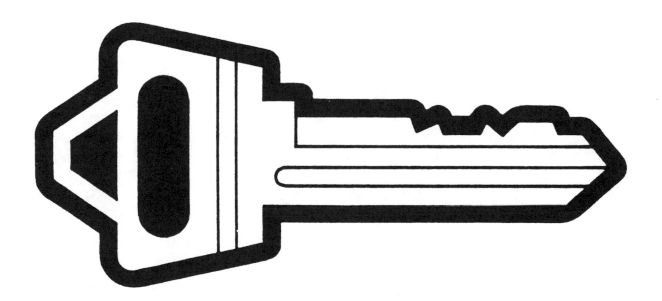

TEACHERS ARE THE KEY FOR THE EFFECTIVE TREATMENT OF ADD

ATTENTION DEFICIT DISORDERS: A GUIDE FOR TEACHERS

Defining Attention Deficit Disorders (ADD)

Attention Deficit Disorder is a syndrome which is characterized by serious and persistent difficulties in three specific areas:

1. Attention span
2. Impulse control
3. Hyperactivity (sometimes)

ADD is a chronic disorder which can begin in infancy and can extend through adulthood while having negative effects on a child's life at home, school, and within his/her community. It is conservatively estimated that 3-5% of our school age population is affected by ADD, a condition which previously fell under the heading of "learning disabled," "brain damaged," "hyperkinetic," or "hyperactive." However, the newer term, attention deficit disorder, was introduced to more clearly describe the characteristics of these children. There are two types of attention deficit disorder, both of which are described below.

Attention Deficit Hyperactivity Disorder (ADHD)

According to the criteria in the Diagnostic and Statistical Manual of the American Psychiatric Association, to diagnose a child as having ADHD s/he must display for six months or more at least eight of the following characteristics before the age of seven.

1. Fidgets, squirms or seems restless
2. Has difficulty remaining seated
3. Is easily distracted
4. Has difficulty awaiting turn
5. Blurts out answers
6. Has difficulty following instructions
7. Has difficulty sustaining attention
8. Shifts from one uncompleted task to another
9. Has difficulty playing quietly
10. Talks excessively
11. Interrupts or intrudes on others
12. Does not seem to listen
13. Often loses things necessary for tasks
14. Frequently engages in dangerous actions

Undifferentiated Attention Deficit Disorder

In this form of ADD the primary and most significant characteristic is inattentiveness; hyperactivity is not present. Nevertheless, these children still manifest problems with organization and distractibility and they may be seen as quiet or passive in nature. It is speculated that Undifferentiated ADD is currently underdiagnosed as these children tend to be overlooked more easily in the classroom. Thus, these children may be at a higher risk for academic failure than those with attention deficit hyperactivity disorder.

Diagnosing Attention Deficit Disorders

Students who have exhibited the characteristics mentioned above for longer than six months may be at risk for having an attention deficit disorder. However, a diagnosis of attention deficit should only be made after ruling out other factors related to medical, emotional or environmental variables which could cause similar symptoms. Therefore, physicians, psychologists, and educators often conduct a multi-disciplinary evaluation of the child including medical studies, psychological and educational testing, speech and language assessment, neurological evaluation, and behavioral rating scales.

Causes of Attention Deficit Disorders

A 1987 Report to Congress prepared by the Intergency Committee of Learning Disabilities attributes the probable cause of ADD to "abnormalities in neurological function, in particular to disturbance in brain neurochemistry involving a class of brain neurochemicals termed 'neurotransmitters'." Researchers are unclear, however, as to the specific mechanisms by which these neurotransmitter chemicals influence attention, impulse control and activity level.

Although many ADD children tend to develop secondary emotional problems, ADD, in itself, may be related to biological factors and is <u>not</u> primarily an emotional disorder. Nevertheless, emotional and behavioral problems can frequently be seen in ADD children due to problems that these children tend to have within their school, home, and social environments. Such characteristics as inattentiveness, impulsivity, and underachievement can also be found in non-ADD students who suffer primarily from emotional difficulties which effect concentration and effort or in those students who simply have motivational deficits leading to diminished classroom attentiveness and performance. Differential diagnosis, therefore, is an essential prerequisite to effective treatment.

Treating Attention Deficit Disorders

Treatment of the ADD child usually requires a <u>multi-modal approach</u> frequently involving a treatment team made up of parents, teachers, physicians, and behavioral or mental health professionals. The four corners of this treatment program are as follows:

Educational Planning   Medical Management

> Multimodal
>
> Treatment Planning

Psychological Counseling   Behavioral Modification

"Hyperactivity with ADD, <u>without treatment</u>, often results in school failure, rejection by peers and family turmoil, all of which can lead to developmental delays and psychiatric complications stemming from low self-esteem and frustration."

Jerry M. Weiner, M.D., *Pres. Amer. Academy of Ch. & Adol. Psychiatry*

N E G A T I V E   C Y C L E

FAILURE
POOR SELF-ESTEEM
FAILURE
POOR SELF-ESTEEM
FAILURE

With this downward cycle in progress ADD can lead to:
     Poor social adjustment
     Behavioral problems
     School failure
     Drop-out and delinquency
     Drug abuse

Using Medication in the Treatment of Attention Deficit Disorders

The use of medication alone in the treatment of ADD is <u>not</u> recommended. As indicated earlier, a multimodal treatment plan is usually followed for successful treatment of the ADD child or adolescent. While not all children having ADD are prescribed medication, in certain cases the proper use of medication can play an important and necessary part in the child's overall treatment.

Ritalin, the most commonly used medication in treating ADD, is a psychostimulant and has been prescribed for many years with very favorable results and minimal side effects. Other psychostimulant medications which are used to treat ADD are Cylert and Dexedrine. In the past several years antidepressant medications such as Tofranil and Norpramine have also proved successful in treating the disorder. All these medications are believed to effect the body's neurotransmitter chemicals, deficiencies of which may be the cause of ADD. Improvements in such characteristics as attention span, impulse control and hyperactivity are noted in approximately 75% of children who take psychostimulant medications. It is important that teachers are informed about all medications that an ADD student may take as teachers need to work closely with the child's parents and other helping professionals in monitoring medication effectiveness.

Medication side effects such as appetite loss, sleep difficulties, and/or lethargy in the classroom, among others, can often be controlled through medication dosage adjustments when reported by the child's parents or teachers.

Teaching Students With Attention Deficit Disorders

The most effective treatment of ADD requires full cooperation of teachers and parents working closely with other professionals such as physicians, psychologists, psychiatrists, speech and educational specialists, etc. In the coordinated effort to ensure success in the lives of children with ADD the vital importance of the teacher's role cannot be overestimated. Dennis Cantwell, M.D. claims, "Anything else is a drop in the bucket when you compare it with the time spent in school."

Recommendations for the Proper Learning Environment

1. Seat ADD student near teacher's desk, but include as part of regular class seating.
2. Place ADD student up front with his back to the rest of the class to keep other students out of view.
3. Surround ADD student with "good role models," preferably students that the ADD child views as "significant others." Encourage peer tutoring and cooperative collaborative learning.
4. Avoid distracting stimuli. Try not to place the ADD student near:

Air conditioner	Heater
High traffic areas	Doors or windows

5. ADD children do not handle change well so avoid:

Transitions	Changes in schedule
Physical relocation	Disruptions
(monitor closely on field trips)	

6. Be creative! Produce a "stimuli-reduced study area." Let all students have access to this area so the ADD child will not feel different.
7. Encourage parents to set up appropriate study space at home with routines established as far as set times for study, parental review of completed homework, and periodic notebook and/or book bag organized.

Recommendations For Giving Instructions to Students

1. Maintain eye contact with the ADD student during verbal instruction.
2. Make directions clear and concise. Be consistent with daily instructions.
3. Simplify complex directions. Avoid multiple commands.
4. Make sure ADD student comprehends before beginning the task.
5. Repeat in a calm, positive manner, if needed.
6. Help ADD child to feel comfortable with seeking assistance (most ADD children won't ask).
7. These children need more help for a longer period of time than the average child. Gradually reduce assistance.
8. Require a daily assignment notebook if necessary.
   a. Make sure student correctly writes down all assignments each day. If the student is not capable of this then the teacher should help the student.

b. Parents and teachers sign notebook daily to signify completion of homework assignments.
c. Parents and teachers may use notebook for daily communication with each other.

Recommendations for Students Performing Assignments

1. Give out only one task at a time.
2. Monitor frequently. Use a supportive attitude.
3. Modify assignments as needed. Consult with Special Education personnel to determine specific strengths and weaknesses of the student. Develop an individualized educational program.
4. Make sure you are testing knowledge and not attention span.
5. Give extra time for certain tasks. The ADD student may work more slowly. Don't penalize for needed extra time.
6. Keep in mind that ADD children are easily frustrated. Stress, pressure and fatigue can break down the ADD child's self-control and lead to poor behavior.

Recommendations for Behavior Modification and Self-esteem Enhancement

Providing Supervision and Discipline

a. Remain calm, state infraction of rule, and don't debate or argue with student.
b. Have pre-established consequences for misbehavior.
c. Administer consequences immediately and monitor proper behavior frequently.
d. Enforce rules of the classroom consistently.
e. Discipline should be appropriate to "fit the crime," without harshness.
f. Avoid ridicule and criticism. Remember, ADD children have difficulty staying in control.
g. Avoid publicly reminding students on medication to "take their medicine."

Providing Encouragement

a. Reward more than you punish in order to build self-esteem.
b. Praise immediately any and all good behavior and performance.
c. Change rewards if not effective in motivating behavioral change.
d. Find ways to encourage the child.
e. Teach the child to reward him/herself. Encourage positive self-talk (i.e., "You did very well remaining in your seat today. How do you feel about that?"). This encourages the child to think positively about him/herself.

Other Educational Recommendations Which May Help Some ADD Students

1. Some ADD students may benefit from educational, psychological, and/or neurological testing to determine their learning style, cognitive ability and to rule out any learning disabilities (common in about 30% of ADD students).
2. Private tutor and/or peer tutoring at school.
3. A class that has a low student-teacher ratio.
4. Social skills training and organizational skills training.
5. Training in cognitive restructuring (positive "self-talk," i.e., "I did that well.").
6. Use of a word processor or computer for school work.
7. Individualized activities that are mildly competitive or non-competitive such as: bowling, walking, swimming, jogging, biking, karate
   Note: ADD children may do less well in team sports
8. Involvement in social activities such as scouting, church groups or other youth organizations which help develop social skills and self-esteem.
9. Allowing the child to play with younger children if that's where they "fit in." Many ADD children have more in common with younger children. The child can still develop valuable social skills from interaction with younger children.

Suggested Reading and References

Books and Pamphlets

Barkley, Russell. *Hyperactive Children*. New York: Guilford Press, 1981.

Canter, Lee & Canter, Marlene. *Assertive Discipline for Parents*. Canter & Associates, Inc., 1553 Euclid St., Santa Monica, CA 90404.

Friedman, Ronald. *Attention Deficit Disorder and Hyperactivity*. Educational Resources, Inc., 1990 Ten Mile Road, St. Clair Shores, MI 48081 ($10.95).

Garfinkel, Barry. *What is Attention Deficit and How Does Medication Help?* Division of Child and Adolescent Psychiatry, Box 95 UMH&C, Harvard Street at East River Road, Minneapolis, MN 55455 (About $2.00).

Parker, Harvey C. *The ADD Hyperactivity Workbook for Parents, Teachers, and Kids*. Impact Publications, Inc., 300 Northwest 70th Avenue, Suite 102, Plantation, FL 33317 ($12.95 plus $2.00 shpg. & hdlg.).

Phelan, Thomas. *ADD-Hyperactivity*. 507 Thornhill Drive, Carol Stream, IL 60188.

Silver, Larry. *The Misunderstood Child*. McGraw Hill, 1984.

Wender, Paul. *The Hyperactive Child, Adolescent and Adult*. Oxford University Press, 1987.

Other References

Diagnostic and Statistical Manual III-R. American Psychiatric Association, Washington, D.C., 1987.

A Report to U.S. Congress. Prepared by Interagency on Learning Disabilities, 1987.

Sunday Gazzette Mail, *Inaccuracies about Ritalin*. John Wender, M.D. January 10, 1988, Charleston, West Virginia.

Acknowledgements

"Attention Deficit Disorders: A Guide for Teachers" was prepared by members of the Education Committee of CH.A.D.D, November 1988.

Education Committee of CH.A.D.D.

Carol Lerner, M.S., Chairperson
Laurie Agopian
Chuck Ansell
Lynn Barker
Claudia Bibace
Nancy Brown
Karen Ford
Mark Milford
Laura Mills
Sandy Mitchell
Jan Morton
Nancy Thornberry

CH.A.D.D. would like to thank and encourage all who are involved with the important task of education. Let us work together today to ensure a bright tomorrow for our children.

For more information on ADD write to: Or contact your local CH.A.D.D. Chapter
CH.A.D.D.
Children with Attention Deficit Disorders
499 N.W. 70th Avenue, Suite 308
Plantation, FL 33317
(305) 587-3700

References

Abikoff, H., & Gittelman-Klein, R., & Klein, D. (1977). Validation of a classroom observation code for hyperactive children. *Journal of Consulting and Clinical Psychology, 45*, 772-783.

Adduci, L. (1991). My Child Couldn't Pay Attention. *Woman's Day*, September, 102 -106.

Alessi, G., & Kaye, J. H. (1983). *Behavior Assessment for School Psychologists*. Kent, OH: National Association of School Psychologists.

Algozinne, B. (1990). *Problem Behavior Management: Educator's Resource Service*. Rockville, MD: Aspen Publishers, Inc.

American Psychiatric Association: *Diagnostic and Statistical Manual of Mental Disorders, Third Edition, Revised,* Washington, DC, American Psychiatric Association, 1987.

Barkley, R. A. (1987). *Defiant Children: A Clinician's Manual for Parent Training*. New York: Guilford Press.

Barkley, R. A. (1990). *Attention Deficit Hyperactivity Disorder: A Handbook for Diagnosis and Treatment*. New York: Gilford Press.

Barkley, R. A. (1991). *Attention-Deficit Hyperactivity Disorder: A Clinical Workbook*. New York: Guilford Press.

Barkley, R. A. (1992). Is EEG Biofeedback Treatment Effective for ADHD Children? A Cautionary Note. Unpublished manuscript.

Barkley, R. A., & Cunningham, C. E. (1979). The effects of methylphenidate on the mother-child interactions of hyperactive children. *Archives of General Psychiatry, 36,* 201-208.

Braswell, L. & Bloomquist, M. L. (1991). *Cognitive-Behavioral Therapy with ADHD Children: Child, Family and School Interventions*. New York: Guilford Press.

CH.A.D.D. (1988). *Attention Deficit Disorders: A Guide for Teachers.*. Plantation, FL: Children with Attention Deficit Disorders.

Conners, C. K. (1989). *Conners' Rating Scales Manual.* North Tonawanda, NY: Multi-Health Systems, Inc.

Conners, C. K. (1990). *Feeding the Brain: How Foods Affect Children.* NY: Plenum Press.

DuPaul, G. J., Rapport, M., & Perriello, L.M. (1990). Teacher Ratings of Academic Performance: The Development of the Academic Performance Rating Scale. *School Psychology Review, 20,* 2, 284 -300.

DuPaul, G.J. (1991). Parent and teacher ratings of ADHD symptoms: Psychometric properties in a community-based sample. *Journal of Clinical Child Psychology, 20,* 245 - 253.

Epstein, M., Singh, N., Luebke, J., & Stout, C. (1991). Psychopharmacological Intervention II: Teacher Perceptions of Psychotropic Medication for Students with Learning Disabilities. *Journal of Learning Disabilities, 24,* 477 - 483.

Feingold, B.F. (1975). *Why your child is hyperactive.* New York: Random House.

Gehret, J. (1990). *Eagle Eyes: A Child's View of Attention Deficit Disorder.* Fairport, NY: Verbal Images Press.

Goldstein S., & Goldstein, M. (1989). *Why Won't My Child Pay Attention?* Salt Lake City, UT: Neurology, Learning and Behavior Center.

Goldstein, S., & Goldstein, M. (1990). *Managing Attention Disorders in Children: A gude for practitioners.* New York: Wiley & Sons.

Goldstein, S., & Goldstein, M. (1990). *Educating Inattentive Children.* Salt Lake City, UT: Neurology, Learning and Behavior Center.

Goldstein, S., & Goldstein, M. (1991). *It's Just Attention Disorder: A Video Guide for Kids.* Salt Lake City, UT: Neurology, Learning and Behavior Center.

Goldstein, S., & Pollock, E. (1988). *Social Skills Training for Attention Deficit Children.* Salt Lake City, UT: Neurology, Learning and Behavior Center.

Gordon, M. *Attention Training System.* DeWitt, NY: Gordon Systems.

Gordon, M. (1983). *The Gordon Diagnostic System*. DeWitt, NY: Gordon Systems.

Gordon, M. (1991). *Jumpin' Johnny Get Back To Work: A Child's Guide To ADHD / Hyperactivity*. DeWitt, NY: GSI Publications.

Gordon, M. (1991). *ADHD / Hyperactivity: A Consumer's Guide*. DeWitt, NY: GSI Publications.

Grant, D., & Berg, E. (1948). *The Wisconsin Card Sort Test: Directions for administration and scoring*. Odessa, FL:

Greenberg, G.S. & Horn, W.F. (1991). *Attention Deficit Hyperactivity Disorder: Questions and Answers for Parents*. Champaign, IL: Research Press.

Ingersoll, B. (1988). *Your Hyperactive Child: A Parent's Guide to Coping with Attention Deficit Disorder*. New York: Doubleday.

Kagan, J. (1966). Reflection-impulsivity: The generality and dynamics of conceptual tempo. *Journal of Abnormal Psychology, 71*, 17 - 24.

Kalan, M. R. (1991). *Superintendent's Task Force Report on Attention Deficit Disorder*. Ft. Lauderdale, FL: Broward County Public Schools.

Kaufman, A. S., & Kaufman, N.L L. (1983). *Kaufman Assessment Battery for Children*. Circle Pines, MN: American Guidance Service.

Levine, Mel. (1990). *Keeping A Head In School*. Cambridge, MA: Educators Publishing Service, Inc.

Lloyd, J. W., & Landrum, T. J. (1990) Self-Recording of Attending to Task: Treatment Components and Generalization of Effects. In T. Scruggs & B.Y.L. Wong (Eds.), *Intervention Research in Learning Disabilities.*. NY: Sringer-Verlag.

Nadeau, K., & Dixon, E. (1991). *Learning To Slow Down and Pay Attention*. Virginia: Chesapeake Psychological Services.

Parker, H. (1994). *The ADD Hyperactivity Workbook for Parents, Teachers and Kids*. 2nd edition. Plantation, FL: Specialty Press, Inc.

Parker, H. (1990). *Listen, Look, and Think*. Plantation, FL: Specialty Press, Inc.

Parker, H. (1991). *The Goal Card Program*. Plantation, FL: Specialty Press, Inc.

Parker, R., & Parker, H. (1992). *Making the Grade: An Adolescent's Struggle with Attention Deficit Disorder*. Plantation, FL: Specialty Press, Inc.

Pelham, W.E., Atkins, M.S., Murphy, H.A., & Swanson, J.. (1984) *A teacher rating scale for the diagnosis of Attention Deficit Disorder: Teacher norms, factor analysis, and reliability*. Unpublished manuscript.

Professional Group for ADD and Related Disorders (PGARD). (1991). *Response From PGARD To the Congressional Notice of Inquiry on ADD*. Unpublished manuscript.

Quinn, P. O. ,& Stern, J. (1991). *Putting On the Brakes*. New York: Magnination Press.

Rosvold, H.E., Mirsky, A. F., Sarason, I., Bransome, E.D., & Beck, L.H. (1956). A continuous performance test of brain damage. *Journal of Consulting Psychology, 20*, 343-350.

Saudargas, R. A., & Creed, V. (1980). *State-Event Classroom Observation System*. Knoxville: University of Tennessee, Department of Psychology.

Shapiro, E.S. (1989). *Academic Skills Problems: Direct assessment and intervention*. New York: Guilford Press.

Shelton, T., & Crosswaite, C. (1992) *Prevention/Treatment Program for Kindergartners with ADHD. CH.A.D.D.ER, 6*, 1992.

Silver, L. (1984). *The Misunderstood Child: A Guide for Parents of LD Children*. New York: McGraw Hill.

Robin, A. L. & Foster, S. L. (1989). *Negotiating Parent-Adolescent Conflict*. New York: Guilford Press.

Rosenfield, S. A. (1987). *Instructional Consultation*. New Jersey: Lawrence Erlbaum Associates, Publishers.

Thomas, S. (1991). Parents' Perspectives:Gaps, Cracks and Craters. *Journal of Child and Adolescent Psychopharmacology, 1*, 251-254.

Virginia Department of Education (1989). *Task Force Report: Attention Deficit Hyperactivity Disorder and the Schools*. Virginia.

Wender, P. H. (1987). *The Hyperactive Child, Adolescent, and Adult:*

Attention Deficit Disorder Through the Life Span. New York: Oxford University Press.

Wirt, R. D., Lachar, D., Klinedinst, J. K., & Seat, P.D. (1984). *Multi-dimensional descripton of child personality: A manual for the Personality Inventory for Children, revised 1984.* Los Angeles: Western Psychological Services.

Zametkin, A.J., Nordahl, T.E., Gross, M., King, A.C., Semple, W.E., Rumsey, J, Hamburger, S., & Cohen, R.M.. (1990). Cerebral Glucose Metabolism in Adults with Hyperactivity of Childhood Onset. *New England Journal of Medicine, 323,* 1361-1366.

Student Worksheets

(Worksheets may be reproduced for classroom use.)

Following Class Rules
Contract

The following class rules will be followed:

_____

_____

_____

If _____
             Student's Name

follows these rules

_____
             Reward

If _____
             Student's Name

does not follow these rules

_____
             Consequence

Date_____

Getting To My Goal
Contract

Today my goal is to:

_____

_____

_____

If _____
              Student's Name

reaches the goal

_____
                    Reward

If _____
              Student's Name

does not reach the goal

_____
                 Consequence

Date_____

Source: The ADD Hyperactivity Handbook for Schools by Harvey C. Parker, Ph.D. This form may be reproduced for classroom use.

Contract

I _____, a student at _____
       name of student   name of school

do hereby declare that I promise to _____

_____ .

I _____, a teacher at _____
       name of teacher   name of school

do hereby declare that in exchange for _____ fulfilling his
                                                 name of student

promise as stated above, I will _____

_____ .

In WITNESS WHEREOF, we have subscribed our names this _____ day
                                                         day

of _____, 19_____.
      month   year

_____
signature of teacher

_____
signature of student

_____
signature of witness

Source: The ADD Hyperactivity Handbook for Schools by Harvey C. Parker, Ph.D. This form may be reproduced for classroom use.

Daily Report

Name _____   Date _____

Rate the child's progress for the day in each of the following areas by filling in the bar to the right of the behavior.

	Fair	Better	Good
Completed work.			
Paid attention.			
Followed class rules.			
Cooperated with others.			
_____			

Additional comments: _____

_____

_____

Teacher Signature_____

Source: The ADD Hyperactivity Handbook for Schools by Harvey C. Parker, Ph.D. This form may be reproduced for classroom use.

_____

_____

Weekly Progress Report

Name _____ Grade _____ Date _____

Teacher _____ Subject _____

<u>Behavior</u>
___ Positive
___ Satisfactory
___ Occasionally disruptive
___ Frequently disruptive

<u>Homework</u>
___ Thoroughly completed
___ Adequately completed
___ Occasionally unprepared
___ Frequently unprepared

<u>Effort</u>
___ Good, Working well
___ Satisfactory
___ Minimal
___ Declining
___ Improving

<u>Test Scores</u>
___ Good
___ Average
___ Poor

<u>Quality of Work</u>
___ Exceptional
___ Adequate
___ Poor

<u>Progress</u>
___ Satisfactory
___ Unsatisfactory
___ Improving
___ Declining

<u>Attention Span</u>
___ Good
___ Fair
___ Poor

Weekly School Report

Name _____   From _____ to _____   Grade _____

Subject	Teacher	Homework	Test Grades	Behavior

Source: The ADD Hyperactivity Handbook for Schools by Harvey C. Parker, Ph.D. This form may be reproduced for classroom use.

SCHOOL-BASED TOKEN PROGRAM

Name _____   Date _____

PERIOD OR SUBJECT

TARGET BEHAVIORS TO EARN POINTS	POINT VALUE	POINTS EARNED DAILY				
Completed classwork	Yes/No					
Completed homework	Yes/No					
Any assignments due?	Yes/No					
Any recent grades?	Yes/No					
Arrived to class on time?	Yes/No					
Parent's Initials ☐ Teacher's Initials						

Write any comments below and initial:

Source: The ADD Hyperactivity Handbook for Schools by Harvey C. Parker, Ph.D. This form may be reproduced for classroom use.

_____

_____

SCHOOL BASED TOKEN PROGRAM

Name _____   Week of _____

TARGET BEHAVIORS TO EARN POINTS	POINT VALUES	POINTS EARNED DAILY				
		MON	TUE	WED	THU	FRI
	+					
	+					
	+					
	+					
TOTAL NUMBER POINTS EARNED						

Menu of rewards or activities to choose from:

_____ = _____ Points

_____ = _____ Points

_____ = _____ Points

Source: The ADD Hyperactivity Handbook for Schools by Harvey C. Parker, Ph.D. This form may be reproduced for classroom use.

SCHOOL-BASED TOKEN PROGRAM

Name _____   Week of _____

PERIOD OR SUBJECT

TARGET BEHAVIORS TO EARN POINTS	POINT VALUES	POINTS EARNED DAILY				
	+					
	+					
	+					
	+					
TOTAL NUMBER POINTS EARNED						

Menu of rewards or activities to choose from:

_____ = _____ Points

_____ = _____ Points

_____ = _____ Points

Source: The ADD Hyperactivity Handbook for Schools by Harvey C. Parker, Ph.D. This form may be reproduced for classroom use.

SCHOOL-BASED TOKEN PROGRAM

Name _____   Week of _____

TARGET BEHAVIORS TO EARN POINTS	POINT VALUES	POINTS EARNED DAILY				
		MON	TUE	WED	THU	FRI
	+					
	+					
	+					
	+					
TARGET BEHAVIORS TO LOSE POINTS		POINTS LOST DAILY				
	-					
	-					
	-					
POINTS EARNED THIS DAY						
BALANCE FROM YESTERDAY						
NEW BALANCE FOR TODAY						
POINTS SPENT TODAY						
TOTAL POINTS LEFT						

Menu of rewards or activities to choose from:

_____ = _____ Points

_____ = _____ Points

_____ = _____ Points

Source: The ADD Hyperactivity Handbook for Schools by Harvey C. Parker, Ph.D. This form may be reproduced for classroom use.

Was I Paying Attention?

Name _____   **Date** _____

Subject_____

Listen to the beep tape as you do your work. Whenever you hear a beep, stop working for a moment and ask yourself, "Was I paying attention?" Mark your answer (√) below and go back to work. Answer the questions on the bottom when you finish.

Was I Paying Attention?	
Yes	No

Was I Paying Attention?	
Yes	No

Did I follow the directions?	Yes	No
Did I pay attention?	Yes	No
Did I finish my work?	Yes	No
Did I check my answers?	Yes	No

Source: The ADD Hyperactivity Handbook for Schools by Harvey C. Parker, Ph.D. This form may be reproduced for classroom use.

I Can Do It!

Name _____   Date _____

Put a √ if you did this.

	Morning	Afternoon
I CAN PAY ATTENTION		
I paid attention to the teacher		
I followed directions		
I finished all my work		
I CAN CONTROL MY BEHAVIOR		
I raised my hand		
I asked permission before getting up		
I cooperated with others		
I CAN KEEP MY THINGS IN ORDER		
My desk was neat		
My work was put away in its place		
My writing was neat		
ADD UP YOUR CHECK MARKS HERE	#	#
Activities I have earned		
_____	_____	_____
_____	_____	_____

Source: The ADD Hyperactivity Handbook for Schools by Harvey C. Parker, Ph.D. This form may be reproduced for classroom use.

I Can Do It!

Name _____   Date _____

Put a √ if you did this.   Subject: _____ _____

I CAN PAY ATTENTION		
I paid attention to the teacher		
I followed directions		
I finished all my work		
I CAN CONTROL MY BEHAVIOR		
I raised my hand		
I asked permission before getting up		
I cooperated with others		
I CAN KEEP MY THINGS IN ORDER		
My desk was neat		
My work was put away in its place		
My writing was neat		
ADD UP YOUR CHECK MARKS HERE	#	#
Activities I have earned		
_____	_____	_____
_____	_____	_____

Source: The ADD Hyperactivity Handbook for Schools by Harvey C. Parker, Ph.D. This form may be reproduced for classroom use.

Writing Reminders

Name _____   **Date** _____

Subject_____

Answer these questions before you begin to write.

Is my pencil sharp?	Yes	No
Am I holding the pencil correctly?	Yes	No
Am I sitting properly?	Yes	No
Is my paper where it should be?	Yes	No
Am I paying attention to neatness?	Yes	No
Am I taking my time when I write?	Yes	No

Source: The ADD Hyperactivity Handbook for Schools by Harvey C. Parker, Ph.D. This form may be reproduced for classroom use.

Raise Your Hand Before Talking

Name _____   **Date** _____

Fill in a circle everytime you raise your hand before talking.

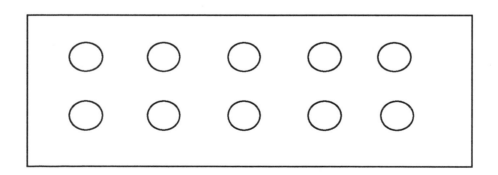

Source: The ADD Hyperactivity Handbook for Schools by Harvey C. Parker, Ph.D. This form may be reproduced for classroom use.

Getting Along With Others

Name_____   Date _____

Choose a skill from those below or select one of your own ideas.

Skill to be practiced today:

_____

Practice in: Classroom   Lunchroom   Schoolyard
(Circle)

Sample Social Skills

1. Giving others a turn

2. Cooperating with others

3. Expressing your ideas or feelings

4. Doing someone a favor

5. Starting a conversation

6. Leading a group

7. Respecting the rights of others

8. Saying you're sorry

9. Ignoring someone's behavior

10. Being polite

Source: The ADD Hyperactivity Handbook for Schools by Harvey C. Parker, Ph.D. This form may be reproduced for classroom use.

Proofreading Checklist

Name _____   Date _____

Assignment _____   Class _____

Check your work to see if you have done the following:

	Yes	No
Heading on paper?		
Margins correct?		
Proper spacing between words?		
Handwriting neat?		
Sentences start with capital letters?		
Sentences end with correct punctuation?		
Crossed out mistakes with only one line?		
Spelling is correct?		

__ I proofread my paper. __ Someone else proofread my paper.

Source: The ADD Hyperactivity Handbook for Schools by Harvey C. Parker, Ph.D. This form may be reproduced for classroom use.